MÉTO
GRAMATICA ~~~~~~
DE LA LENGUA INGLESA

MARÍA ISABEL IGLESIAS
Catedrática de lengua inglesa

GRAMÁTICA SUCINTA DE LA LENGUA INGLESA

EDITORIAL HERDER - BARCELONA
JULIO GROOS - HEIDELBERG

Original de la cubierta de WILL FABER

Vigésima novena edición 1994

Reimpresión 1995

© *Julio Groos - Heidelberg 1961*

ISBN 84-254-0807-5

ES PROPIEDAD   DEPÓSITO LEGAL: B. 37. 409-1995   PRINTED IN SPAIN
LIBERGRAF S.L. - BARCELONA

ÍNDICE

Prólogo VII
Pronunciación... IX
   Las vocales.. X
   Los diptongos... XI
   Las consonantes....................................... XII
   Semivocales.. XIV
Lección primera - El artículo............................. 1
Lección segunda - El número de los substantivos............ 4
Lección tercera - Plurales irregulares..................... 9
Lección cuarta - El adjetivo.............................. 15
Lección quinta - El género................................ 19
Lección sexta - El verbo.................................. 24
Lección séptima - Forma interrogativa y negativa de «to be» y «to have»... 28
Lección octava - Forma interrogativa y negativa del verbo.... 30
Lección novena - Forma interrogativa y negativa del verbo (continuación)... 34
Lección décima - El genitivo.............................. 37
Lección undécima - El pronombre personal.................. 42
Lección duodécima - La forma progresiva del verbo......... 45
Lección decimotercia - Verbos anómalos y defectivos: «can», «may», «must»... 50
Lección decimocuarta - Los números cardinales............. 55
Lección decimoquinta - Los números ordinales.............. 61
Lección decimosexta - El pasado........................... 69
Lección decimoséptima - Grados del adjetivo............... 75
Lección decimoctava - Los tiempos de perfecto............. 83
Lección decimonovena - El participio pasado............... 89
Lección vigésima - Verbos débiles irregulares............. 93
Lección vigésima primera - La voz pasiva.................. 97
Modelos de conjugación.................................... 103
Lista de verbos fuertes y débiles irregulares............. 116
Lección vigésima segunda - El adverbio.................... 119
Lección vigésima tercera - El adverbio (continuación)..... 126
Lista de adverbios de uso más frecuente................... 131
Lección vigésima cuarta - El artículo (ampliación)........ 135
Lección vigésima quinta - Los nombres geográficos......... 142

Lección vigésima sexta - El genitivo y la preposición «of» (ampliación) 151
Lección vigésima séptima - El adjetivo calificativo (ampliación). 156
Lección vigésima octava - Pronombres de relativo 162
Lección vigésima novena - Pronombres interrogativos 167
Lección trigésima - Pronombres reflexivos y enfáticos 171
Lección trigésima primera - Adjetivos y pronombres (ampliación) 178
Lección trigésima segunda - Verbos anómalos y defectivos (ampliación) 187
Lección trigésima tercera - El subjuntivo 195
Lección trigésima cuarta - El infinitivo 201
Lección trigésima quinta - Participio y gerundio 207
Lección trigésima sexta - Verbos impersonales 214
Lección trigésima séptima - Preposiciones 223
Lección trigésima octava - Conjunciones e interjecciones 233
Lección trigésima novena - Auxiliares repetidos 241

PRÓLOGO

Las diez ediciones de la *Gramática sucinta de la lengua inglesa*, de LUIGI PAVIA, aparecidas en el transcurso de treinta años dentro de la colección Gaspey-Otto-Sauer, para el estudio de las lenguas modernas, atestiguan la bondad del método empleado y el acierto que presidió en la adaptación y redacción confiada al mencionado profesor.

Sin embargo, el tiempo transcurrido imponía una revisión profunda que, manteniendo lo que era esencial en el método Gaspey-Otto-Sauer, colocara la obra al nivel de un lector de nuestros días. Resultaba sumamente difícil lograr un perfecto equilibrio entre las dos exigencias impuestas. Por una parte, la de conservar vivas y operantes las cualidades eminentemente pedagógicas del método apuntado. Por otra parte, actualizar los textos utilizados y modernizar las explicaciones teóricas al compás de los grandes progresos realizados en el campo filológico. La Editorial ha tenido el privilegio de poner a contribución para esta delicadísima tarea la competencia y la experiencia docente de una distinguida profesora que, en realidad, brinda a los estudiosos de España e Hispanoamérica una obra que puede considerarse enteramente nueva, aun cuando conserva muchos rasgos fundamentales de la gramática inglesa según el método Gaspey-Otto-Sauer, sobre todo en su versión original alemana.

La autora ha puesto especial cuidado en adoptar, para facilidad del estudioso, el sistema de transcripción fonética, hoy generalizado por la Asociación Fonética Internacional. El principiante hallará condensada en unas pocas páginas la fonología comparada del inglés y el castellano. La clasificación de los fonemas de la lengua inglesa se apoya en la adoptada por el profesor DANIEL JONES en su *Outline of English Phonetics* (Cambridge, [8]1956).

Era no menos urgente actualizar el vocabulario fundamental empleado en la obra, suprimiendo las palabras que habían ido cayendo en desuso y añadiendo el acervo de palabras nuevas que el progreso de la técnica y la transformación operada en la vida moderna han ido constituyendo. Tal actualización del vocabulario ha ido acompañada de un completo remozamiento de la parte práctica, destinada a ejercitar al estudiante y a dotarlo insensiblemente del léxico más indispensable y de los giros más corrientes que le permitan rápidamente iniciarse en la traducción de textos más extensos. En este terreno, la labor realizada por la autora resulta sumamente eficaz. Los ejercicios insisten especialmente en los aspectos gramaticales que, de modo sucinto, el lector encuentra desarrollados en el texto. La repetición de las estructuras básicas, multiplicando los ejemplos, ayuda enormemente el aprendizaje de la lengua, el cual, por otra parte, es facilitado mediante lecturas sabiamente graduadas, fragmentos de diálogo y de conversación sencilla, sobre temas actuales, y fragmentos tomados de la lengua coloquial o de la poesía, destinados especialmente a la memorización. El conjunto se enriquece además con numerosos ejercicios destinados a agilizar al estudiante en la conjugación y uso apropiado de los tiempos y modos verbales. Un vocabulario inglés-español y español-inglés está destinado a facilitar la ejecución de los ejercicios de versión y tema que sucesivamente se proponen al estudiante.

La Editorial espera que la presente obra contribuirá no poco al fin propuesto, que es el de facilitar el estudio y la difusión de la lengua inglesa aprovechando las enormes ventajas que brinda el método Gaspey-Otto-Sauer.

PRONUNCIACIÓN

El alfabeto inglés consta de 26 letras, pero como la escritura inglesa dista mucho de ser fonética, algunas de estas letras representan más de un sonido, en tanto que un sonido dado puede escribirse de muy diversas maneras.

Así tenemos, por ejemplo, que la letra «a» es un fonema distinto, es decir, se pronuncia diferente, en cada una de las palabras «father», «call», «Mary», «man», «was»; en tanto que, a pesar de su ortografía distinta, «ee», «ea», «ei», «ey», «e», «i» son el mismo fonema, o sea tienen idéntico sonido, en «feet», «mean», «receive», «key», «he», «machine». Por lo tanto, siendo la fonética inglesa tan irregular, el uso de una transcripción que la facilite resulta casi indispensable.

Cada grupo o familia de sonidos, esto es, cada uno de los sonidos que ocurren en una palabra junto con las variantes del mismo que puedan tener lugar en determinada secuencia, se llama fonema; y cada fonema se representa por un símbolo determinado tal como se pronuncia independientemente de su ortografía.

El sistema adoptado en esta gramática es el de la Asociación Fonética Internacional, que es el más empleado en Inglaterra; y todas las voces en ella usadas van seguidas de los símbolos que representan su pronunciación exacta.

Las letras del alfabeto inglés, con la pronunciación que corresponde a cada una de ellas, son las siguientes:

A	B	C	D	E	F	G	H	I
ei	*bi:*	*si:*	*di:*	*i:*	*ef*	*dʒi:*	*eitʃ*	*ai*
J	K	L	M	N	O	P	Q	R
dʒei	*kei*	*el*	*em*	*en*	*ou*	*pi:*	*kju:*	*a:**
S	T	U	V	W	X	Y	Z	
es	*ti:*	*ju:*	*vi:*	*'dʌblju:*	*eks*	*wai*	*zed*	

Las vocales

En inglés hay doce vocales puras, o monoptongos, cuyos símbolos fonéticos exponemos a continuación:

1) i: see, tea, people, meet, meter, machine, believe, receive.
2) i did, it, city, before, is, Sunday, money, mountain, manage.
3) e yes, lesson, meant, ready, many.
4) æ bad, man, apple, grammar.
5) a: father, class, car, park, can't, half, laugh, clerk.
6) ɔ on, not, want, dog.
7) ɔ: walk, saw, wall, war, daughter, saucer, before, fourth, door, cord.
8) u pull, should, would, room, took, good.
9) u: too, moon, who, blue, you, to, rude, student *[ju]*.
10) ʌ but, husband, much, son, some, understand, country, colour, enough, sunny.
11) ə: verb, err, burn, sir, thirty, word, work, learn, Turkey, third, early, journey, Blackburn.
12) ə again, o'clock, mother, collect, cinema, theatre, sailor, colour, sentence, colossus, lustrous.

i: La vocal *i:* de «see», «tea» es más larga y cerrada que la «i» española.
i La «i» de «did», «it» es más corta y más relajada que la «i» española. Se parece a la «i» de la palabra española «timbre», pero es aún más abierta.
e La «e» de «let» es siempre breve. Se parece a la «e» española de «papel», pero es algo más abierta.
æ Este fonema no existe en español, pero se aproxima a la «a» palatal de «valle», «baile». Es siempre un sonido breve.
a: Es siempre un sonido largo que se aproxima a la «a» velar de «bajo», pero es más largo y algo más velar.
ɔ Este sonido es siempre breve, mucho más abierto que el de la «o» española y se pronuncia con los labios mucho menos ovalados. Parece un sonido intermedio entre la «a» larga velar y la «o».
ɔ: Es siempre una vocal larga, más abierta que la «o» española de «rosa». Los labios, al pronunciar este fonema, estarán menos abocinados que en la «o» española.
u Sonido breve, como el de la «u» española, pero más abierto.
u: Es una vocal larga; se pronuncia con los labios abocinados y las mandíbulas más cerradas que para la «u» española.
ʌ Este fonema no existe en español. Se parece a la «a» palatal de «padre». En realidad, es un sonido intermedio entre *a:* y *ə:*, y debe adquirirse por imitación directa.
ə: Tampoco tiene equivalencia en español. Es un sonido intermedio entre los de «e», «o», «i», pero no se parece,

en realidad, a ninguno de ellos. Es siempre largo y sólo puede adquirirse por imitación directa.

Muy semejante a la anterior, pero siempre breve y débil. Podría compararse a una expiración sonora de aire. Se emplea con mucha frecuencia en sustitución de otras vocales en sílaba no acentuada. Es, por consiguiente, el fonema más usado en el habla inglesa.

Los diptongos

En inglés hay doce diptongos, cuyos símbolos fonéticos y valor mostramos a continuación:

13) ei they, baby, Spain, vein.
14) ou no, those, only, below, over.
15) ai mine, eye, my, kind.
16) au how, noun, house, out.
17) ɔi boy, noise, choice, employ.
18) iə (empieza con una «i» breve y evoluciona hacia ə) near, here, hear, idea, beer.
19) εə (empieza con una «e» abierta y evoluciona hacia ə) there, pair, pear, care, hair, wear, affair.
20) ɔə (empieza con una vocal muy parecida a ɔː y evoluciona hacia ə) pour, tore, more, store.
21) uə (empieza con una u breve y evoluciona hacia ə) sure, poor, tour.
22) ĭə (se parece al diptongo número 18, pero es siempre átono o débil) audience [ˈɔːdĭəns], variable [ˈvɛərĭəbl], happier [ˈhæpĭə], Victoria [vikˈtɔːrĭə].
23) ŭə (se parece al diptongo número 21, pero es siempre átono o débil) penury [ˈpenjŭəri], neurologist [ˈnjŭəˈrɔlədʒist], arduous [ˈɑːdjŭəs], valuable [ˈvæljŭəbl], usual [ˈjuʒŭəl], puerility [pjŭəˈriliti], influence [ˈinflŭəns].
24) ŭi (siempre débil; es bastante frecuente, pero como se parece a la pronunciación disilábica de «u» seguida de «i», no es necesario que los estudiantes lo diferencien fonéticamente de estos sonidos) valuing [ˈvæljŭiŋ], ruination [rŭiˈneiʃn].

Muchas personas de habla inglesa no suelen diferenciar, en conversación rápida, los diptongos 22 y 23 de los 18 y 21 respectivamente; por lo tanto, en una transcripción fonética amplia suelen transcribirse por el mismo símbolo.

Las consonantes

Los símbolos del alfabeto fonético correspondientes a las consonantes son los siguientes:

1) *p* *p*in, o*p*en, la*p*.
2) *b* *b*e, *b*all, *b*ut, ro*b*.
3) *t* *t*en, *t*ree, po*t*, be*tt*er.
4) *d* *d*id, ma*d*am, *d*o.
5) *k* *c*at, *c*lass, *k*ing, ro*ck*.
6) *g* *g*ive, *g*olf, ba*g*, e*gg*, ea*g*le.
7) *f* *f*ive, sa*f*e, *ph*iloso*ph*y, rou*gh* [rʌf].
8) *v* *v*an, sa*v*e, gi*v*e, pre*v*ent.
9) θ *th*in, no*th*ing, tru*th*.
10) ð *th*ere, wi*th*, hi*th*er.
11) *s* *s*on, *s*poon, *s*leep, *C*icely, cap*s*.
12) *z* *z*oo, play*s*, tree*s*, ea*s*y.
13) ʃ *sh*oe, fi*sh*, *s*ugar, ma*ch*ine.
14) ʒ trea*s*ure, lei*s*ure, presti*g*e.
15) tʃ *ch*in, ea*ch*, pic*t*ure.
16) dʒ *J*ane, a*g*e, bri*dg*e, *G*eorge (es el sonido de «g» y de «j» seguidas de «e», «i»).
17) *h* *h*ave, *wh*o, per*h*aps, *h*ill.
18) *m* *m*an, co*m*e, co*mm*and, swi*m*.
19) *n* *n*o, su*n*, wi*n*dow, *n*i*n*e, *kn*ee.
20) ŋ so*ng*, E*ng*land, lo*ng*er, i*nk*.
21) *r* *r*ed, *r*ock, ve*r*y, Ma*r*y, fa*r* [fɑːˑ].
22) *l* *l*ast, *l*et, fee*l*, fe*ll*, cei*l*ing.

p   Más oclusiva, esto es, se pronuncia con mayor fuerza que la española. Es aspirada al principio de sílaba acentuada, pronunciándose seguida de una ligera expiración del aire: «paper» [pʰeipəˑ]. Es muda en los grupos iniciales «pt», «pn», «ps»: pneumatic [njuˈmætik], psychology [saiˈkɔlədʒi], Ptolemy [ˈtɔləmi].

b   Es muy semejante a la «b» inicial española después de pausa, pero se pronuncia con mayor fuerza que ésta. Es muda en posición final precedida de «m»: dumb [dʌm], y en algunas palabras delante de «t»: debt [det].

t   Se diferencia de la «t» española en que se pronuncia apoyando la punta de la lengua en los alvéolos superiores. Únicamente cuando precede a θ o ð se adelanta la punta de la lengua hasta detrás de los dientes. A principio de sílaba acentuada se pronuncia seguida de una ligera aspiración: time [tʰaim].

d   Se pronuncia con la punta de la lengua contra los alveólos superiores. La punta de la lengua *no* debe tocar los dientes al pronunciarla. La «d» fricativa española de «rueda» no existe en inglés.

k	Semejante a la española. La «k» inicial de sílaba acentuada es también aspirada: come [kʰʌm]. Es muda delante de «n»: knee [niː]. La «x» se pronuncia generalmente [ks]: box [bɔks] (véase la «g»).
g	Semejante a la «g» oclusiva española delante de «a», «o», «u», como, por ejemplo, en la palabra «gallo». La «x» se pronuncia [gz] en el prefijo «ex» seguido de vocal acentuada (se exceptúan las palabras que empiezan por «exc»).
f	Semejante a la española.
v	Se pronuncia apoyando los dientes superiores sobre el labio inferior y expirando el aire por los intersticios entre ambos. La «v» es una consonante sonora. No debe, pues, confundirse con la «f», que es sorda.
θ	Se parece a la «z» española en la palabra «Zamora». Este sonido, como el siguiente, corresponde ortográficamente al grupo «th».
ð	Este sonido no existe en español. Se parece bastante a la «z» de la palabra «hallazgo», o a una «d» fricativa muy exagerada. Es más interdental y menos relajado, no obstante, que el de la «d» española en «moda».
s	Semejante a la «s» española cuando está en posición inicial.
z	Corresponde también a «s» no inicial y a «z» ortográficas: rose [rouz], zoo [zuː]. Es una consonante sonora que no tiene equivalencia en español y debe, por lo tanto, adquirirse por imitación directa. Se parece a la «s» francesa de «maison» y a la catalana de «rosa».
	La «s» ortográfica se pronuncia s en los siguientes casos: en posición inicial: sister ['sistə*]; en el plural y la 3.ª persona del presente de indicativo de los verbos cuando sigue a una consonante sorda, es decir, p, t, k, f, θ: caps [kæps], cats [kæts], takes [teiks]; en posición final precedida de «i, a, o, u, y»: house [haus], this [ðis]. Son excepciones a la regla anterior las flexiones verbales: was [wəz], has [hæz], flies [flaiz], etc., y las palabras his [hiz], as [æz], y unas pocas más. La «c» seguida de «e, i, y» también se pronuncia s: face [feis]. La «s» es muda en algunas palabras, como: isle [ail].
	Se pronuncia z la «s» ortográfica de los plurales cuyo singular termine en vocal o consonante sonora, es decir, todas menos p, t, k, f, θ; también en la 3.ª persona del singular de los verbos cuando éstos terminen en vocal o en consonante sonora; en otras palabras, la «s» final se pronuncia z cuando sigue a «e» no muda.
ʃ	No tiene equivalencia exacta en español, pero su timbre se parece a la fricación de la última parte de la «ch» española de la palabra «techo».
ʒ	Es un sonido parecido al anterior, pero sonoro.
tʃ	Muy semejante a la «ch» española, pero la segunda parte, esto es, la fricación, es más larga y menos aguda que en el sonido español.
dʒ	Muy semejante al anterior, pero sonoro.
h	Es una fricación sorda muy débil que se produce expirando

libremente el aire de los pulmones con la boca ya dispuesta para pronunciar la vocal que le sigue. *No* es una «j» española; su sonido es mucho más suave. Defecto muy corriente entre los españoles que hablan inglés es el de pronunciarla demasiado parecida a la «j».

m   Semejante a la española. Es muda en el grupo «mn»: mnemonic *[niː'mɔnik]*.

n   Semejante a la española. Con frecuencia es silábica con «t» y «d» precedentes, pronunciándose sin ninguna vocal intermedia: button *['bʌtn]*, eaten *['iːtn]*.

ŋ   Sonido muy semejante al de la «n» sonora española de las palabras «cinco», «pongo». Corresponde al grupo «ng» y con frecuencia a «n» delante de «k» y «g».

r   Se pronuncia elevando la punta de la lengua hacia la parte de atrás de los alvéolos superiores y dejándola caer en seguida sin tocarlos y casi sin fricación. Formando los grupos *pr*, *tr*, *kr*, *fr*, *θr*, *ʃr*, la fricación es más acusada. El fonema *r* se pronuncia así cuando le sigue una vocal. *No* se pronuncia nunca delante de una consonante o en posición final, a no ser que la siga una palabra que empiece por vocal.

l   Delante de vocal y del sonido correspondiente al símbolo fonético *j*, es semejante a la «l» española. Delante de consonante y de «e» muda, y en posición final, se pronuncia una «l» velar oscura parecida a la «l» catalana. Esta «l» oscura puede formar sílaba por sí sola sin ninguna otra vocal, es decir, puede ser silábica, como en: people *['pipl]*, table *['teibl]*. La «l» es muda en algunas palabras misceláneas: palm *[paːm]*, half *[haːf]*, walk *[wɔːk]*, could *[kud]*, would *[wud]*, should *[ʃud]*, etc.

Semivocales

La lengua inglesa tiene dos letras semivocales, cuyos símbolos fonéticos son los siguientes:

1) *w*   *w*all, *w*ell, *wh*ere, t*w*elve.
2) *j*   *y*es, *y*oung, n*ew*, p*u*re.

    w   Se pronuncia como una «u» con los labios muy redondeados, pasándose rápidamente a la vocal siguiente. La pronunciación del grupo «wh» como «hw», o simplemente como una consonante sorda, es empleada por mucha gente, especialmente en Escocia, Irlanda y norte de Inglaterra: what *[wɔt ('hwɔt)]*. Es muda delante de «r»: write *[rait]*.

    j   Corresponde a «y» ortográfica. Se pronuncia como una «i» muy breve de la que se pasa rápidamente a la vocal siguiente. Es un poco más relajada y abierta que la «y» española. Con frecuencia se inserta este sonido delante de «ue», «ui», «ew», «eu», «u» cuando la «u» es larga: few *[fjuː]*, new *[njuː]*.

FIRST LESSON   LECCIÓN PRIMERA

El artículo

El artículo determinado «the» es invariable, y se usa esta única forma para el masculino, femenino, singular y plural. Se pronuncia [ðə] delante de consonante; delante de vocal que no tenga el sonido [juː] y en forma enfática, se pronuncia [ði].

the pupil ðə 'pjuːpil	el alumno	the arm ði 'aːm	el brazo
the wall ðə 'wɔːl	la pared	the ink ði 'iŋk	la tinta
the new book	el libro	the old book	el libro
ðə 'njuː 'buk	nuevo	ði 'ould 'buk	viejo
the unit ðə 'juːnit	la unidad		

Delante de «h» aspirada se pronuncia también [ðə], pero delante de «h» muda se pronuncia [ði].

the house ðə 'haus	la casa	the hour ði 'auə*	la hora

El artículo indeterminado es «a» [ei, ə]; pero se cambia en «an» [ən] delante de «h» muda, de vocal cuyo sonido no sea [juː] y de «y» semiconsonante.

a pupil ə 'pjuːpil	un alumno	an arm ən 'aːm	un brazo
a house ə 'haus	una casa	an hour ən 'auə	una hora
a unit ə 'juːnit	una unidad	an uncle ən 'ʌnkl	un tío
a new book	un libro	an old book	un libro
ə 'njuː 'buk	nuevo	ən 'ould 'buk	viejo

El artículo indeterminado no tiene plural, pero en su lugar se usa un adjetivo indefinido:

some 'sʌm pupils	algunos alumnos	any 'eni pupils	algunos alumnos

TO BE tu bi: ser o estar		
I am *ai æm* yo soy, estoy	we are *wi: a:* *	nos. somos, estamos
you are *ju: a:* * tú eres, estás	you are *ju: a:* *	vos. sois, estáis
he is *hi: iz* él es, está	they are *ðei a:* *	ellos son, están
she is *ʃi: iz* ella es, está		
it is *it iz* ello es, está		

Corrientemente se usa en forma abreviada:

I'm *ai(ə)m*	we're *wiə* *
you're *juə* *	you're *juə* *
he's *hi:z*, she's *ʃi:z*, it's *its*	they're *ðeiə* *

Forma interrogativa		Forma negativa	
Am I?	¿Soy yo?, ¿estoy yo?, etc.	I am not.	Yo no soy, estoy, etc.
Are you?		You are not.	
Is he?		He is not.	
Is she?		She is not.	
Is it?		It is not.	
Are we?		We are not.	
Are you?		You are not.	
Are they?		They are not.	

Words Vocabulario

and *ænd, ənd*	y	on *ɔn*	en, encima de, sobre
book *buk*	libro	platform *'plætfɔ:m*	plataforma
ceiling *'si:liŋ*	techo	pupil *'pju:pil*	alumno, -a
door *dɔ:* *	puerta	room *ru:m*	habitación
England *'iŋglənd*	Inglaterra	schoolroom *'sku:lru(:)m*	clase
floor *flɔ:* *	suelo	table *teib(ə)l*	mesa
here *hiə* *	aquí	teacher *'ti:tʃə* *	profesor
in *in*	en	that *ðæt*	ese, esa, aquel-lla
ink *iŋk*	tinta	there *ðɛə* *	allí
map *mæp*	mapa	this *ðis*	este, esta
master *'ma:stə* *	maestro, amo	too *tu:*	también
no *nou*	no	wall *wɔ:l*	pared, muro
not *nɔt*	no	what? *(h)wɔt*	¿qué?
of *ɔv, əv*	de		

where *(h)wɛə**	dónde	window *'windou*	ventana
who *hu:*	quien	yes *jes*	sí

Nota. El verbo «ser» precedido del adverbio «there» forma el impersonal «haber»:

there is *ðɛər iz, ðɛəz*   hay (singular)
there are *ðɛər a:*, ðɛərə**   hay (plural)
is there?   ¿hay?
there is not   no hay

Exercise   Ejercicio

Who are you? I am a pupil. Where are you? I am in the room. Who is in the room? The teacher is in the room and I am in the room, too. Where is the pupil? He is in the schoolroom. Who is he? He is the teacher. Are you the teacher? No, I am not the teacher: I am the pupil. What is that? That is the window and this is the door. And what is that? It is a map. Here is a map, too. Where is the map? The map is on the wall. It is a map of England. Here is a table. On the table there is a book. Is this ink? Yes, this is ink and that is the map. Where is the book? The book is on the table, the table is on the platform, the platform is in the schoolroom, the schoolroom is in the school, and the school is in England. Is the map on the table? No, it is not; it is on the wall. Is there a book on the floor? No, it is not on the floor; it is on the table. Where is the ceiling? The ceiling is there.

Who are you? I'm a pupil. Is this a book? No, it's not; it's a map. I'm a pupil and you're a teacher. Is she the teacher? No, she isn't; she's a pupil.

Conversation   Conversación

Where is the book? Where is the door? Where is the map? Where is the wall? Where is the master? Where are you? What is there on the table? What is there on the floor? What is there on the wall? Is there a map on the table? Where is the map? Who are you? Are you the pupil? Is he the teacher? Is she here? Is the window in the ceiling? Where is the window?

Ejercicio

¿Dónde estamos? Estamos en la clase. ¿Están ellos también en la clase? Sí, ellos están también en la clase. ¿Dónde está la puerta? La puerta está en la pared. Esto es una ventana. La habitación está en el colegio. Encima de la mesa hay un libro. En el suelo no hay un libro; el libro está en la mesa. Eso es un mapa, eso es una ventana y aquello es una ventana. El profesor está aquí y el alumno está allí. ¿Dónde está el profesor? Está aquí, y el alumno también está aquí. ¿Están el alumno y el profesor en clase? Sí, están aquí. ¿Dónde estás tú? Estoy aquí, y ella también está aquí. ¿Dónde está el mapa de Inglaterra? Está en la pared.

Conjugate:

a] I am in the schoolroom, you are in..., etc
b] Am I in the room? Are you in...?, etc.
c] Where am I? Where are you?, etc.
d] Where am I? You are in the room, etc.
e] Where are you? I am on the platform, etc.

SECOND LESSON   LECCIÓN SEGUNDA

El número de los substantivos

El plural de los nombres en inglés se forma añadiendo una «s» al singular. Dicha «s» se pronuncia de distinta manera según la letra en que termine el singular. La regla es la siguiente: *a)* cuando el singular termina en *p, t, k, f, th*, la «s» del plural es sorda, parecida a «s» castellana; *b)* si el singular termina en vocal o en las demás consonantes, la «s» del plural es sonora.

Singular

map *mæp*   mapa
hat *hæt*   sombrero
book *buk*   libro
plate *pleit* plato
roof *ru:f*   tejado
cap *cæp*   gorra

Plural

maps *mæps*
hats *hæts*
books (etc.)
plates
roofs
caps

El número de los substantivos

Singular		Plural
cab *kæb*	coche	cabs *kabz*
bed *bed*	cama	beds (etc.)
leg *leg*	pierna, pata	legs
boy *bɔi*	niño	boys
name *neim*	nombre	names

Las palabras que terminan en *s*, *ss*, *sh*, *ch*, *x*, *z* forman el plural añadiendo la sílaba «es» [*iz*], cuya «s» se pronuncia sonora. Las que terminan en *e* muda precedida de *s*, *c*, *z*, *g* suprimen dicha *e* antes de añadir la sílaba «es».

Singular		Plural
class *klaːs*	clase	classes *klaːsiz*
dish *diʃ*	plato, fuente	dishes *diʃiz*
box *bɔks*	caja	boxes *bɔksiz*
watch *wɔtʃ*	reloj	watches *wɔtʃiz*
nose *nouz*	nariz	noses *nouziz*
sponge *spʌndʒ*	esponja	sponges *spʌndʒiz*
piece *piːs*	pedazo	pieces *piːsiz*
face *feis*	cara	faces *feisiz*

Las palabras terminadas en *o* precedida de consonante forman el plural añadiendo la sílaba «es». Si la *o* está precedida de vocal toman solamente una «s». Algunas palabras extranjeras terminadas en *o* precedida de consonante añaden sólo «s».

Singular		Plural
potato *pə'teitou*	patata	potatoes *pə'teitouz*
tomato *tə'maːtou*	tomate	tomatoes *tə'maːtouz*
echo *'ekou*	eco	echoes *'ekouz*
hero *'hiərou*	héroe	heroes *'hiərouz*
duo *'dju(ː)ou*	dúo	duos *'dju(ː)ouz*
halo *'heilou*	aureola	halos *'heilouz*
tobacco *tə'bækou*	tabaco	tobaccos *təbækouz*

Algunos nombres de origen sajón terminados en *f* o en *fe* cambian la *f* en «v» antes de tomar la sílaba «es».

Singular		Plural
calf *kaːf*	ternera	calves *kaːvz*
elf *elf*	duende	elves (etc.)
leafe *liːf*	hoja	leaves
loaf *louf*	pan (uno entero)	loaves
self *self*	mismo	selves

Singular		Plural
sheaf ʃiːf	gavilla	sheaves
shelf ʃelf	estante	shelves
staff staːf	palo	staves
thief θiːf	ladrón	thieves
wharf wɔːf	muelle	wharves
wolf wulf	lobo	wolves
wife waif	esposa	wives
life laif	vida	lives
knife naif	cuchillo	knives

Los nombres terminados en *y* precedida de consonante cambian aquélla en «i» antes de añadir la terminación «es». Cuando la *y* está precedida de vocal añaden simplemente una «s».

Singular		Plural
sky *skai*	firmamento	skies *skaiz*
body *bodi*	cuerpo	bodies (etc.)
lady *leidi*	señora	ladies
boy *bɔi*	niño, muchacho, chico	boys *bɔiz*
day *dei*	día	days (etc.)
key *kiː*	llave	keys

Nota: «House» [haus] tiene el plural «houses» [hauziz].

TO HAVE *hæv* tener o haber

Yo tengo, yo he, etc.	*¿Tengo yo?, ¿he yo?*, etc.
I have *hæv*	have I?
you have	have you?
he ⎫	⎧ he?
she ⎬ has *hæz*	has ⎨ she?
it ⎭	⎩ it?
we have	have we?
you have	have you?
they have	have they?

Nota: En la conversación, se abrevia ordinariamente de la siguiente manera:

«I've», por «I have»; «you've», por «you have»; «we've», por «we have»; «they've», por «they have».

El número de los substantivos

La forma negativa se hace poniendo el adverbio «not» después del verbo: «I have not» [ai hæv nɔt], «you have not», etc., que ordinariamente se contrae en «haven't» [hæv(ə)nt], «hasn't» [hæz(ə)nt].

Words

also 'ɔ(:)lsou	también
behind bi'haind	detrás
bench bentʃ	banco
blackboard 'blækbɔ:d	pizarra
box bɔks	caja
bring briŋ	traer
but bʌt	pero
chair tʃɛə*	silla
chalk tʃɔ:k	yeso
class kla:s	clase
classroom 'kla:sru(:)m	clase (habitación, aula)
count kaunt	contar
desk desk	pupitre, escritorio
duster 'dʌstə*	borrador
exercise 'eksəsaiz	ejercicio
exercise-book 'eksəsaizbuk	cuaderno
for fɔ:*, fə*	para, por

form fɔ:m	clase, forma
girl gə:l	niña, muchacha
how many 'hau 'meni	¿cuántos?
in	en
only 'ounli	sólo, solamente
our auə*	nuestro, nuestra, -os, -as
pen pen	pluma
pencil pensil	lápiz
pencil-case 'pensilkeis	plumier
penholder 'penhouldə*	mango
satchel 'sætʃəl	cartera
school sku:l	colegio, escuela
schoolroom 'sku:lru(:)m	clase, aula
sponge spʌndʒ	esponja
under 'ʌndə*	debajo

Numerals — Numerales

Cardinal numbers — Cardinales

1 one wʌn
2 two tu:
3 three θri:
4 four fɔ:*
5 five faiv
6 six siks

7 seven 'sevən
8 eight eit
9 nine nain
10 ten ten
11 eleven i'levən
12 twelve twelv

Reading exercise — Lectura

We are at school. This is our school. Our school has four walls, two windows and a door. There are four walls and a ceiling. There is also a door. There are desks for the pupils. There is also a platform. It is for the teacher. One, two, three, four. How many walls are there in the classroom? Four. In the classroom there are four walls. Are

there many doors? There is only one door and one window.
Behind the desk there is a chair. Bring the chair. The chair
is for the teacher. Bring the master the chalk. What has the
master on the table? He has books, a pen, a pencil and
chalk. Behind the chair there is a window. The blackboard
is behind the desk and the bench is behind the table. The
pupil has a satchel for the books. We also have satchels
for our books, and for our pens and pencils and rubbers.
In the classroom there is a blackboard for the pupils and
under the blackboard there is chalk. There is a box for the
chalk, the sponge and the duster.

Conversation

Where are you? Who is in the schoolroom? What is
there in a schoolroom for the teacher? Who is the teacher?
How many windows are there in this room? How many
pencils are there here? How many pupils are there in that
class? Have you a satchel? Has the teacher a satchel, too?
How many books have you here? Have you three pencils?
Where is the chalk? How many pencils have you in your
pencil box? Are you a boy or a girl? Is the teacher a boy?
Are you in the classroom?

Ejercicio

Nuestra clase tiene cuatro paredes, una ventana y dos
puertas. ¿Cuántas ventanas tiene la clase? Tiene sólo una.
Tiene también una mesa y diez pupitres. La mesa es para
el profesor; los pupitres son para los niños. Los alumnos
tienen un banco, un pupitre y una cartera para los libros,
los lápices y la goma de borrar. La niña tiene un cuaderno.
Nosotros también tenemos cuadernos. Son nuestros cuadernos. Debajo de la pizarra están la esponja y un borrador
en una caja. ¿Dónde está la pizarra? Está detrás de la
mesa del profesor. El profesor tiene la tiza; los alumnos tienen plumas y tinta. ¿Tienen los alumnos tiza? No, ellos
tienen sólo plumas y lápices.

Conjugate:

    a) I have an exercise book, you have..., etc.
    b) How many books have you?, has he?, etc.
    c) I have not a pencil, you have not..., etc.

THIRD LESSON   LECCIÓN TERCERA

Plurales irregulares

a) Los siguientes nombres forman el plural añadiendo la sílaba «en»:

Singular		Plural
ox ɔks	buey	oxen ɔksən
cow kau	vaca	cows kauz
child tʃaild	niño, -a	children tʃildrən
brother 'brʌðə*	hermano	brothers o brethren 'brʌðəz, 'breðrin

«Brethren» se refiere a hermanos o miembros de una cofradía o sociedad.

b) Algunas palabras sufren un cambio en la vocal y no toman sufijo alguno:

Singular		Plural
man mæn	hombre	men men
woman 'wumən	mujer	women 'wimin
tooth tu:θ	diente	teeth ti:θ
foot fut	pie	feet fi:t
louse laus	piojo	lice lais
mouse maus	ratón	mice mais
goose gu:s	ganso	geese gi:s

c) Algunos nombres tienen el plural igual al singular:

swine swain	puerco	grouse graus	gallina silvestre
deer diə*	ciervo	salmon 'sæmən	salmón
sheep ʃi:p	cordero	cod kɔd	bacalao

Así decimos: «a deer, a herd of deer (un rebaño de ciervos); a sheep, a flock of sheep» (un rebaño de ovejas), etc.

d) Algunas medidas, pesos y distancias se suelen usar sin flexión de plural:

a 3 mile walk mail wɔ:k	un paseo de 3 millas
a 5 foot wall fu:t wɔ:l	una pared de 5 pies
a 5 pound note paund nout	un billete de 5 libras

e) Hay palabras que, aun cuando por su forma son del singular, se usan siempre con sentido plural:

people *'pi:pl*	gente
poultry *'poultri*	aves de corral
cattle *'kætl*	ganado
gentry *'dʒentri*	nobleza, aristocracia

f) Hay nombres que se usan siempre como plurales aunque originalmente son singulares:

alms *a:mz*	limosna
riches *ritʃiz*	riqueza
skates *skeits*	patines

g) Por el contrario, otros nombres que son verdaderos plurales se emplean como si fueran singulares:

means *mi:nz*	medios
news *nju:z*	noticias

h) Un número de palabras varias suelen emplearse en plural casi siempre. Son nombres de cosas que constan de más de una parte, o que indican pluralidad:

trousers *'trauzez*	pantalones
spectacles *'spektəklz*	lentes
scissors *'sizəz*	tijeras
ashes *æʃiz*	ceniza
thanks *θæŋks*	gracias
sweets *swi:ts*	caramelos

i) Algunas palabras terminadas en *ics*, y que se refieren a ciencias o enfermedades, aun cuando son plurales, se suelen emplear como si fuesen singulares:

politics *'politiks*	política
physics *'fiziks*	física
hysterics *his'teriks*	histerismo

j) Los nombres propios y los apellidos forman el plural regularmente:

there are many Cæsars *meni si:zəz*	hay muchos Césares
the four Georges *dʒɔ:dʒis*	los cuatro Jorges
the Morrises *'mɔrisiz*	los Morris
the Wilsons *'wilsnz*	los Wilson

Plurales irregulares

k) Los adjetivos de nacionalidad, cuando se usan nominalmente, tienen el plural regular, a excepción de los que terminan en *ch*, *sh*, *ese*, *ss*, que son invariables:

French *frentʃ*	francés	Swiss *swis*	suizo
English *'iŋgliʃ*	inglés	Portuguese *'pɔːtjuˈgiːz*	portugués
Chinese *'tʃaiˈniːz*	chino	Japanese *'dʒæpəˈniːz*	japonés

l) Los nombres de nacionalidad que terminan en *man* lo cambian por «men»:

Singular *Plural*
Englishman *'ingliʃmən*   inglés   Englishmen *'ingliʃmən(-men)*
Frenchman *'frentʃmən*   francés   Frenchmen *'frentʃmən*
Scotsman *'skɔtsmən*   escocés   Scotsmen *'skɔtsmən*
Irishman *'aiərɪʃmən*   irlandés   Irishmen *'aiərɪʃmən*

Nota: La terminación *man* en la palabra «German» no corresponde al sufijo «hombre», sino a la terminación de «germano», y por lo tanto su plural será «Germans».

m) Algunas palabras tienen un doble plural con distinto significado:

Fish *fiʃ*
 { Fish, peces, pescado.
 { Fishes *fiʃiz*, distintas clases de peces.

Cloth *klɔθ*
 { Clothes *klouðz*, prendas de vestir.
 { Cloths *klɔθs*, paños sin confeccionar.

Penny *peni*
 { Pennies *peniz*, piezas de un penique.
 { Pence *pens*, valor propiamente dicho.

n) Las palabras compuestas forman el plural de acuerdo con las reglas siguientes:

La «s» del plural se añade a la palabra que sea sustantivo o que haga el oficio de tal. Si las dos palabras fueran sustantivos se pondrá en plural la que no se use como calificadora:

Singular
father-in-law *'faːðərinlɔː*   suegro
son-in-law *'sʌninlɔː*   yerno

Plural
fathers-in-law *'faːðəzinlɔː*
sons-in-law *'sʌnzinlɔː*

Singular		Plural
step-son 'stepsʌn	hijastro	step-sons 'stepsʌnz
commander-in-chief	comandante	commanders-in-chief
kə'maːndərin'tʃiːf	en jefe	kə'maːndəzin'tʃiːf

Unos cuantos nombres generalizados por la costumbre son excepción a la regla anterior, aunque también pueden seguirla:

Singular		Plural
spoonful 'spuːnful	cucharada	spoonfuls 'spuːnfulz
handful 'hændful	puñado	handfuls 'hændfulz
etc.		

Hay cuatro nombres que pueden considerarse como plurales dobles:

Singular		Plural
man-servant mæn 'səːvənt	criado	men-servants men 'səːvənts
woman-servant 'wumən 'səːvənt	criada	women-servants 'wimin 'səːvənts
Lord-justice lɔːd'dʒʌstis	presidente del tribunal	Lords-justices 'lɔːdz'dʒʌstisiz
Knight templar 'nait 'templə*	templario	Knights templars 'naits 'templəz

o) Los objetos que van en pares son generalmente plural y se les anteponen las palabras «a pair of» [ə pɛə* əv] «un par de»:

a pair of gloves ə pɛə* əv glʌvz   un par de guantes
a pair of tongs ə pɛə* əv tɔŋz   un par de tenazas

p) Cierto número de palabras tomadas directamente del latín, griego u otras lenguas modernas se usan con su plural de origen:

Singular		Plural
datum 'deitəm	dato	data 'deitə
analysis ə'næləsis	análisis	analyses ə'næləsiːz
crisis 'kraisis	crisis	crises 'kraisiːz
cherub 'tʃerəb	querubín	cherubim 'tʃerəbim

No obstante, se tiende a regularizarlos.

Plurales irregulares

Nota. Los nombres o adjetivos de nacionalidad se escriben con mayúscula: He is English.

Words

animal 'æniməl	animal	small smɔːl	pequeño
big *big*	grande	these ðiːz	estos, estas
doctor 'dɔktə*	médico	tree *triː*	árbol
green *griːn*	verde	very 'veri	muy
red *red*	rojo	white (h)wait	blanco

Exercise

The children have a fish. The wolf has sharp teeth. The wives of these men are here. The book has leaves. The tree has leaves, too. The leaves of the tree are green but the leaves of the book are not green: they are white. The roof of the house is red. The roofs of these houses are not red; they are green. Mice are small animals. They have white teeth. That child is small. He has only one tooth. These knives are not big. That man is a teacher. These men are not teachers; they are doctors. The child has a goose. It is a very big goose. There are very small geese, too. They are all white. Is that a woman? Yes, that is a woman. In this room there are two women, three men and five children.

Ejercicio

Las hojas de los árboles son verdes. ¿Son verdes también las hojas de los libros? No, las hojas de los libros son blancas. El niño tiene un palo muy grande. Los niños tienen dos pequeños ratones. Los gansos tienen dos patas, pero los perros tienen cuatro. El niño tiene un pie encima de la silla. ¿Cuántos pies tiene el niño? ¿Cuántas patas tiene un gato? El niño tiene un ganso blanco. ¿Cuántos gansos tiene el niño? Tiene solamente uno. ¿Tiene usted un hermano? Sí, tengo un hermano. Hay dos hombres en la casa; también hay un niño, dos niñas y tres mujeres. Encima de la mesa hay tres cajas. Esta caja es para lápices; esta caja es para la tiza y aquella caja es para la esponja y el borrador.

Pasado del verbo TO BE

Yo era o estaba

I was wɔz, wəz	we were
you were wɛə*, wə*	you were
he was	they were
I was not (etc.)	yo no era
Was I? (etc.)	¿era yo?

Pasado del verbo TO HAVE

Yo tenía o había

I had hæd, həd	we had
you had	you had
he had	they had
I had not (etc.)	yo no tenía
Had I? (etc.)	¿tenía yo?

En la conversación ordinaria las formas de estos verbos se abrevian como sigue: «wasn't» [wɔz(ə)nt] en lugar de «was not»; «weren't» [wɛənt] en lugar de «were not»; «hadn't» [hæd(ə)nt] en lugar de «had not».

Nota: «There was, there were», «había»; «was there?, were there?», «¿había?»; «there was not, there were not», «no había».

Reading exercise

Was that the teacher? No, that was not the teacher; that was a pupil. Where was the school? The school was in England. Was there a book on the table? Yes, on the table there was a book. Had you a map? Yes, I had a map. Had the pupils books? Yes, they had. Was the map on the floor? No, the map was not on the floor; it was on the wall. The teacher was not here; the pupil was there. She had a book in the classroom. Where was the map of England? The map of England was there. Had he an uncle? Yes, he had an uncle. Had the house a roof? The house had a roof. The houses had roofs. The chairs were in the room. Was the table in this room? No, it was not in this room. It was in that room.

Conversation

Where is the ceiling? Have you a staff? Where is the child? Are these knives big or small? Have you any teeth? Are teeth white? Are there any leaves on the trees? Are the leaves green? Are the leaves of books green or white? Have you a goose? Where is the roof? Are mice big animals? Has the small child a tooth? How many teeth have you?

Conjugate:

a) I had a big knife, etc.
b) Had I a white mouse?, etc.
c) I had not any brothers, etc.

FOURTH LESSON LECCIÓN CUARTA

El adjetivo

El adjetivo calificativo es invariable y precede al sustantivo. El adjetivo debe ir necesariamente seguido de un sustantivo o, en su defecto o para evitar repetición, del pronombre indefinido «one». Cuando el adjetivo sea predicado seguirá al verbo:

the good boy	el niño bueno
the big books	los libros grandes
I have a red pencil and a green one.	Tengo un lápiz rojo y uno verde.

pero diremos:

the child is good	el niño es bueno
the book is big	el libro es grande

Los adjetivos posesivos son los siguientes:

my *mai*	mi	our *auə**	nuestro, -a, -os, -as
your *juə**, *jɔː**	tu	your	vuestro, -a, -os, -as
his *hiz*	su (de él)	their *ðɛə**	su (de ellos), sus
her *həː**	su (de ella)		
its *its* (1)	su		

(1) Se refiere siempre a animales o cosas

Los adjetivos demostrativos son los siguientes:

this *ðis*	este, esta	these *ðiːs*	estos, estas
that *ðæt*	aquel, -lla; ese, esa	those *ðouz*	aquellos, -as; esos, esas

yon *jɔn*
yonder *'jɔndə* } aquel (a lo lejos)

Nota: Generalmente, «aquel» se traduce por «that over there».

this book is red these books are red
that book is red those books are red

yonder house is white
that house over there is white

El futuro de los verbos se forma por medio de los auxiliares «shall» [*ʃæl, ʃəl*] para la primera persona singular y plural, y «will» [*wil*] para las restantes. El condicional se forma con los auxiliares «should» [*ʃud*] para las primeras personas singular y plural, y «would» [*wud*] para las restantes:

Futuro	Condicional
Yo seré, estaré, etc.	*Yo sería, estaría, etc.*
I shall be	I should be
you will be	you would be
he will be	he would be
we shall be	we should be
you will be	you would be
they will be	they would be

El futuro y condicional de todos los verbos en inglés se construye según el anterior modelo.

La forma negativa se hace intercalando el adverbio de negación «not» entre el auxiliar y el verbo; y la forma

El adjetivo

interrogativa alternando el orden del sujeto y auxiliar respectivamente.

I shall not be.	No seré, no estaré.
Shall I be?	¿Seré yo? ¿estaré yo?
I should not be.	Yo no sería, estaría.
Should I be?	¿Sería yo? ¿estaría yo?

Nota; «Shall», pasado «should», es también un verbo defectivo que significa «debo» (véase pg. 188, «verbos anómalos»).

Conjugate:

a) I shall be diligent.
b) I should not be lazy.
c) Shall I have a new hat?
d) I shall not have a new book.
e) Should I be here?

Words

bad *bæd*	malo
black *blæk*	negro
blue *blu:*	azul
boot *bu:t*	bota
brown *braun*	marrón
cap *kæp*	gorra
clean *kli:n*	limpio
collar *kɔlə**	cuello
colour *kʌlə**	color
diligent *'dilidʒənt*	diligente, aplicado
dirty *'də:ti*	sucio
good *gud*	bueno
gray, grey *grei*	gris
green *gri:n*	verde
hat *hæt*	sombrero
idle *'aidəl*	perezoso
large *la:dʒ*	grande
lazy *leizi*	perezoso
look at *luk æt*	mira
I think so *ai θiŋk sou*	creo que sí
new *nju:*	nuevo
now *nau*	ahora
old *ould*	viejo
open *'oupən*	abierto
or *ɔ:*, ə**	o
paper *'peipə**	papel
piece *pi:s*	pedazo
quite *kwait*	completamente
red *red*	rojo, encarnado
shoe *ʃu:*	zapato
show me *ʃou mi*	enséñame, muéstrame
shut *ʃʌt*	cerrar
small *smɔ:l*	pequeño
tie *tai*	corbata
to-morrow *tə'mɔrou*	mañana
very *'veri*	muy
what? *(h)wɔt*	¿qué?
white *(h)wait*	blanco
wide *waid*	ancho (completamente)
yellow *'jelou*	amarillo

Exercise

This paper is white; that paper is not white. There are many colours. There is green paper and red paper. Look at that piece of paper. What colour is it?

This one is red, but that one is blue. What colour is this? It is black; it is red. He had a green tie and a white collar. It is very clean; it is not dirty. These girls had some old hats. Her hat was old but she has a new one now. Those boys have grey caps; their caps are grey, but her hat is not grey, it is red. Show me your shoes. What colour are they? They are brown. They are not black. They are not white. My tie is very old; your tie is new. Here is a good pen. It is your pen. My pen is not good; it is bad. Is this your room? Yes, it is. It is a large room. It has two windows. One of the windows is open now. It is wide open. The door is not open; it is shut. Good boys are diligent; bad boys are lazy. Are you a diligent or a lazy boy? I am a very good boy.

Conversation

What colour is the paper? Is your hat white? Is chalk red? And my pencil? And your tie? What colour is this book? And this door? Is this a collar? Where are your shoes? Are they brown? Is the window shut? Is it open? Are you diligent or lazy? Is the wall blue? Is it yellow? What colour is it?

Ejercicio

Mira: esto es un libro. Yo tengo un libro en la mesa y vosotros tendréis un libro encima del pupitre. Mi libro es azul. Vuestro libro no es azul. ¿De qué color es vuestro libro? Es encarnado y blanco. Esta corbata es nueva. Mira, ¡es también azul! Enséñame tu pluma. ¿Es nueva? Mi pluma no es nueva, es vieja. Mi pluma no es gris, es encarnada. Aquellas niñas tendrán zapatos nuevos. Serán marrón. ¿Quiénes son aquellos niños? Son mis alumnos. Tendrán plumas y cuadernos para sus ejercicios. Los cuadernos serán verdes, y las plumas, grises. ¿Tendrás tú también cuadernos nuevos para tu clase? Sí, creo que sí. ¿Estará abierta la puerta de la clase? Ahora está cerrada, pero mañana estará abierta.

FIFTH LESSON   LECCIÓN QUINTA

El género

En inglés, el género coincide con el sexo natural, o con la ausencia del mismo si se refiere a cosas inanimadas. Por lo tanto, son del género *masculino* o *femenino* todas las personas o animales de uno u otro sexo; del *neutro* todas las cosas en general. Hay además un género llamado *común* para indicar nombres que convienen indistintamente a uno u otro sexo.

Modos de denotar el género. a) Con distinta palabra para el masculino y el femenino; b) añadiendo una palabra que denote el género; c) por medio de la terminación *ess* añadida al masculino:

a) man *mæn* hombre
boy *bɔi* niño, muchacho
father *faːðə** padre
husband *'hʌsbənd* marido
brother *'brʌðə** hermano
nephew *'nevjuː* sobrino
uncle *ʌŋkl* tío
son *sʌn* hijo
king *kiŋ* rey
gentleman *'dʒent(ə)lmən* caballero, señor
male *meil* macho
boar *bɔə** cerdo
bull *bul* toro; ox buey
cock *kɔk* gallo
dog *dɔg* perro
drake *dreik* ánade (macho)
gander *'gændə** ganso, ánsar
ram *ræm* carnero, ariete
stag *stæg*, hart *haːt* ciervo
horse *hɔːs* caballo
fox, zorro

woman *'wumən* mujer
girl *gəːl* niña, muchacha
mother *'mʌðə** madre
wife *waif* esposa
sister *'sistə** hermana
niece *niːs* sobrina
aunt *aːnt* tía
daughter *'dɔːtə** hija
queen *kwiːn* reina
lady *'leidi* dama, señora

female *'fiːmeil* hembra
sow *sau* cerda
cow *kau* vaca
hen *hen* gallina
bitch *bitʃ* perra
duck *dʌk* ánade (hembra)
goose *guːs* gansa, oca (hembra)
ewe *juː* oveja
hind *haind* cierva
mare *mɛə** yegua
vixen, zorra

b) man-servant *səːvənt* criado
man-cook -*kuk* cocinero
orphan-boy *ɔːfən-* huérfano
male-child, niño

maid-servant *meid-* criada
woman-cook, cocinera
orphan-girl, huérfana
female-child, niña

boy-pupil ʹpjuːpl discípulo
male-elephant ʹelifənt elefante
cock-sparrow ʹspærou gorrión
he-goat gout macho cabrío, chivo
peacock ʹpiːkɔk pavo real
buck-rabbit ʹbʌk-ræbit conejo

girl-pupil, discípula
female-elephant, elefanta
hen-sparrow, gorriona
she-goat, cabra
peahen, pava real
doe-rabbit dou- coneja

c) abbot ʹæbət abad
actor ʹæktə* actor
author ʹɔːθə* autor
baron ʹbærən barón
duke djuːk duque
emperor ʹempərə* emperador
giant dʒaiənt gigante
God gɔd Dios
heir ɛə* heredero
hero ʹhiərou héroe
jew dʒuː judío
master ʹmaːstə* amo
negro ʹniːgrou negro
poet ʹpouit poeta
prince prins príncipe
shepherd ʹʃeped pastor
traitor ʹtreitə* traidor
lion ʹlaiən león
tiger ʹtaigə* tigre (macho)

abbess ʹæbis abadesa
actress ʹæktris actriz
authoress ʹɔːθəris autora
baroness ʹbærənis baronesa
duchess ʹdʌtʃis duquesa
empress ʹempris emperatriz
giantess, giganta
goddess, diosa
heiress ʹɛəris heredera
heroine ʹherouin heroína
jewess, judía
mistress ʹmistris ama
negress ʹniːgris negra
poetess ʹpouitis poetisa
princess prinʹses princesa
shepherdess ʹʃepədis pastora
traitress, ʹtreitris traidora
lioness, leona
tigress ʹtaigris tigre (hembra)

NB. Widower ʹwidouə* viudo; widow ʹwidou viuda.

Los nombres cuya pronunciación en el femenino no está indicada se pronunciarán como en el masculino más la terminación *ess*, que se pronuncia [is].

Nota: Como se verá, algunas palabras sufren una ligera modificación antes de añadir la sílaba «ess».

Son del género común:

parent ʹpɛərent padre, madre
 (plur.: parents, los padres)
cousin kʌzn primo, -a
friend frend amigo, -a
neighbour ʹneibə* vecino, -a
relation riʹleiʃen ⎱ pariente
relative ʹrelətiv ⎰
companion kəmʹpænjən compañero, -a

admirer ədʹmaiərə* admirador, -ra
traveller ʹtrævlə* viajero, -a
teacher ʹtiːtʃə* maestro, -a
witness ʹwitnis testigo
child tʃaild niño, -a (plur.: children ʹtʃildrən puede expresar «niños» y «niñas», «hijos» e «hijas»)

En ocasiones, las cosas inanimadas pueden personificarse, en cuyo caso, en lugar del pronombre neutro que

El género

les correspondería, adoptan el masculino o femenino, «he», «she». Por ejemplo:

> sun *sʌn* sol — masculino o neutro
> moon *mu:n* luna — femenino
> ship *ʃip* buque — femenino

Nota: Suelen personificarse como masculino las fuerzas más poderosas de la naturaleza como el sol, los vientos, los ríos, etc.; los fenómenos naturales violentos, tempestades, etc.; el tiempo en general, el día y la noche, etc.; también las pasiones y acciones violentas, el amor, el miedo, la guerra, etc. Son femenino, cuando se personifican, las fuerzas más suaves de la naturaleza, cuanto implica fertilidad, atracción y captación, los sentimientos no violentos y las pasiones inferiores. También son femenino los barcos, la máquina del tren.

A los tres géneros del sustantivo corresponden los pronombres personales y posesivos siguientes:

Caso nominativo	Caso objetivo	Pron. poses. (3.ª pers.)
Singular		
he *hi:* él	him *him* le, a él	his *hiz* su, sus
she *ʃi:* ella	her *hə:** la, le, a ella	her *hə:** su, sus
it *it* él, ella (ello)	it *it* le, la, lo; a él, a ella, a ello	its *its* su, sus
Plural		
they *ðei* ellos, ellas	them *ðem* los, las; les; a ellos, a ellas	their *dɛə** su, sus

Las voces «caballero» o «señor», «señora», «señorita» se traducen respectivamente por:

a) «Mr.» [*mistə**], «Mrs.» [*misiz*], «Miss» [*mis*], antes del apellido.

b) «Sir» [*sə:**], «Madam» [*mædəm*], que se emplean en el caso vocativo sin nombre; con «Miss», aun en tal caso, se suele emplear el nombre.

c) «Gentleman», «lady», «young [*jʌŋ*] lady», se usa en la 3.ª persona sin nombre.

Ejemplos:

a) Here is Mr. (*o* Mrs., *o* Miss) Smith.
   Aquí está el señor (*o* la señora, señorita) Smith.
b) Yes, sir (*o* Madam, *o* Miss Smith).
   Sí, señor (*o* señora, señorita).
c) This gentleman (*o* lady, *o* young lady) wishes to speak to you.
   Este caballero (*o* señora, señorita) desea hablar a usted.

Words

because *bi'kɔz*	porque	love *lʌv*	amor
dangerous *pèligroso* 'deindʒərəs	peligroso	many *'meni*	muchos
		meat *mi:t*	carne (para comer)
dog *dɔg*	perro		
domestic *do'mestik*	doméstico	mutton *'mʌtən*	carne de cordero
— animal *'ænimәl*	animal doméstico	obedient *o'bi:djənt*	obediente
donkey *'dɔŋki*	jumento, burro	obey *o'bei*	obedecer
eat *i:t*	comer	over *'ouvə**	sobre
faithful *'feiθful (fəl)*	fiel	pig *pig*	cerdo
farm *fa:m*	granja	pork *pɔ:k*	carne de cerdo
flesh *fleʃ*	carne (del ser vivo)	us *ʌs, əs*	nos, a nosotros
		veal *vi:l*	ternera
friend *frend*	amigo	watch *wɔtʃ*	reloj
goat *gout*	cabra	— over	vigilar
him *him*	le, la; a él, a ella	wild *waild*	silvestre, salvaje

Reading exercise

Look: There is one man in that field. He looks at that child. There are two, three children. There is also a woman and an old man. There are many animals: a cock, a hen and many chicken, a goose, a duck, a drake and a pig. Yes; there are many animals because it is a farm. In the farm there is a man and a woman. They are husband and wife; they have many children; they are boys and girls. There is also a little child. The eldest boy is the heir of the farm. They have a girl-cousin who is an orphan and is here now. There are also many servants in the farm. Look at them: Five men-servants and six maid-servants or women-servants. The man is their master and the woman is their mistress.

Some animals are called domestic animals. The chief are the horse, the donkey, the dog and the cat. The ox, the pig, the sheep, the goat and the cow are also domestic animals. Oxen, pigs and sheep give us meat for food. The flesh of the ox is beef and the flesh of the calf is veal. There is also mutton and pork; they are very nice to eat. Horses and donkeys are beasts of burden because they carry burdens for us. The dog is a good friend of children and children love dogs. They are very faithful to their master, and they are very obedient, too. Dogs and cats catch mice. There are also other animals that are not domestic and they are the lion, the tiger, the bear and the wolf. These animals are very dangerous for men and women. They are wild animals.

Conversation

How many men are there in that field? Are there two or three? Are there some children, too? What have they? Is a chicken big? and a pig? and a lamb? Who are the master and mistress of the house? and of the farm? Have the children any cousins? Are they boy-cousins or girl-cousins? Are there many servants in the farm? How many servants are there?

Ejercicio

¿Quién hay en la granja? En la granja hay muchos hombres y mujeres. Hay mucha gente. También hay muchos animales. ¿Cuántos animales hay en la granja? ¿Cuáles son? Son un perro, un gato, muchos pollitos, un cerdo, un caballo y muchos otros. El pastor cuida los carneros y ovejas en el campo. En el campo hay también muchos conejos. En algunos campos hay zorras que son muy malas para los animales domésticos. También hay animales salvajes, que son los leones y los tigres.

Conjugate:

a) I shall not have a big dog.
b) I should be in the farm.
c) Shall I be a tall man?

SIXTH LESSON LECCIÓN SEXTA

El verbo

En inglés hay dos conjugaciones: una débil y otra fuerte. La primera forma el pasado y el participio añadiendo la sílaba «ed» o «d» al infinitivo. La segunda se forma por medio de cambios internos que consisten generalmente en el cambio de la vocal en el pasado y la adición del sufijo «en», «n» o «ne» en el participio, con o sin cambio de vocal. Al aprender un verbo debe aprenderse el enunciado, pues por el infinitivo solo no es posible saber a cuál de las dos conjugaciones pertenece. El enunciado de un verbo consiste en las tres formas principales del mismo, base de los tiempos compuestos, esto es, infinitivo, pasado y participio.

Infinitivo		*Pasado*	*Participio*
to come *kʌm*	venir	came *keim*	come *kʌm*
to speak *spi:k*	hablar	spoke *spouk*	spoken *'spoukən*
to stand *stænd*	estar de pie, alzarse	stood *stud*	stood *stud*
to leave *li:v*	dejar	left *left*	left *left*
to write *rait*	escribir	wrote *rout*	written *'ritn*
to see *si:*	ver	saw *sɔ:*	seen *si:n*
to watch *wɔtʃ*	vigilar	watched *wɔtʃt*	watched *wɔtʃt*
to use *ju:z*	usar	used *ju:zd*	used *ju:zd*
to go *gou*	ir	went *went*	gone *gɔn*
to do *du:, du*	hacer	did *did*	done *dʌn*
to say *sei*	decir	said *sed*	said *sed*
to look *luk*	mirar	looked *lukt*	looked *lukt*

Presente del verbo débil **TO WALK** *wɔ:k* andar

Yo ando o paseo, etc.

I walk *wɔ:k*	we walk
you walk	you walk
he walks *wɔ:ks*	they walk
she walks	
it walks	

El verbo   25

Presente del verbo fuerte TO WRITE *rait* escribir
Yo escribo, etc. I write *rait*　　　　　we write you write　　　　　　you write he writes *raits*　　　they write she writes it writes

Nótese que la tercera persona del singular añade una «s» o la sílaba «es» siguiendo la misma regla de ortografía dada para el plural de los sustantivos (lecc. 2, p. 4 s).

El presente de todos los verbos, excepto de los defectivos y anómalos, se conjuga según el anterior modelo. Los verbos impersonales se conjugan sólo en la 3.ª persona.

El complemento sigue siempre al verbo, tanto si es nombre como si es pronombre.

　　　　I see the boy　　　　veo al niño
　　　　I see him　　　　　　le veo
　　　　I leave the book　　　dejo el libro
　　　　I leave it　　　　　　lo dejo

El infinitivo va precedido de la preposición «to» (excepto cuando sigue a ciertos verbos que se verán más adelante); ej.: «to open, to write».

El gerundio y el participio de presente se forman añadiendo la terminación *ing* al infinitivo: «walking, writing, looking», «andando, escribiendo, mirando». Con frecuencia se traducen por el infinitivo castellano.

La segunda persona del imperativo es igual al infinitivo sin preposición y no lleva pronombre. Las demás toman el pronombre del caso objetivo. «Go», «ve»: «let him go», «vaya él»; «let them go», «vayan ellos».

Después de preposición, el infinitivo castellano se traduce por gerundio en inglés, excepto cuando la preposición sea «to» = «a»:

　　　　before *bifɔ:** writing　　　　antes de escribir
　　　　after *a:ftə** going　　　　　　después de ir
　　　　I begin to read *bi'gin tu ri:d*　empiezo a leer

Words

back [1] *bæk*	espalda	place *pleis*	sitio, lugar
come *in*	entrar	put *put*	poner
clean *kli:n*	limpio	read *ri:d*	leer
finished *'finiʃt*	listo, terminado	seat *si:t*	asiento
from *frɔm, frəm*	de, desde	sentence *'sentəns*	oración, frase
get up *'get ʌp*	levantarse	shut *ʃʌt*	cerrar
good-bye *'gud'bai*	adiós	sir *sə:*	señor
good morning *'mɔ:niŋ*	buenos días	stand up	levantarse
Henry *'henri*	Enrique	take *teik*	tomar, sacar
home *houm*	casa, hogar	take out	sacar
into *intu*	en, dentro de	them *ðem, ðəm*	a ellos, les
John *dʒɔn*	Juan	then *ðen*	entonces
look at *luk æt, ət*	mirar a	to *tu:, tə*	a, para
me *mi:*	a mí, me	up *ʌp*	arriba
now *nau*	ahora	what	lo que
open *'oupən*	abrir	William *'wiljəm*	Guillermo
out of *aut ɔv, əv*	fuera de	wipe *waip*	limpiar, borrar
		with *wið*	con

Reading exercise

Good morning, children. Come in. Good morning, Mr. Williams. Shut the door and open the window. You see, now the door is shut and the window is open. Now, you will stand before the blackboard and write your exercise. Now, take your books and open them. Read the exercise. It is a long exercise but it is useful for you. After reading, go to the blackboard and take the chalk. Write with the chalk. Write your lesson. John, you will write after me. Mary will read what you write. Now, William, will you take the sponge and wipe out this exercise? Now I get up from my chair and go to the window. From the window I speak to you. I open the window. Mary, what is that? Is it a book? Yes, it is. Watch me, and see what I do. I take a piece of chalk. I go to the blackboard. John watches his teacher; he reads the sentences on the board. All the pupils read them. One of the pupils leaves his seat and goes to the door. He goes out of the room. He comes into the room. You do not leave the room, you look at your tea-

---

1. «Back», detrás de un verbo de movimiento, indica que la acción se realiza en sentido contrario: «to go», «ir»; «to go back», «volver»; «to give», «dar»; «to give back», «devolver».

cher. Henry wipes out the board, puts the chalk into the box, and goes to his place. Now, boys and girls, the lesson is finished. Shut your books and put them in your satchels. Go home now. Good-bye, children. Good bye, Mr. Williams. Good-bye, sir.

Conversation

Where are the boys? Who takes the books? Who is Mr. Williams? Where is the box? Are the pupils in their seats? Is the teacher behind the table? Are the pupils in class? What is there in the satchels? And on the tables? Who shuts the door? Is the window open? Is the blackboard clean? Who writes the sentences on the blackboard? Who watches the teacher? Who reads the lesson?

Conjugate:

a) I see the trees from the window, etc.
b) I shut the book, etc.
c) I walk to the door, etc.

Exercise

I write and you watch. Now, you write and I watch. Mary also watches. The pupils read the sentences that the teacher writes on the board. Then the teacher says: Henry, go to the blackboard and wipe it with the duster. Henry wipes it out and walks back to his seat. Now, Henry, leave the duster in the box. Henry is back in his place and the board is clean. Now, children, go home. Good-bye. Till to-morrow [*til tə'mɔrou*].

Ejercicio

¡Buenos días, muchachos! Entren en la clase. La puerta está abierta. Cierren la puerta y siéntense. Mary va a la pizarra, coge un pedazo de tiza y escribe un ejercicio. Juan mira y lee lo que ella escribe en la pizarra. La niña lo borra después.

Nosotros vamos a la clase, entramos y decimos: «¡Buenos días, Sr. Williams!» El profesor dice: «¡Buenos días, muchachos! Entren y cierren la puerta. Abran la ventana.

Saquen los libros y pónganlos encima de la mesa. Lean la lección y escriban el ejercicio en la pizarra. Miren las oraciones que yo escribo. Ahora cierren los libros y vayan a casa. ¡Adiós, muchachos!» «¡Adiós, Sr. Williams!»

SEVENTH LESSON   LECCIÓN SÉPTIMA

Forma interrogativa y negativa de «to be» y «to have»

am I not?	have I not?
are you not?	have you not?
is he not?	has he not?
are we not?	have we not?
are you not?	have you not?
are they not?	have they not?

Corrientemente estas formas se contraen como sigue: «isn't» [iz(ə)nt] por «is not», «aren't» [a:nt] por «are not», «haven't» [hævnt] por «have not», «hasn't» ['hæznt] por «has not»:

she isn't here	ella no está aquí
he hasn't a pencil	él no tiene un lápiz
they aren't in the room	ellos no están en la habitación
isn't he in London?	¿no está en Londres?
aren't you Spanish?	¿no es usted español?
haven't I a book	¿no tengo yo un libro?

Words

again ə'gein	otra vez, de nuevo	play plei	jugar, tocar (instrumento)
collect kə'lekt	recoger	pronounce prə'nauns	pronunciar
distinct, -ly dis-'tiŋkt -li	con claridad	properly 'prɔpəli	bien
English iŋgliʃ	inglés	reading 'ri:diŋ	leyendo
finish finiʃ	terminar	repeat ri'pi:t	repetir
first fə:st	primero	sit sit	sentarse
gay gei	alegre	sit down sit daun	sentarse
German dʒə:mən	alemán	slow, -ly slou -li	despacio
give giv	dar	speak spi:k	hablar
go on 'gou‿'ɔn	siga adelante	spell spel	escribir, deletrear
happy hæpi	feliz	stand stænd	alzarse, estar de pie
letter letə*	carta, letra		
phrase freiz	frase	—up ʌp	levantarse

translate	traducir	well *wel*	bien
træns'leit		while *wail*	mientras
up *ʌp*	arriba	work *wə:k*	trabajo
way *wei*	camino, manera		

Phrases of school-life

1. Stand up. Sit down. 2. Open your books. Read the first sentence. 3. Repeat this word. Say it again. 4. Go on. Finish the sentence. Translate it. 5. What is this word in English? 6. Spell the word «window». — W-i-n-d-o-w. 7. How many letters has this word (are there in this word)? — It has six letters. 8. Give me the sponge. 9. Read slowly. Speak distinctly. Pronounce properly. 10. Collect the exercise books.

Reading exercise

Henry writes with a pencil. He takes his book and reads his lesson. He then shuts the book and opens his exercise book. He writes a sentence. Then he translates the sentence. The teacher watches the pupils and sees what they write. John, look at the blackboard ; it is dirty. Clean it! He cleans the blackboard and goes back to his place. The teacher puts the chalk and the duster back into the box. Mary sits down and writes her lesson. Mary, get up and walk to the table. Take a book and open it. Mary takes the book, opens it and reads a sentence. She reads distinctly and slowly, and pronounces very well. William, aren't you reading your lesson? No; I haven't a book. The teacher writes a sentence and you read it. Aren't you reading the sentence? Yes, we are reading it.

Work and play

Work while you work, and play while you play.
That is the way to be happy and gay.

Ejercicio

Enrique está escribiendo su lección. ¿Qué está haciendo Enrique? Está escribiendo. Yo estoy leyendo. ¿Estoy leyendo el ejercicio? No; no estoy leyendo; estoy escribiendo. ¿Quién está escribiendo? Enrique está escribiendo. ¿Está María escribiendo? No, no está escribiendo ahora, está yendo a la pizarra y borrando el ejercicio. ¿Estás leyendo un libro? No, no estoy leyendo un libro. Juan está leyendo, pero yo estoy escribiendo un ejercicio.

Conjugate:

- *a)* I haven't a book, etc.
- *b)* Haven't I an English book, etc.
- *c)* I'm not in the room.

To learn by heart

Infinitivo		*Pasado*	*Participio*
to walk *wɔːk*	andar	walked *wɔːkt*	walked
to give *giv*	dar	gave *geiv*	given *'givn*
to take *teik*	tomar, coger	took *tuk*	taken *'teikən*
to run *rʌn*	correr	ran *ræn*	run *rʌn*
to tell *tel*	decir	told *tould*	told *tould*
to study *'stʌdi*	estudiar	studied *'stʌdid*	studied

EIGHTH LESSON   LECCIÓN OCTAVA

Forma interrogativa y negativa del verbo

La forma interrogativa del presente de indicativo se hace anteponiendo al infinitivo el auxiliar «do» [*duː*], seguido del sujeto correspondiente, excepto en la tercera persona del singular, en la que «do», al tomar la «s» característica de dicha persona, se convierte en «does» [*dʌz, dəz*]. La forma negativa se hace con el mismo auxiliar, precediendo al adverbio de negación «not»:

Hablo yo?, etc.

do I speak? *duː ai spiːk*   do we speak?
do you speak?   do you speak?
does he speak?   do they speak?

Yo no hablo, etc.

I do not speak   we ⎫
you do not speak   you ⎬ do not speak
he does not speak?   they ⎭

Nota: Todos los verbos, exceptuando los auxiliares, anómalos y defectivos, se conjugan en sus formas interrogativa y negativa según el anterior modelo.

Cuando la oración comienza con un pronombre interrogativo en nominativo se omite el auxiliar «do»:

> Who opens the window? ¿Quién abre la ventana?
> Which girl is your sister? ¿Cuál de las niñas es tu hermana?

Pero diremos·

> What do you say? ¿Qué dice usted?

porque «what» no es nominativo.

También con el imperativo se emplea el auxiliar «do» en las formas negativas, incluso con los verbos «to be» y «to have»:

> Do not (don't) write! ¡No escribas!
> Do not (don't) be a fool *fu:l.* No seas tonto.

En general, al hacer referencia a partes del cuerpo u objetos de uso personal se emplea en inglés el adjetivo posesivo en lugar del artículo:

> Take *your* book and study *your* lesson. Coge el libro y estudia la lección.
> He had *his* book in *his* hand. Tenía el libro en la mano.

To learn by heart

Infinitivo		*Pasado*	*Participio*
to finish *'finiʃ*	acabar	finished *'finiʃt*	finished
to live *liv*	vivir	lived *livd*	lived
to love *lʌv*	amar	loved *lʌvd*	loved
to send *send*	enviar	sent *sent*	sent

Words

always *ɔ:lweiz, -wəz*	siempre	of course *əv 'kɔ:s*	naturalmente
		dog *dɔg*	perro
arm *a:m*	brazo	each *i:tʃ*	cada
at times *æt taimz*	a veces	eye *ai*	ojo
between *bi'twi:n*	entre (dos)	eyebrows *'aibrauz*	cejas
body *'bɔdi*	cuerpo	eyelashes *'ailæʃiz*	pestañas
brown *braun*	marrón	face *feis*	cara, rostro
chew *tʃu:*	masticar	fair hair *'feə'hɛə**	pelo rubio
colour *'kʌlə**	color	feel *fi:l*	sentir

finger ˈfiŋgə*	dedo	lips *lips*	labios
food fuːd	alimento	mouth mauθ	boca
gums gʌmz	encías	nose nouz	nariz
hand hænd	mano	palate ˈpælit	paladar
head hed	cabeza	part paːt	parte
hear hiə*	oir	people piːpl	gente
hold hould	aguantar, sostener	right rait	derecha
		smell smel	olor, oler
how hau	como	taste teist	gusto, sabor
inside ˈinˈsaid	dentro	thumb θʌm	pulgar
keep kiːp	guardar, conservar	toe tou	dedo del pie
		tongue tʌŋ	lengua
left *left*	izquierda	which (h)witʃ	cual
leg *leg*	pierna, pata	why (h)wai	por qué
limbs limz	miembros	yawn jɔːn	bostezar

Reading exercise

The human body consists of head, trunk and limbs. Look at me! Do you see me? This is my face and this is my head. I have two eyes, a nose and a mouth. Inside my mouth I have teeth, gums, a tongue and a palate. We see with our eyes, hear with our ears, smell with our nose, taste with our mouth and feel with our hands. We also eat with our mouth, and we bite with our teeth, that is, we chew our food. At times we open our mouth very wide, and then we yawn. Over the eyes we have the eyebrows. We also have eyelashes. Some people have blue eyes; others have not blue eyes, they have brown eyes and brown hair. English people have fair hair. Men have two arms and two legs. Animals have four legs. Men and women and children have a right hand and a left one and they have five fingers on each hand and five toes on each foot. We walk with our legs and feet; we do things with our hands; we write with our right hand; some people write with their left hand, but not many.

I walk in the garden and I look at the trees. Do you also walk in the garden? Yes, I also walk in the garden. What is this? This my head. And what is that? That is my face. These are my eyes, this is my nose and this is my mouth. My lips are red. These are my lips.

How many ears have you? I have two ears. I hear with my ears. Have you a right hand? Yes, I have a right hand and a left one. What do you do with your right hand? I write with my right hand. What do you do with your eyes? I see with my eyes. Do you see with your mouth? No, with my mouth I speak; I do not see with my mouth. Have you toes and fingers? Yes, I have ten toes and ten fingers. How many fingers and how many toes have you? I have ten toes; five on each foot. And I have ten fingers also.

Conversation

Have you blue eyes? Do you see with your eyes? With what do you speak? With what do you hear? Do you go to school? Do you walk home from school? How many legs has a cat? Does your friend have brown hair? What colour is your hair?

Ejercicio

¿Cuántas manos tienes? Tengo dos manos y dos pies. ¿Qué haces con los ojos? Veo con los ojos, oigo con los oídos, como con la boca y huelo con la nariz. El niño tiene la boca abierta. Abre la boca y cierra los ojos. ¿Con qué mano escribes? Escribo con la mano derecha. ¿De qué color son los dientes? Los dientes son de color blanco. Comemos con la boca y mordemos con los dientes. ¿Cómo coges la pluma? Cojo la pluma con el pulgar y los dedos, naturalmente. Tenemos diez dedos en las manos. Cinco en cada mano. En cada pie tenemos cinco dedos. Las personas tienen cabeza, cuerpo, brazos, piernas y pies. ¿Tiene el perro brazos? No, el perro tiene cuatro patas.

Conjugate:
- a) Do I go to school in the afternoon (tarde)?
- b) Do I write with my left hand?
- c) Do I shut my book?

Words

above ə'bʌv	arriba, sobre	chin tʃin	barbilla
ajar ə'dʒaː*	entreabierta	grass graːs	yerba
as æz, əz	como	jar dʒaː*	jarro, -a; tarro
because bi'kɔːz	porque	king kiŋ	rey
blackberry 'blækbəri, -beri	mora (fruta)	like laik	como, semejante, gustar
but bʌt, bət	pero, sino	riddle 'ridəl	acertijo
cobbler 'kɔblə*	zapatero remendón	snow snou	nieve
cherry 'tʃeri	cereza	when (h)wen	cuando

Exercise

Riddles

a) White as snow, but it isn't snow. Green as grass, but it isn't grass. Red as a cherry, but it isn't a cherry. Black as ink, but it isn't ink. (A blackberry.) b) When is a door not a door? — When it is ajar. c) Why is a cobbler like a king? — Because his nose is above his chin.

Conversation

How many riddles are there in this exercise? What is black as ink? What colour is the grass?, and a cherry? Who is like a king? What is above your mouth? Why are you like a king? Where do you put your books when the lesson is finished? Who cleans the board when it is dirty? What do you say when you leave the classroom?

Ejercicio

Mi perro es blanco y castaño. Tengo un ratón blanco como la nieve. ¡Cierra la puerta! No la dejes entreabierta. Mi hermana está siempre alegre porque es muy feliz.

Cierra los ojos. Ábrelos de nuevo (otra vez). No abras la ventana. Abre la puerta. No veo porque tengo los ojos cerrados. No termino el ejercicio aquí porque lo terminaré en casa. ¿Dónde vives? ¿No vives en Londres? No, antes vivía en Londres, pero ahora vivo en Manchester.

NINTH LESSON   LECCIÓN NOVENA

Forma interrogativa y negativa del verbo (cont.)

Generalmente, en la conversación usual, las formas interrogativa y negativa del presente de indicativo suelen contraerse. «Do not» se contrae en «don't» [*dount*], y «does not», en «doesn't» [*'dʌznt*].

The children don't walk to school.	Los niños no van andando al colegio.
He doesn't write his exercise.	Él no escribe su ejercicio.

Forma interrogativa y negativa del verbo

Nota: Obsérvese que delante de la palabra «school» se omite el artículo cuando no se refiere a un edificio determinado.

La forma interrogativo-negativa sigue las reglas de los elementos que la componen:

> Don't I study my lesson every *evəri* day? ¿No estudio mi lección todos los días?
> Doesn't he work well? ¿No trabaja bien?

Words

difficult *'difikəlt*	difícil	once *wʌns*	una vez
down *daun*	abajo	please *pli:z*	por favor
enough *i'nʌf*	bastante	quickly *kwikli*	de prisa, rápidamente
fifteen *'fif'ti:n*	quince		
four times *'fɔ: taimz*	cuatro veces	Summer *sʌmə**	verano
		thirteen *'θə:'ti:n*	trece
fourteen *'fɔ:'ti:n*	catorce	three times *taimz*	tres veces
next *nekst*	próximo	twice *twais*	dos veces

To learn by heart

Infinitivo		*Pasado*	*Participio*
to call *kɔ:l*	llamar	called *kɔ:ld*	called
to get *get*	obtener	got *gɔt*	got
to know *nou*	saber, conocer	knew *nju:*	known *noun*
to learn *lə:n*	aprender	learned *lə:nt*	learned
to like *laik*	gustar	liked *laikt*	liked
to listen *'lisn*	oir, escuchar	listened *lisnd*	listened
to play *plei*	jugar	played *pleid*	played
to stand up *stænd ʌp*	levantarse	stood up *stud ʌp*	stood up

Reading exercise

Come in, children. Don't stand up. Sit down. Don't open your exercise books, now. Do not write, please. Write (write down) what I tell you. Write once. Don't write it twice. It is enough. Once, twice, three times. Now, don't write it again; translate it. Learn it. Mary, how do you spell the word pencil? Spell it please. Do not translate it, but finish the sentence. It is enough, please. What is the Spanish for this word? Read it; don't write, it. Translate it please. Don't translate it but read it again distinctly. Now, get up and go to the blackboard. Don't go to the window. Write this word. Now, listen to me. Don't read quickly. Read slowly. Thirteen, fourteen, fifteen. Why don't you pronounce this word distinctly? Because it's very dificult. Go to your place, Mary. Don't sit down. We shall finish the lesson. Say good bye, and leave the room.

Exercise

They don't speak. Do they speak? Does he translate? You don't translate. We play. Don't you play? We don't play. She stands. Doesn't she stand? No; she doesn't stand. Do they finish their lesson? No; they don't. Do we go now? No, you don't. Yes, you do. Who doesn't go? We don't. Do you? Yes, we do. Who watches? The girl and the boy do. Doesn't he watch? Yes, he does. No, he doesn't.

Nota: Obsérvese que en las contestaciones se repite siempre el auxiliar empleado en la pregunta: «Does he watch? —Yes, he does; no, he doesn't.»

Ejercicio

Hablo. No hable. ¿Quién habla? Ella habla. Ella no habla. ¿Qué escribes? No escribo. ¿Te levantas? No. ¿Quién se levanta. Mary se levanta. ¿Quién viene? Yo. Yo, no. Siéntese usted. Nosotros no vamos. ¿Viene usted? No, yo no voy. Enrique vendrá. ¿Vienes, Enrique? Sí, voy. No digas esto. ¿Qué es esto? No sé. ¿Adónde van ustedes? A casa.

Conversation

Do you stand up when the teacher comes into the room? Do you write your exercises? What do you say when you come into a room for the first time? Do you say good morning? What do you say when you leave a room? Where do you go every morning? Does he speak English with his teacher? Do you speak English with your teacher? Why don't you always speak English? Do you speak Spanish? Why don't you speak English to me? Do you speak English with your English friends? Will you speak English next Summer? What do you say? What does he say?

To learn by heart

If your face wants[1] to smile[2], let[3] it.
If it doesn't, make[4] it.

1. Want *wɔnt* querer. 2. Smile *smail* sonreír. 3. Let *let* permitir.
4. Make *meik* hacer.

TENTH LESSON LECCIÓN DÉCIMA

El genitivo

En inglés, para expresar posesión o pertenencia se emplea el caso genitivo, que se forma añadiendo una «s» precedida de apóstrofo al nombre del poseedor. También puede hacerse por medio de la preposición «of», como en castellano. Cuando se usa el genitivo propiamente dicho, el orden de las palabras en la frase se altera, poniéndose en primer lugar el poseedor, seguido de apóstrofo y «s», y a continuación el objeto poseído sin artículo.

the girl's mother	la madre de la niña
the boy's book	el libro del niño
these men's hats	los sombreros de los hombres

La «s» del genitivo se omite, conservando, no obstante, el apóstrofo:

a) Después del sustantivo plural terminado en «s»:

these girls' mother	la madre de estas niñas
these boys' pens	las plumas de estos niños

b) Cuando la última sílaba del sustantivo singular empieza y termina en «s»:

Moses' law *'mouziz lɔ:* la ley de Moisés

c) Cuando la última sílaba del sustantivo termina en «s» o en «ce» seguido de la palabra «sake»:

for goodness' *'gudnis* sake *seik*   por (amor de) Dios
for conscience' sake   en conciencia

Pero si el nombre tiene una sola sílaba se conserva la «s» del genitivo:

> Bess's secret *si:krit* el secreto de Bess

Como ya se ha visto, los plurales que no terminan en «s» toman normalmente la «s» precedida de apóstrofo:

> the children's books   los libros de los niños

El genitivo se emplea:

a) Con nombres de persona:

> Mr. Brown's garden   el jardín del señor Brown
> Mary's cat   el gato de María

b) Con nombres que denotan persona:

> my sister's book   el libro de mi hermana
> this boy's brother el hermano de este muchacho

c) Con nombres que denotan seres animados:

> the dog's tail *teil*   el rabo del gato
> the cat's paws *pɔ:z*   las garras del gato

d) Con algunos nombres personificados:

> England's army *'iŋglǝndz a:mi*   el ejército de Inglaterra
> life's difficulties *'laifs 'dificǝltis*   las dificultades de la vida

e) Con algunos nombres que indican tiempo, medida, espacio y algunas cosas que se quiera dignificar:

> to-morrow's paper   el periódico de mañana
> 3 ounzes' weight   tres onzas de peso
> two miles' walk *mailz wɔ:k*   un paseo de dos millas
> duty's call *'dju:tiz kɔ:l*   la llamada del deber
> the Sun's rays *sʌnz 'reiz*   los rayos del sol

Los nombres compuestos y los grupos de palabras forman el genitivo en la última palabra del grupo:

> my father-in-law's house   la casa de mi suegro
>   *'fa:ðǝrin lɔ:z haus*
> Brown and Son's office *'ɔfis*   la oficina de Brown e hijos
> the boy and the girl's books   los libros del niño y de la niña

El genitivo

Generalmente, las palabras «house», «church» [tʃəːtʃ] «iglesia», «store» [stɔː*] «almacén», «shop» [ʃɔp] «tienda», y unas cuantas más, suelen omitirse después de un genitivo:

I am at my sister's	estoy en casa de mi hermana
I go to mass to St. Paul's	voy a misa a San Pablo
I am at the baker's 'beikəːs	estoy en la panadería

El genitivo propiamente dicho solamente puede usarse en los casos antedichos; en todos los demás debe usarse la preposición «of», como en castellano:

| the door of the room | la puerta de la habitación |
| the leaves of the tree | las hojas del árbol |

Words

ball *bɔːl*	pelota	doctor *'dɔktə**	médico
big *big*	grande	have you been?	¿ha estado usted?
by *bai*	por, junto a	letter *'letə**	carta
dentist *'dentist*	dentista	tailor *'teilə**	sastre

Exercise

Mary's book is on the table. My sister's little cat is white. John's house is by the river. That is my brother's hat. This house is my parents'. This is my brother's house. I am at the doctors'. He is at the dentist's. Cats' eyes are green. My father's pen is not here. To-day's paper is on the table. The dog is man's friend. That man is my father's friend. He reads his sister's letter. A girls' school. Have you been at the tailor's? Is this Peter's ball? Is this gentleman Mary's father? Are you my brother's friend? They are not here; they are at my sister's. My friend's dog is very big. The girl's pencil is not on the table; it is in the box.

To learn by heart

Infinitivo		*Pasado*	*Participio*
to be	ser	was	been
to have	tener	had	had
to stay *stei*	estar, permanecer	stayed	stayed
to smell *smel*	oler	smelt	smelt
to pick	coger, recoger	picked	picked
to sit	sentarse	sat	sat

Words

America ə'merikə	América	Margaret ma:gərit	Margarita
American ə'merikən	americano, -a	Mary 'mɛəri	María
Anne æn	Ana	name neim	nombre
birthday 'bə:θdei	cumpleaños	none nʌn	ninguno
bring briŋ	traer	often ɔfn	a menudo
call kɔ:l	llamar	on ɔn	encima, sobre
family 'fæmili	familia	Peter 'pi:te*	Pedro
give giv	dar	picture 'piktʃə*	cuadro, dibujo, película
grandchildren 'grændtʃildrən	nietos	present 'prezənt	regalo, presente
grandfather 'grænd'fa:ðə*	abuelo	Richard ritʃəd	Ricardo
grandmother 'grænd'mʌðə*	abuela	send send	mandar, enviar
grandparents 'grænd'pɛərənts	abuelos	so sou	así, por lo tanto
Jane dʒein	Juana	so much sou mʌtʃ	tanto
Kate keit	Catalina	sometimes 'sʌmtaimz	a veces
live liv	vivir	Spain spein	España
lot lɔt	lote, cantidad	tell tel	decir
lots of	muchos, -as	Thomas tɔməs	Tomás
		very far 'veri fa:*	muy lejos

Reading exercise

I live in England. My name is Richard, but my parents, my family and my friends call me Ted. Mother doesn't call me Ted; she calls me Teddy. She likes Teddy. I have one brother and two sisters. My brother's name is John, and my sisters' are Margaret and Kate. My father is a doctor, and we live in Chester. My father's brother is uncle Peter and father's sister is aunt Anne. But we don't call her «aunt Anne» but Aunty. My uncle's wife is also my aunt and their children are my cousins and my parents' nephews and nieces. Their names are Charles, Peter, Jane and Gwen. They don't live here; they live in London but sometimes they come to see us and they stay with us at home. One of my aunts doesn't live in England; she lives in America. Another aunt lives in Spain. Sometimes they come to England for their holidays but not very often because it is very far. When they come they bring very nice presents. It is nice to give and to have nice presents. I like to give other people presents. My parents and my grandparents gave me a very nice pen for my birthday. My grandfather is very old. So is my grandmother. We are their grandchildren (nietos). They love us very much and bring lots of things when they come to see us.

Conversation

What is your name? Have you a large family? How many brothers and sisters are you? What are your sisters' names? What are your brothers' names? Do your family and friends call you Edward? What do they call you? Have you any cousins? Do they live with you? When is your birthday? Do your parents give you a present for your birthday? Do you get any presents from your friends? What do you call your uncle's wife? And your mother's mother? And your mother's brother? Have you many friends? Do you live in England? Do your cousins live in America? What is your father? What is your mother's name? Will you be a doctor, too? If you will not be a doctor, what will you be?

Ejercicio

El nombre de mi hermano es Ricardo (mi hermano se llama ...). ¿Cómo te llamas tú? ¿De quién son estos lápices? El hermano de mi madre es alto. Dime, ¿quién es la hermana de tu padre? La hermana de mi padre es mi tía. ¿Escribes cartas a tus amigos? ¿Cómo se llama tu madre? Mi madre se llama (su nombre es) María. ¿Cuándo es el cumpleaños de tu hermana? ¿Cuándo es tu cumpleaños? Mi cumpleaños es mañana. ¿Viven tus primos en América? No, mis primos no viven en América. Viven en Inglaterra. ¿Tienen tus abuelos muchos nietos? No, no tienen muchos nietos. Sólo tienen dos, Ricardo y Ana. ¿Te hacen regalos tus abuelos? Sí, me hacen muchísimos regalos. Mis tías también me mandan regalos a veces. Mis primos no me mandan regalos, pero me escriben cartas muy largas. ¿Cómo se llama tu primo? Se llama Tomás. Dime tu nombre. Mi nombre es Juan.

ELEVENTH LESSON LECCIÓN UNDÉCIMA

El pronombre personal

Nominative (Sujeto)	Objective (Compl. dir., ind.)	Genitive (Posesivo)	Reflexive and emphatic (Reflexivo y enfático)
Yo, tú, etc.	*Me, a mí*, etc.	*Mío*, etc.	*Yo mismo*, etc.
I *ai*	me *mi:*	mine *main*	myself *mai'self*
you	you	yours *jɔ:z, juez*	yourself *jɔ:'self, juə'self*
he	him	his *hiz*	himself *him'self*
she	her	hers *hə:z*	herself *hə:'self*
we	us	ours *'auəz*	ourselves *auə'selvz*
you	you	yours *jɔ:z, juez*	yourselves *jɔ:'selvz, juə'selvz*
they	them	theirs *ðɛəz*	themselves *ðəm-'selvz*

En inglés, cuando un verbo tiene dos complementos, uno en acusativo y otro en dativo, puede ocurrir: *a)* que ambos complementos sean pronombres; *b)* que ambos sean nombres; *c)* que uno sea nombre y el otro pronombre.

Si los dos complementos fuesen nombres puede construirse la oración de dos formas: 1) precediendo el complemento directo (acusativo) al indirecto con la preposición «to» (dativo); 2) poniendo el complemento indirecto inmediatamente después del verbo, *sin preposición*, y a continuación el complemento directo, también sin preposición alguna. Esta segunda forma es más usada que la primera, que suele usarse para mayor énfasis.

1) I give a present to my sister   doy un regalo a mi hermana
2) I give my sister a present   doy a mi hermana un regalo

Ambas construcciones pueden usarse también indistintamente en el caso de que el acusativo fuese nombre y el dativo pronombre. Así tendremos:

I give a present to her   le doy un regalo (a ella)
I give her a present   le doy un regalo

El pronombre personal

Pero si el dativo fuese nombre y el acusativo pronombre, éste debe preceder siempre al dativo con preposición:

> I give it to my sister   lo doy a mi hermana

Si ambos complementos fuesen pronombres, también el acusativo ha de preceder al dativo con preposición:

> I give it to her   (se) lo doy a ella

Exercise

I see you. You watch us. They tell me. Did you give them a book? Look at them. Don't look at them. We write to you. He leaves me. Did you read it? Do you like that book? Give it to me. Don't look at me. Look at him. Speak to us. Tell the girls. She gave it to her. Mary brought a book for her sister. Mary brought her sister a book. The girls give a present to their brother. The girl gives her brother a present. Did you take it to her? No, I didn't take it to her; I took it to her sister. He gave me a book for my birthday. He gave it to me. Who gave you a pencil? Who sent him a present? Mary loves her mother. Peter loves his and Jane loves hers. We love ours and yours. We study our lesson; you study yours. Tell him good-bye. Say good-morning to your mother. Give it to them. Give them an apple (manzana). Give an apple to them. Read the letter to her. Read her a book. He gives her a letter; she gives it to him.

Words

all ɔːl	todo, -s	fruit-tree 'fruːttriː	árbol frutal
apple 'æpl	manzana	full ful	lleno
apple-tree 'æpltriː	manzano	garden 'gaːdn	jardín
		grow grou	crecer
Autumn 'ɔːtəm	otoño	kitchen 'kitʃin	cocina
all sorts ɔːl sɔːts	toda clase	lily 'lili	lirio
bean biːn	habichuela	lovely 'lʌvli	lindo, bonito
beautiful 'bjuːti-ful, -fəl	hermoso	not yet nɔt'jet	todavía no
		pansy 'pænzi	pensamiento
cabbage 'kæbidʒ	col	pea piː	guisante
cherry-tree 'tʃeritriː	cerezo	pear pɛə*	pera
		pick pik	coger, recoger
chickens 'tʃikinz	pollitos	plum plʌm	ciruela
flower 'flauə*	flor	plum-tree plʌm-triː	ciruelo
fruit fruːt	fruta		

ripe *raip*	maduro	taste *teist*	sabor
rose *rouz*	rosa (flor)	to have a nice time *tu hæv ə 'nais taim*	pasarlo bien, divertirse
spring *spriŋ*	surgir, primavera		
still *stil*	todavía, aún		
strawberry *'strɔːbəri*	fresas	tree *triː*	árbol
		unripe *'ʌn'raip*	verde (fruta)
Summer *'sʌmə**	verano	vegetable(s) *'vedʒitəbəl(z)*	verdura
sure *ʃuə**	seguro		
sweet *swiːt*	dulce	violet *'vaiəlit*	violeta

Reading exercise

We live in the country. We have a very nice house with a beautiful garden full of very nice flowers. In Spring and Summer, violets, pansies, an lilies grow in our garden and the roses look lovely. Smell these roses. Pick one, please. Doesn't it smell sweet? Don't you like to smell roses? Look at these trees over there! They are fruit trees. That is an apple tree. It is full of apples. Do you see that one over there? It is a pear-tree. The plums grow on a plum-tree. They are ripe. These pears are not yet ripe; they are unripe. The apples in that tree over there are not ripe because they are Winter apples. I don't like unripe fruit. It is not good to eat. That is why I don't take one of these apples. I like strawberries very much. Do you like them, too? Look at that cherry-tree. Aren't the cherries nice and red? Eat one, please. Do you like it? Doesn't it taste nice? At the back of the house there is a kitchen garden full of vegetables; there are potatoes, tomatoes, cabbages, beans and peas. We also have many animals and to watch over the house we have dogs. Do you like our garden? Isn't it a nice garden? We love it. If you like it, come and stay with us. We shall go for walks, we shall eat all sorts of fruits and we shall have a very nice time.

Conversation

Where do you live? Is there a garden behind your house? What is there in your garden? Do you like the smell of roses? What colour are roses? When is fruit ripe? Do you like fruit? What grows on fruit-trees? When do you pick apples? What colour are apples? Do you like strawberries? Do they taste good? Do you have a dog?

Ejercicio

Vivimos en una casa blanca con un gran jardín. Hay una huerta detrás de la casa, donde crecen verduras de todas clases. Me gustan las flores. ¿Te gustan a ti las violetas? ¿No son bonitas las rosas? Coge una pera, es muy buena, te gustará. Mira estas manzanas. Son manzanas de invierno. ¿Te gustan las manzanas de invierno? Las peras no están aún maduras. No las comas, porque están verdes. Aquel cerezo está muy hermoso tan cubierto de cerezas. Están muy bonitas y son muy buenas. Toma una.

Conjugate:

a) I pick an apple, you pick..., etc.
b) Do I like cherries, do you like...?, etc.
c) I do not eat unripe fruit, you do not eat..., etc.

TWELFTH LESSON   LECCIÓN DUODÉCIMA

La forma progresiva del verbo

La forma progresiva o continua del verbo, formada con el verbo «to be» seguido del participio de presente del verbo que se conjuga, denota que la acción se está desarrollando, que no está terminada.

Presente: *Yo estoy escribiendo*, etc.	
I am writing 'raitiŋ	we are writing
you are writing	you are writing
he is writing	they are writing
Pasado: *Yo estaba escribiendo*, etc.	
I was writing	we were writing
you were writing	you were writing
he was writing	they were writing

Las formas en «ing» de los verbos siguen las reglas de ortografía usuales.

a) Si el infinitivo termina en «e», se omite dicha «e» antes de añadir la terminación del participio de presente:

    to write   escribir   writing   escribiendo

b) Si el verbo termina en «ie», se cambiará dicha «ie» en «y» antes de añadir la terminación «ing»:

    to lie *lai*   mentir   lying *laiiŋ*   mintiendo

c) Si termina en «y» precedida de consonante, se añadirá directamente la terminación:

    to study   estudiar   studying   estudiando

d) Si el verbo termina en sílaba breve acentuada, se doblará la última consonante antes de tomar la terminación «ing»; si la última sílaba no está acentuada, se añadirá directamente la terminación:

to sit *sit*	sentarse	sitting	sentándose
to eat *i:t*	comer	eating	comiendo
to visit *'vizit*	visitar	visiting	visitando

El presente progresivo de los verbos suele llamarse *presente actual*, e indica que la acción está teniendo lugar *ahora*. También puede indicar un futuro inmediato. El presente llamado *habitual* es el presente simple del verbo, e indica hábito o costumbre, así como una verdad universal o un hecho presente o futuro, si queda claro del contexto:

    birds fly *bə:dz flai*   los pájaros vuelan
    a bird is flying over the house   un pájaro vuela por encima de la casa

El pasado progresivo puede traducirse por el imperfecto de indicativo castellano:

    I was writing   yo escribía, yo estaba escribiendo
    I was eating   yo comía, yo estaba comiendo

La forma progresiva suele abreviarse de ordinario en la conversación:

    I'm going home   voy a casa
    aren't you going home?   ¿no vas a casa?
    I wasn't going home   no iba a casa
    weren't you going home?   ¿no ibas a casa?

Uso de los indefinidos «every» [*'evri*] «cada», «todos»; «each» [*i:tʃ*], «cada»; «all» [*ɔ:l*] «todos»:

«Every» se usa siempre acompañando a un nombre o a un cardinal y denota cada uno de los miembros de un todo en sentido general y en conjunto.

| I told every boy to come to-morrow | dije a todos los niños que viniesen mañana |

«Each» se refiere a cada uno por separado:

| I told each boy to come | dije a cada uno de los niños que viniera (a cada uno por separado) |

«All», en sentido limitado, va seguido del artículo y se refiere a un plural:

| I told all the children to come | dije a todos los niños que viniesen |

En sentido general, «all» no va seguido de artículo:

all men are mortal *'mɔːtl* todos los hombres son mortales

Words

home *houm*	casa, hogar	holiday *'hɔlidei*	día de fiesta
afternoon *'aːftə'nuːn*	tarde	because *bi'kɔz*	porque
morning *'mɔːniŋ*	mañana	night *nait*	noche

Exercise

I am writing my lesson. Are you writing your exercise? Where are you going? I am going to school. Aren't you going to school this afternoon? No, I am not going to school this afternoon because it is a holiday. Are you going for a walk? No, I'm not going for a walk. Are you eating apples? Yes, I am eating apples. Mary is not eating apples; she doesn't like apples. Are you having a lesson now? Yes, I am having a lesson now. I always have a lesson in the afternoon. Were you studying when he came? No, I wasn't studying; I was reading. We were running home. They were looking at these trees. They were looking at the sky. Every boy was looking at the blackboard. What is Mary eating? She is eating an apple. Peter was leaving the room when his friend came in.

Words

after 'a:ftə*	después	provisions prə'viʒənz	provisión
at æt	a, en	rain rein	lluvia
at work ət'wə:k	trabajando	shine ʃain	brillar
bee bi:	abeja	shop ʃɔp	tienda
buy bai	comprar	sky skai	cielo
carefully 'kɛəfuli	cuidadosamente	soar sɔ:*	elevarse
copy 'kɔpi	copiar	so much sou mʌtʃ	tanto
day dei	día	sun sʌn	sol
geography dʒi'ɔgrəfi	geografía	sunny 'sʌni	soleado
hay hei	heno	sunshine sʌnʃain	sol
high hai	alto	teach ti:tʃ	enseñar
history 'histəri	historia	thing θiŋ	cosa
how hau	como	to-day tə'dei	hoy
hum hʌm	zumbar	to-morrow tə'mɔrou	mañana
it is cold it is kould	hace frío	the day after — ðə dei 'a:ftə*	pasado mañana
it is hot it is hɔt	hace calor	to learn how to speak tə lə:n hau tə spi:k	aprender a hablar
lark la:k	alondra		
learn lə:n	aprender		
lesson 'lesn	lección		
listen 'lisn	escuchar	town taun	pueblo, ciudad
little 'litl	pequeño	what a pity! wɔt ə piti!	¡qué lástima!
make meik	hacer		
morning 'mɔ:niŋ	mañana	yesterday 'jestə:dei	ayer
in the —	por la mañana		
office 'ɔfis	oficina	the day before bi'fɔ:*—	anteayer
proverb 'prɔvə:b	proverbio		

Nota: Los adjetivos de nacionalidad se escriben con mayúscula, así como los días de la semana, los meses del año y las estaciones.

English, French [frentʃ] francés; Monday [mʌndi] lunes; Spring [spriŋ] primavera.

Reading exercise

We are having a lesson. We are sitting at our desks and listening to what the teacher is telling us. He is giving us an English lesson and we are learning how to pronounce English. We have many lessons every day; we are learning English, French, History and Geography. Our teacher pronounces the words for us, and we pronounce them after him. He is not sitting; he is standing by the table. We are all looking at him and repeating the words after him. He shows us how to pronounce the words properly. Each pupil reads a sentence very carefully and he tells him how to read it well. Then each boy writes one sentence until he knows it. Then he copies it again.

Look, it is raining! The boys are shutting the windows because it is raining. The sky was blue this morning, but now it is not. The sun isn't shining and it is cold. Does it rain much here? Yes, it rains very much and very often. What a pity! I like the sun so much! While I am working my sister is learning her lessons at home and mother is buying food and provisions in the shops in the town and my father is in his office.

Conversation

Where are you? Are you listening to your teacher? What is he teaching you? Are you sitting or standing? Are you a teacher? Are you having an English lesson now? Will you be having one to-morrow? Is your sister studying at home? When do you shut the window? Is it raining now? Was it raining this morning? Was it raining yesterday when you came to school? Do you always study your lessons at home after school? Do you get up when your teacher comes into the room? Are you getting up now? Is it raining now? Is it sunny? Is it cold? Was it cold yesterday?

> Spring is coming, spring is coming!
> Hark! the little bee is humming.
> See! the lark is soaring high
> In the blue and sunny sky.

Proverbs.

After rain comes sunshine.
Make hay while the sun shines.

Ejercicio

¿Adónde vas? Voy a casa. Voy a comprar comida para mañana porque es fiesta. Después voy al cine. ¿Vas al cine todas las fiestas? No, todas no. Solamente algunas. Estoy leyendo un libro muy bonito. ¿Qué comes (estás comiendo)? Como manzanas. ¿Comes frutas todos los días? Sí, todos los días como frutas. ¿Estabas estudiando cuando yo vine?

No, cuando viniste no estudiaba; leía un libro. Yo voy al colegio; mi hermana estudia en casa. Mi padre va al despacho todos los días, y mi madre trabaja en casa. Hoy, mi padre no trabaja en el despacho porque es fiesta. Esta tarde no iré al cine porque está lloviendo. Llueve mucho. ¡Qué lástima! No me gusta que llueva. Me gusta el sol. Cierra la ventana. Está lloviendo y hace mucho frío.

To learn by heart

Infinitivo		Pasado	Participio
to eat *i:t*	comer	ate *et*	eaten *'i:tn*
to read *ri:d*	leer	read *red*	read *red*
to buy *bai*	comprar	bought *bɔ:t*	bought *bɔ:t*
to learn *lə:n*	aprender	learnt *lə:nt*	learnt *lə:nt*

Conjugate:
  a) I am eating an apple.
  b) I was reading a book.
  c) I was not listening to you.

THIRTEENTH LESSON
LECCIÓN DECIMOTERCIA

Verbos anómalos y defectivos: «can», «may», «must»

CAN	MAY
Presente: *Yo puedo*, etc.	
I can *kæn*	I may *mei*
you can	you may
he can	he may
we can	we may
you can	you may
they can	they may

«Can» y «may» sólo se conjugan en presente y pasado. El pasado de «can» es «could» [*kud*], y el de «may» es «might» [*mait*], para todas las personas. Estos verbos se llaman también anómalos por tener una serie de peculiaridades comunes a todos los de su clase:

  a) La tercera persona del singular del presente no tiene la «s» característica de este tiempo: «he can», «he may».

b) Las formas interrogativa y negativa de estos verbos no toman «do» como los demás verbos: «can I?», «may I?», «I cannot» [kænɔt], «I may not» [mei nɔt]. La costumbre ha unido verbo y negación, que suelen contraerse: «I can't» [ka:nt].

c) Estos verbos toman un complemento en infinitivo sin el «to», de este modo: «he can write», «he may go».

«Can» significa poder en el sentido de facultad, habitualidad, condición del sujeto para hacer algo. Los tiempos de que carece se expresan por medio de «to be able» ['eibl] «ser capaz», «poder», esto es, el verbo «to be» seguido del adjetivo «able».

| I can open the door. | Puedo abrir la puerta. |
| I shall be able to open the door. | Podré abrir la puerta. |

«Can» se usa también con el significado de saber hacer algo:

Can you play *plei* the piano *pjænou?* ¿Sabe usted tocar el piano?

«May» expresa permiso, posibilidad de hacer algo. Los tiempos de que carece se conjugan con la forma «to be allowed» [ə'laud] «ser permitido (permitir)», «poder».

May I open the window?	¿Puedo abrir la ventana?
You will be allowed to learn English.	Te permitirán (podrás) aprender inglés.
He can speak English.	Él sabe hablar inglés.

MUST

Presente: *Yo debo*, etc.

I must *mʌst*	we must
you must	you must
he must	they must

«Must» expresa obligación ineludible, necesidad de hacer algo. Puede también expresar deducción de que un hecho debe de haber tenido lugar.

we must study	debemos estudiar
we must eat	debemos comer
he must be in London now	debe de estar en Londres ahora

«Must not» suele abreviarse: «mustn't» [mʌs(ə)nt]. Para los tiempos de que carece suele usarse «to be obliged» [ə'blaidʒd], o «to have to», en el tiempo correspondiente.

Uso de algunas preposiciones

«In» expresa situación en un lugar; también hace referencia a una extensión de espacio o tiempo prolongada.

I am in the room.	Estoy en la habitación.
In England.	En Inglaterra.
In Winter.	En invierno.

«At» hace referencia a una pequeña extensión de espacio o tiempo. También indica proximidad con contacto actual o no.

He is not at home.	No está en casa.
He came at four o'clock ə'klɔk.	Vino a las cuatro.
He goes to school at eight o'clock in the morning.	Va al colegio a las ocho de la mañana.
She sits at the table.	Se sienta a la mesa.

«In» indica también posición en reposo en o dentro de algo.

The pencil is in the box.   El lápiz está en la caja.

«Into», «en, dentro de», indica movimiento hacia un lugar y reposo en él:

I put the pencil into the box.   Pongo el lápiz dentro de la caja.

«On» significa «sobre», «encima de», con contacto:

The book is on the table.   El libro está encima (sobre) de la mesa.

Words

afraid (be — of) ə'freid	temer, tener miedo	like *laik*	como
against ə'geinst	contra	neither... nor 'naiðə* nɔː*	ni... ni
asked aːskt	preguntado	not at all 'nɔt ət 'ɔːl	en absoluto
at first ət'fəːst	al principio		
blind *blaind*	ciego	please *pliːz*	por favor
close *klouz*	cerrar	ride *raid*	montar (a caballo, en bicicleta, etc.)
deaf *def*	sordo		
difficult 'difikəlt	difícil		
difficulty	dificulta	slowly *slouli*	despacio, lentamente
dumb *dʌm*	mudo		
deaf and —	sordomudo	succeed sək'siːd	tener éxito, salir bien (una cosa)
easy *iːzi*	fácil		
Englishman 'iŋgliʃmən	inglés	time *taim*	tiempo, vez
		try *trai*	intentar, tratar
gentle, gently 'dʒentl, -tli	suave, dulcemente	understand ʌndə'stænd	comprender

Reading exercise

People can speak, hear and see. When a man can't see he is blind; when he can't hear he is deaf and when he can't speak he is dumb. There are people who can neither hear nor speak and they are called deaf and dumb. We call lame a man who cannot walk well and bald a man who has very little hair on his head. Can you understand these sentences? The children who cannot understand them must study them because they are very easy. English is not at all difficult. Don't be afraid to pronounce this word. Try it. Try it again. If you don't succeed the first time try again, and you will be able to do it because it is not difficult. You must try to pronounce like an Englishman. Speak slowly and gently.

Once a boy wanted to ride his bycicle in the garden of his father's friend and he asked him: «Sir, may you ride a bycicle in the garden?» And the gentleman answered: «I may, but you may not.»

May I open the window if it is not raining? Yes, but if it begins to rain, you must close it again.

Words

beggar *begə**	pordiosero	never *'nevə**	nunca
cake *keik*	pastel	put off *'put'ɔ(:)f*	posponer
choose *tʃu:z*	escoger	Roman *'roumən*	romano
chooser *'tʃu:zə**	el que escoge, exigente	Rome *roum*	Roma
		stone *stoun*	piedra
drink *driŋk*	beber	throw *θrou*	echar, arrojar
glass *gla:s*	vaso	till *til*	hasta
lead *li:d*	conducir, llevar	water *'wɔ:tə**	agua
lie *lai*	tumbarse, echarse	umbrella *ʌm'brelə*	paraguas

Proverbs.

Never put off till to-morrow what you can do to-day.
You cannot eat your cake and have it.
Beggars cannot (may not, must not) be choosers.
As you make your bed, so you must lie on it.
People who live in glass houses must not throw stones.
When you are in Rome, you must do as the Romans do.
You may lead a horse to the water, but you cannot make it drink.

Conversation

Can a blind man see [*blaind mæn si:*]? What do you call the man who cannot see? What do you call a man who cannot speak? Can you speak English? When do you speak English? Must you speak English when you are with your teacher? What must you do when it rains? Can you open the window? Are you allowed to go to the garden to play? What must you speak when you are in England?

Ejercicio

Yo no puedo ir. ¿Puedes ir tú? Creo que no, porque debo estudiar la lección. ¿Cuándo podrás ir? Podré ir mañana. Debes procurar entender lo que dice el profesor y pronunciarlo despacio. Tengo que (debo) ver a Juan. ¿Sabes dónde vive? Si quieres verle debes ir a Londres, porque vive allí. ¿Qué ves (puedes ver) desde la ventana? Veo (puedo ver) el jardín. ¿Puedes verlo tú? No, desde aquí no puedo verlo.

Los chicos que no entiendan esta frase deben traducirla y repetirla. No es difícil, en absoluto. No tengáis miedo. Probad una vez, varias (algunas) veces y tendréis éxito.

To learn by heart

Infinitivo		*Pasado*	*Participio*
to shine ʃain	brillar	shone ʃɔn	shone ʃɔn
to teach tiːtʃ	enseñar	taught tɔːt	taught tɔːt
to show ʃou	mostrar, enseñar	showed ʃoud	shown ʃoun
to ride raid	montar, cabalgar	rode roud	ridden 'ridn

Conjugate:

The sun does not shine to-day, etc.
I cannot ride a bycicle, etc.
I must study my lessons every day, etc.

FOURTEENTH LESSON
LECCIÓN DECIMOCUARTA

Los números cardinales

(Véanse los doce primeros números en la lecc. 2.ª)

13 thirteen *'θəːˈtiːn*	70	seventy *sevənti*
14 fourteen *'fɔːˈtiːn*	80	eighty *eiti*
15 fifteen *'fifˈtiːn*	90	ninety *nainti*
16 sixteen *'siksˈtiːn*	100	a hundred *əˈhʌndrid*
17 seventeen *'sevənˈtiːn*	101	one (a) hundred and one
18 eighteen *'eiˈtin*	129	one (a) hundred and twenty-nine
19 nineteen *'nainˈtiːn*	200	two hundred
20 twenty *twenti*	300	three hundred
21 twenty-one *'twntiˈwʌn*	1 000	a thousand *θauzənd*
22 twenty-two *'twentiˈtuː*	1 500	fifteen hundred
23 twenty-three *'twentiˈθriː*	2 000	two thousand
30 thirty *θəːti*	2 500	two thousand five hundred
31 thirty-one *'θəːtiˈwʌn*	100 000	a (one) hundred thousand
40 forty *fɔːti*	1 000 000	a (one) million *miljən*
50 fifty *fifti*	2 000 000	two million(s)
60 sixty *siksti*	0	nought *nɔːt*

Nótese que entre la decena y la unidad no se emplea la conjunción «and», como en castellano. Después de millón, mil y cien, los números que sean inferiores a cien deben ir precedidos de la conjunción «and». Por lo tanto, si en la cantidad hubiera decenas, la conjunción «and» precederá a éstas; si no las hubiese, precederá a las unidades.

> 1 343 one thousand three hundred and fourty three
> 3 204 three thousand two hundred and four
> 1 001 one thousand and one

Las palabras «million», «thousand» y «hundred» son invariables. Se usan, empero, en plural cuando hacen el oficio de sustantivos colectivos.

> Are there many books in this library?   ¿Hay muchos libros en esta biblioteca?
> Yes, there are several hundreds.   Sí, hay varios centenares.

Antes de la preposición «of» también se usan en plural:

> Hundreds of boys.   Centenares de muchachos.

Words

addition ə'diʃən	suma	multiplication	multiplicación
subtraction	resta	mʌltipli'keiʃən	
səb'trækʃən		division di'viʒən	división

Addition:

    What is two plus *plʌs* two (2+2)? ¿Cuánto es dos más dos?
    Two plus two is four; two and two are four; two added to two make four.

Subtraction:

    What is three minus *mainəs* one? ¿Cuánto es tres menos dos?
    Three minus one is two; one from three leaves two: one from three is two.

Multiplication:

    What is three times four? ¿Cuánto son tres por cuatro?
    Three times four are twelve.

Once one is one.	Uno por uno es uno.
Twice two are four.	Dos por dos son cuatro

Nota: «One time» se contrae en «once», «una vez»; «two times», en «twice».

Division:

What is twelve divided by three *divaidid bai θri:?*	¿Cuánto es doce entre tres?
Twelve divided by three is four.	Doce entre tres es cuatro.
How many times does three go into thirteen?	¿Cuántas veces cabe tres entre trece?
Three goes four times into thirteen and leaves one left over.	Tres entre trece cabe a cuatro y sobra uno.

La multiplicación suele abreviarse diciendo, por ejemplo: «four fours are sixteen» (4×4=16).

Ejercicio práctico.

What is:	7 plus 8?	What is:	3 times 3?
	3 + 7?		2 × 5?
	9 + 2?		5 × 8?
	5 + 2?		3 × 6?
	4 + 4?		8 × 4?
	6 + 1?		2 × 2?
What is:	6 minus 2?	What is:	10 divided by 2?
	8 − 5?		13 : 3?
	9 − 3?		15 : 2?
	12 − 4?		40 : 5?
	4 − 1?		32 : 4?

Los números cardinales

Nótense las expresiones:

the last *ðə la:st*	el último
the last but one	el penúltimo
the last but two	el antepenúltimo
the two first	los dos primeros
the two last	los dos últimos
both	ambos
all three	los tres
every second *'evri 'sekənd*	cada dos
every third	cada tres
every other one	alterno, uno sí y uno no
twice *tuais*	dos veces
three times	tres veces
once a week *wʌns ə wi:k*	una vez a la semana
twice a month *tuais ə mʌnθ*	dos veces al mes

Words

add *æd*	sumar, añadir	multiplied *'mʌltiplaid*	multiplicado
added *'ædid*	sumado, añadido	multiply *'mʌltiplai*	multiplicar
addition *ə'diʃən*	suma, adición	nest *nest*	nido
already *ɔ(:)l'redi*	ya	nothing *'nʌθing*	nada
and so on *ənd sou ɔn*	etcétera	nought *nɔ:t*	cero
arithmetic *ə'riθmətik*	aritmética	number *'nʌmbə**	número
becomes *bi'kʌmz*	deviene, se hace	odd *ɔd*	impar
count *kaunt*	contar	ordinal *'ɔ:dinl*	ordinal
divide *di'vaid*	dividir	over *ouvə**	sobre
divided *di'vaidid*	dividido	pleasant *'pleznt*	agradable
dozen *'dʌzən*	docena	plus *plʌs*	más
draw *drɔ:*	dibujar, trazar, arrastrar	rule *ru:l*	regla
		ruler *'ru:lə**	regla
even *'i:vən*	pares, incluso	several *'sev(ə)rəl*	varios
example *ig'za:mpəl*	ejemplo	snows *snouz*	nieva
		spell *spel*	deletrear, escribir
figure *'figə**	cifra, número		
goes into *gouz intu*	cabe a	straight *streit*	recto
		subtract *səb'trækt*	restar
gross *grous*	gruesa (medida)		
know *nou*	saber, conocer	subtracted *səb'træktid*	restado
leave *li:v*	dejar, restar		
line *lain*	línea	up to *ʌp tu, tə*	hasta

Exercise

Three is a number; the next number is four. After four comes five. Add two to ten and you will have twelve. Five fours are twenty, and three times two are six. Now count from ten to thirty. 10 and 30 are figures. Numbers are called figures. Multiply three by three and you will have nine. We call twelve a dozen and twelve dozen make a gross. Can you tell me the four rules? What have you if you subtract three from three? Three from three leaves nothing. The even numbers are two, four, six, and so on; the odd numbers are one, three, five, and so on. Write with words: 205, 473, 1954, 6 892, 221, 1 102, 1 103 157, 84, 75. All these numbers are called cardinal numbers. We have already learned the cardinal numbers, but we do not know yet the ordinal numbers. We shall learn the ordinal numbers in the next lesson.

Conversation

Can you count in English? What are the first three odd numbers? How many hands have you? How many books are there on the table? Can you divide 15 by three? How many times does 5 go into 40? Count from 1 up to 15. Can you spell million? 3? 12? What is another word for 12? How many legs have you? and the table? and a horse? Can you draw a straight line under the figures? Why do you draw a straight line under the figures? Can you write English numbers? Do you know how to spell 15? Can you write 2? How many fingers have people? And how many toes? Have you five fingers in each hand? Can you multiply 5 by 6? What is 7 by 3? How many times does 5 go into 40? If you take 5 from 7, how many have you left?

El tiempo se expresa en inglés por medio del verbo «to be» en forma impersonal:

What is the weather like *'weðə* laik?*	¿Qué tiempo hace?
It is very cold *kould.*	Hace mucho frío.
It is very hot *hɔt.*	Hace mucho calor.
It is very windy *windi.*	Hace mucho viento.

La sensación de frío y calor también se expresa con el verbo «to be» en la persona y tiempo correspondientes:

I am very cold.	Tengo mucho frío.
I was very hot.	Tenía mucho calor.

También la edad se expresa con el verbo «to be», añadiendo el adjetivo «old» al número o a la indicación de tiempo:

I am 16 years old. Tengo 16 años.
The baby is 3 months old. El niño tiene 3 meses.
This church is a hundred years Esta iglesia tiene cien años.
old 'tʃəːtʃ is ə hʌndrid jeːˑs ould.

The seasons 'siːznz **Las estaciones**

| Winter 'wintə* | invierno | Summer 'sʌmə* | verano |
| Spring spriŋ | primavera | Autumn 'ɔːtəm | otoño |

The months of the year mʌnθs ɔv ðə jəː* **Los meses del año**

January 'dʒænjuəri	enero	July dʒu(ː)'lai	julio
February 'februəri	febrero	August 'ɔːgəst	agosto
March maːtʃ	marzo	September səp'tembə*	septiembre
April 'eiprəl	abril	October ɔk'toubə*	octubre
May mei	mayo	November no'vembə*	noviembre
June dʒuːn	junio	December di'sembə*	diciembre

Words

afternoon 'aːftə'nuːn	tarde
at æt, ət	a, en
begin bi'gin	empezar
blow blou	soplar
bring forth 'briŋ fɔːθ	brotar, sacar
clouds klaudz	nubes
cold kould	frío
common 'kɔmən	común, corriente
end end	fin
equal 'iːkwəl	igual
first fəːst	primero
fortnight 'fɔːtnait	quincena
freezes 'friːziz	hiela
hour auə*	hora
leap-year 'liːpjəː*	año bisiesto
mid-day 'middei	mediodía
midnight 'midnait	medianoche
minute 'minit	minuto
month mʌnθ	mes
night nait	noche
noon nuːn	mediodía
o'clock ə'klɔk	contracción de «of the clock», «del reloj»
one	la una
only 'ounli	solamente
part paːt	parte
rainbow 'reinbou	arco iris
season 'siːzən	estación (del año)
second 'sekənd	segundo
shower 'ʃauə*	chaparrón
some sʌm	algún, alguno
sometimes 'sʌmtaimz	a veces
swallow 'swɔlou	golondrina
time taim	tiempo
warm wɔːm	caluroso, templado
weather 'weðə*	tiempo
week wiːk	semana
wind wind	viento

Reading exercise

The year has four seasons. The first month of the year is January and it is a very cold month. February is also very cold and sometimes there is a lot of rain. Rain is water that comes from the clouds. February has only 28 days, but every four years it has 29 and then it is called leap-year.

The other months have 30 or 31 days. After Winter comes Spring. In Spring we open the windows and the air comes into the room. Sometimes it rains but it is only a shower and the air is clearer after. The swallows come and make their nests in Spring. The first month of Summer is July. It is very hot, and very pleasant. When Autumn comes the weather is cold, the afternoons are not so long and soon it becomes very cold, the wind blows and it rains a lot. Sometimes it freezes and snows. Then the year is at an end.

Conversation

What are the names of the four seasons? How many days has a month? and a year? and a week? Have all months thirty days? Which months have 31 days? Which months are very cold? When is it very windy? When do swallows come? Do they stay here in Winter? Does the sun shine when it rains? What comes out after rain? How many days has the week? Which are the months of the year? Does the sun shine at mid-day? and at mid-night? How many hours has a day? How many minutes has an hour? When does Autumn begin? Is it one o'clock now? Is it raining now? Did it rain yesterday? Is it warm to-day? Was it cold yesterday? Does it freeze often?

Ejercicio

El año tiene 365 días y el año bisiesto tiene 366. Los meses tienen 30 ó 31 días, pero febrero tiene 28. En los años bisiestos, febrero tiene 29. Dos semanas o 14 días son una quincena. El año tiene 52 semanas, y la semana tiene 7 días.

Enero es el primer mes del año. Hay cuatro estaciones en el año: invierno, primavera, verano y otoño. En invierno hace mucho frío, nieva a menudo y a veces hiela. Después viene la primavera. Los meses de primavera son: abril, mayo y junio. Ya no nieva; el tiempo es más templado y al mediodía hace calor. A veces llueve mucho en abril, pero es bueno. Las frutas maduran ahora y hay flores en los jardines. En verano hace mucho calor, y las golondrinas hacen sus nidos en los árboles. Con el mes de octubre viene el otoño. Los días ya no son largos, empieza a hacer frío y el año se acaba.

To learn by heart

Infinitivo		Pasado	Participio
to draw *drɔː*	dibujar, arrastrar	drew *druː*	drawn *drɔːn*
to know *nou*	saber, conocer	knew *njuː*	known *noun*
to begin *biˈgin*	empezar	began *biˈgæn*	begun *bigʌn*

Conjugate:

a) I do not write a letter
b) Shall I write my exercise?
c) Did I begin my lesson?

FIFTEENTH LESSON
LECCIÓN DECIMOQUINTA

Los números ordinales

Los ordinales se forman añadiendo la terminación «th» al cardinal, excepto los tres primeros números, que tienen una palabra distinta, y el 5, 9 y 12, en los que el cardinal sufre una ligera modificación antes de tomar la terminación «th». Los terminados en «y» cambian ésta en «ie» antes de la terminación.

1st	the	first *fəːst*	22nd	the	twenty-second
2nd	»	second *ˈsekənd*	23rd	»	twenty-third
3rd	»	third *θəːd*	24th	»	twenty-fourth
4th	»	fourth *fɔːθ*	25th	»	twenty-fifth
5th	»	fifth *fifθ*	30th	»	thirtieth *θəːtiiθ*
6th	»	sixth *siksθ*	31st	»	thirty-first
7th	»	seventh *ˈsevənθ*	40th	»	fortieth
8th	»	eighth *eitθ*	50th	»	fiftieth
9th	»	ninth *nainθ*	60th	»	sixtieth
10th	»	tenth *tenθ*	70th	»	seventieth
11th	»	eleventh *iˈlevənθ*	80th	»	eightieth
12th	»	twelfth *twelfθ*	90th	»	ninetieth
13th	»	thirteenth *ˈθəːˈtiːnθ*	100th	»	hundredth *ˈhʌndrətθ*
14th	»	fourteenth *ˈfɔːˈtiːnθ*	101st	»	hundred and first
15th	»	fifteenth *ˈfifˈtiːnθ*	102nd	»	hundred and second
16th	»	sixteenth *ˈsiksˈtiːnθ*	103rd	»	hundred and third
17th	»	seventeenth *ˈsevnˈtiːnθ*	200th	»	two hundredth
18th	»	eighteenth *ˈeiˈtiːnθ*	210th	»	two hundred and tenth
19th	»	nineteenth *ˈnainˈtiːnθ*	1 000th	»	thousandth *ˈθauzətθ*
20th	»	twentieth *twentiiθ*	2 000th	»	two thousandth
21st	»	twenty-first			

Los numerales fraccionados o quebrados se expresan como se indica a continuación:

1/2	a half *ha:f* (*o* one half)
1/3	a third (*o* one ...)
1/4	a fourth, a quarter *'kwɔ:tə** (*o* one ...)
1/5	a fifth (*o* one ...)
1/6	a sixth (*o* one ...)
1/16	a sixteenth (*o* one ...)
3/5	three fifths
8/12	eight twelfths
58/100	fifty-eight hundredths
300/1 000	three hundred thousandths
27/164	twenty-seven one hundred and sixty fourths

Puede también emplearse el artículo determinado cuando lo requiera el caso: «the half», «the third», «the four fiftieths». «Half», «medio», «mitad», tiene el plural «halves»: «two halves», «dos mitades». Cuando expresa cantidad lleva pospuesto el artículo:

I lost half the money and waited half an hour.	Perdí la mitad del dinero y esperé media hora.

Con los nombres de peso, medida y tiempo no se emplea «fourth», sino «quarter».

Los números mixtos se expresan como en castellano, pero anteponiendo el artículo indeterminado «a» a la fracción cuando es singular:

A quarter of a pound *paund*.	Un cuarto de libra.
A quarter of a mile *mail*.	Un cuarto de milla.
Six yards and a half *ja:ds ənd ə ha:f*.	Seis yardas y media.

Se usan los ordinales para expresar:

a) Orden en general:

You are the second.	Eres el segundo.
Chapter the first *'tʃæptə* ðə fɔ:st*.	Capítulo primero.

b) Cronología:

George the sixth *dʒɔ:dʒ ðə siksθ*.	Jorge VI.
The twentieth century.	El siglo XX.

c) Fechas:

London, April, the 21st *'lʌndən eipril ðə 'twenti fɔ:st*.
Chester, May, the 2nd *'tʃestə* mei ðə 'sekənd*.

Los números ordinales

Los números que indican el año no suelen leerse como cifra, sino por cientos:

1956
- *como numeral:* one thousand nine hundred and fifty six
- *como fecha:* nineteen hundred and fifty six, *o bien* nineteen fifty-six

La fecha del mes puede preguntarse de dos maneras:

What is the date, to-day? *deit, tə 'dei?*	¿Qué fecha es hoy?
What day of the month is it to-day? *mʌnθ iz it tə 'dei?*	¿Qué día del mes es hoy?

The days of the week

Sunday *'sʌndi*	domingo	Thursday *'θəːzdi*	jueves
Monday *'mʌndi*	lunes	Friday *'fraidi*	viernes
Tuesday *'tjuːzdi*	martes	Saturday *'sætədi*	sábado
Wednesday *'wenzdi*	miércoles		

Delante de los días de la semana el artículo se sustituye por «on» (en), «last» (último, pasado) y «next» (próximo).

Las estaciones del año y los meses, como los días de la semana, se escriben con mayúscula.

He will come on Monday.	Vendrá el lunes.
In Winter it is very cold.	En invierno hace mucho frío.
In May there are many flowers.	En mayo hay muchas flores.

Nota: «On Monday», el lunes; «in Spring», en la primavera; «at Easter», por Pascua; «at Christmas» [*'krismәs*], por Navidad.

either *aiðə**, *iːðə** ... or *ɔː**	o ... o.
neither *naiðə** ... nor *nɔː*	ni ... ni.

Take one or the other.   Toma uno u otro.
Take neither the one nor the other.   No tomes ni uno ni otro.

Words

age *eidʒ*	edad	Christmas *'krismәs*	Navidad
at *æt, әt*	a, en	— Day	día de Navidad
Bank Holiday *bæŋk 'hɔlidei*	uno de los cuatro días de fiesta legal cada año	— Eve *iːv*	víspera de Navidad
born *bɔːn*	nacido	Easter *'iːstә**	Pascua de Resurrección
Boxing Day *'bɔk-siŋ dei*	día de san Esteban	— Sunday *'sʌndi*	domingo de Pascua
bring *briŋ*	traer	Good Friday *gud 'fraidi*	viernes santo
but *bʌt, bәt*	pero		
but once *wʌns*	sólo una vez		

great *greit*	grande	New Year *'nju: 'jə:*	año nuevo
greet *gri:t*	felicitar, saludar	New Year's Day	día de año nuevo
happy *'hæpi*	feliz	− − Eve	día último de año
hence *hens*	desde aquí	people *'pi:pl*	gente
holiday *'hɔlidei*	día de fiesta	rest *rest*	descanso
instead of *ins-'ted əv*	en lugar de	day of −*dei əv*	día de descanso
just *dʒust*	justamente	return *ri'tə:n*	regreso
last *las:t*	último pasado	week day	día de la semana
many happy returns of the day *'meni hæpi ri'tə:ns əv ðə dei*	muchas felicidades, por muchos años	Whitmonday *'wit'mʌndi*	lunes de Pentecostés
		Whitsuntide *'witsntaid*	Pentecostés
Midsummer day *'midsʌmə'dei*	el 24 de junio	− sunday	domingo de Pentecostés
		wish *wiʃ*	deseo

Reading exercise

The week has seven days. In England, Sunday is the first day of the week. Saturday is the last. Tuesday is the third and Friday is the sixth. On week days we work but on Sunday we don't work because it is a holiday. The year has fifty-two weeks and the week has six working days and one holiday. The year begins on the first of January, so we call it New Years' Day. The last day of the year is December, 31st, so we call it New Year's Eve. There are some great holidays in the year. One of these is December the twenty-fifth. It is Christmas Day, and the day before it is also very great because Christ was born on the night of that day, many years ago. Boxing Day is also a holiday, and it is on December the 26th. Sometimes we write Xmas., instead of Christmas. On Christmas Day we greet our friends with Christmas cards and we say to them Merry Christmas and Happy New Year. Another great holiday is Easter, which is in the Spring. Holy Week is the week before Easter, and on that week Thursday and Friday are called Mondy Thursday (Jueves Santo) and Good Friday. Whitsuntide is seven weeks after Easter and it is also a holiday. There are also 4 holidays in the year called Bank Holidays and on these days everywhere is closed. Midsummer's Day is June, 24th, and it is a very nice holiday. Once a year it is our birthday. My birthday is on May the 10th. On that day they will give me many presents and all my friends will wish me many happy returns of the day.

Los números ordinales

Conversation

How many days has the week? Do you work all the days of the week? What do we call the 25th of December? What do we say on our friends' birthday? Do we greet our friends at Christmas? When is your birthday? How many months are there in a year? What do we call the last day of the year? Do you like to go out on Midsummer's night? When do you have a holiday? Do you work during the holidays? Do you give presents to your friends for their birthday? Who gives you presents for your birthday? When is Christmas? When is Boxing day? Is your birthday in May? When is your sister's birthday? Do you go home for your holidays?

Ejercicio

El año tiene 365 días. Algunas veces tiene 366 y entonces se llama bisiesto. Durante la semana trabajamos, pero el domingo es fiesta, y los días de fiesta no trabajamos; por lo tanto, el domingo es día de descanso. El 25 de diciembre es Navidad. Navidad es una fiesta muy bonita. Por Navidad felicitamos a nuestros amigos y les mandamos tarjetas de Navidad. También por Año Nuevo les deseamos muchas felicidades. El día de Noche Buena hay una misa (mass) a medianoche que se llama Misa del Gallo (Midnigth Mass). Me gusta mucho ir a esta misa y todos los años, el día de Noche Buena, voy a ella. Hoy es el último día de diciembre. ¿Sabes cómo llamamos a este día? Le llamamos día de Noche Vieja, o último día del año, o víspera de Año Nuevo. ¿En qué día empieza el año? El primer día del año es el día de Año Nuevo o el primero de enero. ¿Cuántos días tiene la semana? ¿el mes? ¿el año? ¿Trabajas todos los días de la semana? Yo trabajo todos los días de la semana menos el domingo. El domingo voy al cine o voy de paseo con mis amigos.

To learn by heart

Christmas comes but once a year.
But when it comes it brings good cheer *tʃiə** (alegría).

Escribir con palabras: 8.º, 13.º, 25.º, 23 de enero, 1 de junio, 2 de agosto, 3 de abril.

La hora se expresa en inglés con números cardinales. Para indicar los minutos que pasan de la hora, esto es, a la derecha del reloj, se dice «past», y para indicar los que faltan para la hora siguiente, o sea a la izquierda del reloj, se dice «to»; el cuarto de hora es «a quarter» [kwɔ:tə], y la media «half past» [ha:f pa:st]. Para preguntar la hora se usan corrientemente dos expresiones:

What time is it?	¿Qué hora es?
What is the time?	¿Qué hora es?

Las horas se expresan siempre con relación al meridiano. A partir, pues, de medianoche, la primera hora de la madrugada se expresará añadiendo después del número que la indique las letras *a. m.*, que significan «ante meridiem»; y a partir del mediodía, esto es, de la una de la tarde hasta las 12 de la noche las letras *p. m.*, que significan «post meridiem», es decir, después del meridiano: «it is 4 a. m.», «it is 4 p. m.».

En lugar de decir las 12 del mediodía suele decirse «midday» [middei] o «noon» [nu:n], y «midnigth» [midnait] en lugar de las 12 de la noche o las 24.

It is 5 minutes past 12.	Son las 12 y cinco.
It is 10 minutes to 12.	Son las 12 menos 10.
It is a quarter past 12.	Son las 12 y cuarto.
It is a quarter to 12.	Son las 12 menos cuarto.
It is half past 12.	Son las 12 y media.
It is 4 a. m.	Son las 4 de la mañana.
It is 6 p. m.	Son las 6 de la tarde, o las 18.

También puede abreviarse diciendo: «it is 5 past 12», «it is 10 to 12».

Con frecuencia después de la hora exacta se añade la expresión «o'clock» [ə'klɔk], que es una abreviación de «of the clock», «del reloj»: «it is 5 o'clock».

Nótense las expresiones: A long time ago. Hace mucho tiempo. In two hours time. Dentro de dos horas.

Words

according to ə'kɔ:diŋ	según, de acuerdo con	by *bai*	por, junto a
before *bi'fɔ:**	antes	clock *klɔk*	reloj
both *bouθ*	ambos	dial *daiəl*	esfera
		dot *dɔt*	punto

Los números ordinales

exactly *ig'zæktli*	exactamente	right *rait*	derecha
face *feis*	cara, esfera	is —	está bien (del reloj: va bien)
fast *fa:st*, is —	adelantado, está —	round *raund*	redondo, alrededor
gain *gein*	adelantar, ganar		
hand *hænd*	mano, manecilla	school clock	reloj del colegio
long—, short—	minutero, horario	short *ʃɔ:t*	corto
hang *hæŋ*	colgar	set (the watch)	poner el reloj en hora
home *houm*	casa, hogar	set ðə wɔtʃ	
keep good time	tener buen hora, ir bien	slow *slou;* is —	despacio; va atrasado (del reloj)
late *leit*	tarde	strike *straik*	dar la hora, golpear
listen *'lisən*	escuchar		
long *lɔŋ*	largo	stroke *strouk*	campanada, golpe
lose *lu:z*	perder, atrasar	tell *tel*	decir
mark *ma:k*	marcar	too *tu:*	también
nearly *'niəli*	casi	usually *'ju:ʒuəli*	generalmente
past *pa:st*	pasado	watch *wɔtʃ*	reloj (pequeño, de bolsillo, pulsera, etc.)
pocket *'pɔkit*	bolsillo		
point *pɔint*	punto		
repair *ri'pɛə**	reparar, componer	worn *wɔ:n*	llevado, usado
		wrong *rɔŋ*	equivocado, mal

Reading exercise

Clocks and watches tell us the time. If we want to know the time we look at them. Watches are worn on the wrist. Clocks hang usually on the wall or stand on a table. On this table there is a clock; it is round. On a white dial you can see two hands, a long one and a short one. The long one points out the minutes; the short one the hours. Around the dial there are twelve figures which mark the hours and between (entre) the figures there are some little black strokes or dots which mark the seconds. Can you tell me what time it is? Yes; it is twenty past five. I don't know if my watch keeps good time. I think it is a little fast. What time do you make it? I make it a quarter past five. Then you are fast. Yours is right. It is neither fast nor slow. Listen! It is striking a quarter, now. Look! My watch is wrong; it gains five minutes every day. I must take it to be repaired. Now I shall set it like yours. I have set mine like the school clock; I think that was right, because usually it keeps good time. Many watches and clocks lose a few minutes every day; others gain them. When a watch loses we say it is slow and when it gains we say it is fast. Show me your watch. The short hand points to six and the long hand points to 4. What time is it? It is twenty past six. It is very late. We must go home. Must you go, too? No, I can stay; it is not late for me. By my watch it is not twenty past six. Then you are slow. Set you watch and put it right.

Conversation

When you want to know the time what do you do? Is a watch big or small? and a clock? What tells you the time? My watch is neither fast nor slow, and yours? Does the church-clock lose or gain? What do you call the face of a clock? What do you see on the dial? How many figures are there on a dial? Show me your watch. Tell me the time. Is that the right time? Isn't your watch a little fast? Is it slow? What time is it when the small hand points to 2 and the long one to 12? Do you go to the school or do you go to the office? At what time do you go to school? At what time do you go to the office? Do you carry your watch in your pocket? Do you hear the church clock when it strikes the hour? How many times does it strike when it is seven o'clock?

Ejercicio

¿Qué hora es ahora? Son las tres y cuarto. Son las cinco y media; las 7 y diez; las 11 menos cinco. Las 12 del mediodía. Las doce de la noche. ¿Va bien este reloj? No; va un poco atrasado. ¿Y el tuyo? Sí, el mío va bien. No atrasa ni adelanta. El de la iglesia no va bien; adelanta cinco minutos todos los días. ¿Qué hora es cuando la manecilla pequeña señala las 12 y la larga está en las seis? ¿Cuántos números tiene el reloj? El reloj tiene doce números que son las horas. Entre las horas hay unos puntos que son los segundos. La hora tiene 60 minutos y un minuto sesenta segundos. Encima de la mesa hay un reloj. Cuando queremos saber qué hora es, lo miramos. A veces es temprano y nos quedamos leyendo; otras veces es tarde y vamos al colegio o a la oficina. Yo salgo a las 8 y media para ir al colegio. Mi hermana sale a las 8, y mi hermano pequeño, a las 9 y cuarto. Mi padre sale muy temprano para ir al despacho (office). Mi madre sale más tarde. Generalmente sale a las 11 y media y va a comprar cosas para comer y para la casa. ¿Cuántas horas tiene el día? El día tiene doce horas de día y doce de noche. Esto es, 24 horas. Tenemos que salir dentro de 5 minutos o llegaremos tarde al colegio. Oye. Ahora está dando la hora en el reloj de la iglesia. Pon tu reloj en hora como éste porque va bien. No adelanta ni atrasa. ¿Qué hora es ahora? Son las dos y 25 de la tarde. No es muy tarde. A las tres iré a estudiar.

To learn by heart

Infinitivo		Pasado	Participio
to wear wɛə*	usar, llevar (puesto)	wore wɔː*	worn wɔːn
to teach tiːtʃ	enseñar	taught tɔːt	taught tɔːt

SIXTEENTH LESSON
LECCIÓN DECIMOSEXTA

El pasado

Como dejamos ya dicho (lección 6), el pasado de los verbos se forma de distinta manera según sea un verbo débil o fuerte. Los verbos débiles añaden el sufijo «ed» al infinitivo.

Pasado del verbo débil TO WALK, andar
Yo andaba, anduve, etc.
I walked   we walked
you walked   you walked
he walked   they walked

Hay que tener en cuenta las siguientes reglas de ortografía y fonética:

a) Si el infinitivo termina en «e», dicha «e» se omite antes de añadir la terminación «ed»: «live, lived; arrive, arrived».

b) Si termina en sílaba breve acentuada, terminada en consonante simple, se duplica dicha consonante antes de tomar la terminación «ed»: «permit, permitted; prefer, preferred».

c) Si termina en «y» precedida de consonante, se cambiará ésta en «i» antes de añadir la terminación «ed»: «cry, cried; say, said». Pero si la «y» está precedida de vocal sigue la regla general: «reply, replied; play, played».

La terminación «ed» se pronuncia de distinta manera según los casos.

a) Cuando sigue a una «t» o a una «d» se pronuncia [*id*]: «want» [*wɔnt*], «wanted» [*wɔntid*]; «divide» [*divaid*], «divided» [*divaidid*].

b) Cuando sigue a una consonante sorda se pronuncia [*t*]: «knock» [*nɔk*], «knocked» [*nɔkt*]; «place» [*pleis*], «placed» [*pleist*].

c) Cuando el verbo termina en cualquier otra consonante o vocal se pronuncia simplemente [*d*]: «live» [*liv*], «lived» [*livd*]; «call» [*kɔ:l*], «called» [*kɔ:ld*].

Hay también una serie de verbos débiles irregulares cuya terminación «ed» se cambia en «t» o en «d», con o sin modificación de la vocal interna: «feel» [*fi:l*], «felt» [*felt*]; «bend» [*bend*], «bent» [*bent*]; «buy» [*bai*], «bought» [*bɔ:t*]

Los verbos fuertes forman el pasado por un cambio de la vocal radical: «write, wrote; speak, spoke; come, came».

Pasado del verbo TO WRITE, escribir
Yo escribía, escribí, etc.
I, you, he } wrote   we, you, they } wrote

La forma interrogativa del pasado de los verbos se hace anteponiendo al infinitivo el auxiliar «did» (pasado de «do»), seguido del sujeto; la forma negativa, intercalando dicho auxiliar, seguido del adverbio «not», entre el sujeto y el infinitivo:

Did I walk?	¿Andaba yo?, ¿anduve yo?
Did he come?	¿Vino él?, ¿venía él?
I did not walk.	Yo no andaba, yo no anduve.
He did not come.	Él no vino, él no venía.

Nota importante: No debe olvidarse que en las formas interrogativa y negativa el verbo está *siempre* en infinitivo. Es el auxiliar «did» el que indica que el tiempo es pasado. La forma interrogativo-negativa es una combinación de las anteriores:

>   Did I not walk?   ¿No andaba yo?, ¿no anduve yo?
>   Did I not write?   ¿No escribía yo?, ¿no escribí yo?

En conversación ordinaria estas formas se contraen:

>   I didn't walk   I didn't write.
>   Didn't I walk?   Didn't I write?

La preposición «por» puede traducirse de muy diversas formas. Véanse los ejemplos siguientes:

>   by plane *plein*   por avión
>   by train *trein*   por tren, en tren
>   along the street ə'lɔŋ ðə striːt   por la calle
>   in the country   por el campo
>   out of the window   por la ventana
>   for you   por ti, para ti
>   over the sea 'ouvə* ðə siː   por el mar

Nótese la diferencia: «at home», «en casa (en el hogar)»; «in the house», «en la casa (el edificio)».

Words

afford ə'fɔːd	permitirse	lose luːz	perder
alone ə'loun	solo	money 'mʌni	dinero
answer 'aːnsə*	responder	pass paːs	pasar
at work ət wəːk	trabajando	since sins	ya que (desde)
by car bai kaː*	en coche	smile smail	sonrisa
companions	compañeros	stopped stɔpt	se paró
kəm'pænjənz		through θruː	por, a través
country 'kʌntri	país, campo	travelling	viajando
field fiːld	campo	'trævliŋ	

Reading exercise

Once a king was travelling by car through his country. As he passed a field he saw that there was only one woman at work. The king stopped the car went to the woman and said to her: I see that you are working alone. Where are your companions? The woman answered: They went to see the king. I also wanted to go and see the king, but as I have six children I can't afford to leave my work. So I could not go. When the king heard this, he said to the woman with a smile: «Tell your friends that since you cannot go and see the king, the king came here to see you.» And he gave the woman some money for her children.

Conversation

Where did the king go? How did he travel? Whom did he see in the fields? What was the woman doing? Were there many people working in the fields? What did the king ask? What did the woman say? Did she also want to see the king? Why didn't she go to see the king? What did the king tell her to tell her companions? What did the king give her? Do you often walk in the country? What do you see out of the window? Did you study your lesson for to-day? (hoy). Did you give your friend a present for her birthday? Did you go to school last Saturday? Did you want to go to the pictures last night?

Ejercicio

Un rey viajaba en coche por el campo. En un campo había una mujer. La mujer estaba sola. Sus compañeros no estaban trabajando con ella. El rey preguntó a la mujer dónde estaban sus amigos. Los amigos fueron a ver al rey. La mujer no pudo ir a ver al rey porque tenía que (had to) trabajar. La mujer tenía que trabajar porque tenía 6 hijos. El rey sonrió cuando la mujer le dijo adónde fueron sus amigos. El rey le dijo a la mujer que el rey venía a verla a ella. También le dio dinero. El dinero que el rey le dio era para sus hijos.

Words

bed *bed*	cama	flight *flait*	vuelo
go to —	ir a la cama	fly *flai*	volar
bird *bə:d*	pájaro	healthy *helθi*	sano, saludable
cure *kjuə**	curar	no *nou*	no, ningún
early *ə:li*	temprano	pain *pein*	dolor
everything	todo	pains (pl.)	dificultades (pl.)
evriθiŋ		power *pauə**	poder

El pasado

rise *raiz*	levantarse	in time ˈwelθi	a tiempo
save *seiv*	ahorrar	wealthy ˈwelθi	rico
stay *stei*	detener	wise *waiz*	prudente, sabio
stitch *stitʃ*	punto	without *wiðˈaut*	sin
tick *tik*	golpear, tictac	worm *wəːm*	gusano

Time flies.

> Sixty seconds make a minute,
> Sixty times the clock ticks in it;
> Sixty minutes make an hour,
> To stay its flight we have no power.

Proverbs.

> Time is money.
> Time cures everything.
> A stitch in time saves nine.
> The early bird catches the worm.
> Early to bed and early to rise makes a man healthy, wealthy and wise.
> No gains without pains.

El futuro del verbo «haber» impersonal se hace con el futuro del verbo «to be», al que se antepone, como para los demás tiempos, el adverbio «there»: «there will be», «habrá».

Conjugate:

> There will be flowers in the Spring.
> There will not be any flowers in the Winter.
> Will there be any flowers in the Summer?

Words

bill *bil*	cuenta	menu ˈmenjuː	menú
clear *kliə**	claro	nearly *niə*li*	casi
— soup *suːp*	sopa líquida, clara	oatmeal ˈoutmiːl	avena
		once *wʌns*	una vez
course *kɔːs*	plato (¹)	out *aut*	fuera
chips *tʃips*	patatas fritas	pleased *pliːzd*	complacido
despair *disˈpɛə**	desesperado	pointed ˈpɔintid	señaló
dine *dain*	comer	poor *puə**	pobre
England ˈiŋglənd	Inglaterra	quit *kwit*	largarse, salir de
feel hungry	sentir hambre	restaurant	restaurante
fellow ˈfelou	muchacho, chico	ˈrestərɔŋ	
fish *fiʃ*	pescado	Spaniard ˈspæn-	español
French *frentʃ*	francés	jəd	
hand *hænd*	alargar	suddenly ˈsʌdnli	de pronto

(¹) En el sentido de 1.ᵉʳ plato, 2.º plato, ... de una comida

there and then *allí mismo* ðɛə* ənd ðen	too much *tuː* demasiado mʌtʃ
to go into *tu gou* entrar 'intu	with himself consigo mismo wið him'self

Reading exercise

There was once a Spaniard who was travelling in England but he had no knowledge of the English language. One evening at seven o'clock he passed a restaurant and he suddenly felt hungry. So, he went into the restaurant, sat down and the waiter gave him the menu. As he could not speak English he pointed to the first line, then to the second, then to the third course. Very pleased with himself, he waited and after a time the waiter placed before him a clear soup. After that, the waiter placed before him another soup, this time, a vegetable soup; and when the waiter brought him the third course; it was another soup. The poor fellow was nearly in despair when the waiter handed him the bill. This was too much for him. He paid, got up and left the restaurant. Just opposite, there was a shop; he bought some fish and chips and he ate them there and then.

Conversation

Where was the Spaniard travelling? Could he speak English? Why did he go into the restaurant? Did he point to the menu? What did the waiter bring him the first time? and the second? and the third? Was he very pleased with the soups? What did the waiter hand him afterwards? What did he do before he went out? What did he see? What die he buy there?

Ejercicio

Una vez viajaba yo por Inglaterra. Comprendo el inglés bien, pero no lo hablo muy bien todavía. Vi un restaurante y, como sentía hambre, entré y pedí pescado y patatas fritas. Las comí, pedí la cuenta y salí del restaurante muy satisfecho.

Un muchacho francés que no hablaba inglés entró en un restaurante para comer. Le presentaron el menú y él señaló los tres primeros platos. Eran tres sopas. Una sopa clara, una sopa de verdura y una sopa de avena. El pobre chico se largó del restaurante desesperado.

Conjugate: future and conditional; a) *interrog.,* b) *negat.:*

to pay *tu pei*	paid *peid*	paid *peid*	pagar
to feel *tu fi:l*	felt *felt*	felt *felt*	sentir
to dine *tu dain*	dined *daind*	dined *daind*	comer

SEVENTEENTH LESSON
LECCIÓN DECIMOSÉPTIMA

Grados del adjetivo

El comparativo de superioridad y el superlativo relativo se forman:

a) Añadiendo al adjetivo positivo «er» para el primero, «est» para el segundo.

b) Anteponiendo al adjetivo positivo respectivamente «more» [*mɔ:**] «más», «the most» [*moust*] «el (la, los, las) más».

Ejemplos:

cold	frío	cold*er*	más frío	the cold*est*	el más frío
thin	delgado	thinn*er*	más delgado	the thinn*est*	el más delgado
beautiful	bello	*more* beautiful	más bello	the *most* beautiful	el más bello

Forman el comparativo en «er» y el superlativo en «est» los siguientes adjetivos:

a) Los monosílabos:

cold, colder, coldest — frío, más frío, el más frío
dark *da:k*, darker *da:kə**, darkest *da:kist* — oscuro, más oscuro, el más oscuro

b) Unos cuantos bisílabos y trisílabos terminados en «ow», «er», «y», «e», «l» silábica y otras consonantes:

Positivo		Compar.	Superl.
happy *hæpi*	feliz	happier *hæpiə**	the happiest *hæpiəst*
wise *waiz*	sabio, prudente	wiser *waizə**	the wisest *waizist*
lovely *'lʌvli*	bonito, delicado	lovelier *'lʌvliə**	the loveliest *'lʌvliəst*
handsome *'hænsəm*	hermoso, bello	handsomer *'hænsəmə**	the handsomest *'hænsəməst*
yellow *jelou*	amarillo	yellower *jelouə**	the yellowest *jelouist*
clever *klevə**	listo	cleverer *klevərə**	the cleverest *klevərist*
easy *i:zi*	fácil	easier *i:ziə**	the easiest *i:ziist*
gentle *'dʒentl*	suave	gentler *dʒentə**	the gentlest *dʒentlist*
quiet *'kwaiət*	quieto, tranquilo	quieter *kwaitə**	the quietest *kwaiətist*
common *'kɔmən*	común, corriente	commoner *'kɔmənə**	the commonest *'kɔmənist*

Los adjetivos de dos o más sílabas forman el comparativo y el superlativo añadiendo las terminaciones «more» [*mɔ:**] y «most» [*moust*] al grado positivo del adjetivo.

Positivo		Compar.	Superl.
frugal *fru:gəl*	frugal	more frugal	the most frugal
learned *lə:nid*	docto, culto	more learned	the most learned
striking *'straikiŋ*	sorprendente, asombroso	more striking	the most striking
terrible *'terəbl*	terrible	more terrible	the most terrible
sensible *'senθibl*	juicioso, sensible	more sensible	the most sensible
virtuous *'və:tʃwəs*	virtuoso	more virtuous	the most virtuous
candid *kændid*	cándido	more candid	the most candid

Para añadir las terminaciones propias del comparativo y superlativo se siguen las reglas de ortografía usuales: las palabras agudas terminadas en sílaba breve doblan la consonante final antes de tomar la terminación; las palabras terminadas en «y» precedida de consonante cambian la «y» en «i» antes de tomar la terminación correspondiente; las palabras terminadas en «e» muda suprimen dicha «e» antes de tomar la terminación correspondiente:

Positivo		Compar.	Superl.
fat *fæt*	gordo	fatter	the fattest
big *big*	grande	bigger	the biggest
dry *drai*	seco	drier *draiə**	the driest
lazy *'leizi*	perezoso	lazier	the laziest
noble *'noubl*	noble	nobler	the noblest
fine *fain*	hermoso, fino	finer	the finest

Forman el comparativo y superlativo del mismo modo:

sad	sæd	triste	sly slai		astuto
hot		caliente	naughty 'nɔːti		travieso
wet		húmedo	red		rojo

Los grados de inferioridad («menos ..., el, la, los, las menos») se forman con «less» en el comparativo y «the least» [liːst] en el superlativo, antepuestos al adjetivo; v. gr.:

happy feliz	less happy	menos feliz;	the least happy el menos feliz
easy iːzi fácil	less easy	menos fácil	the least easy el menos fácil

En las comparaciones, tanto de superioridad como de inferioridad, los dos términos se unen por medio de la conjunción «than» [ðæn] «que», y se ponen ambos en el mismo caso (como en castellano).

You are stronger than I.	Usted es más fuerte que yo.
My sister is taller tɔːlə* than your mother.	Mi hermana es más alta que tu madre.
It is often less easy to obey ə'bei than to command kə'maːnd.	Muchas veces es menos fácil obedecer que mandar.
You love him more than me, and less than her.	Usted le quiere a él más que a mí, y menos que a ella.
She was prettier, more accomplished and less vain than her friend.	Era más bonita, más distinguida y menos vana que su amiga.

Asimismo se emplea «than» para traducir la expresión «de lo que» después de una comparación.

He appears ə'piə*z better than he really riəli is.	Parece mejor de lo que realmente es.
It was higher haiə* than we thoght θɔːt.	Era más alto de lo que creíamos.

Las preposiciones «de, entre», etc., después de un superlativo relativo, se traducen por las correspondientes inglesas «of, among», pero cuando se habla de un lugar «de» se traduce siempre por «in».

Henry is the most diligent of (o among) my pupils; he is the cleverest boy in his class.	Enrique es el más diligente de (entre) mis discípulos; es el muchacho más hábil (inteligente) de su clase.
Mary mɛəri is the ugliest 'ʌgliəst girl in the town.	María es la muchacha más fea de la ciudad.

La comparación de igualdad se forma con «as [æz] ... as», «tan ... como», etc., en las cláusulas afirmativas, y con «so ... as», «tan ... como», etc., en las negativas. Aquí también el segundo término debe estar en el caso del primero.

Joan is as beautiful as Mary, but she is not so good as she.	Juana es tan hermosa como María, pero no es tan buena como ella.
They love you as much as us.	Os quieren tanto como a nosotros.
They do not love you so much as us.	No os quieren tanto como a nosotros.

NB. En las cláusulas interrogativas e interrogativo-negativas se emplea siempre «as ... as». Ej.:

Is he not as idle *aidl* as you?   ¿No es tan perezoso como tú?

El superlativo absoluto se forma generalmente mediante los adverbios «very» [*veri*] y «much» [*mʌtʃ*] «muy, mucho».

«Very» se emplea con los adjetivos y adverbios positivos, y con los participios de presente; «much», con los comparativos y los participios pasivos.

Very happy.	Muy feliz.
He is a very idle child.	Es un niño muy perezoso.
She was a very interesting old woman.	Era una vieja interesantísima.
He acted very meanly *'miːnli*.	Obró muy mezquinamente.
That teacher is much loved by his pupils.	Ese maestro es muy amado por sus discípulos.
Sophy *'soufi* was much stronger *'strɔŋgə** and much more diligent than she.	Sofía era mucho más fuerte y diligente que ella.

En los demás casos en que se encuentre, «mucho» se traduce también por «much». El plural de «much» es «many» y precede a los nombres en plural.

Me quiere mucho.	He loves me much.
Mucho pan.	Much bread.
Muchas mujeres.	Many women.

En lugar de «very» y «much» (excepto con los comparativos) se puede usar «most», que da más fuerza a la expresión. En algunos casos se emplea la forma en «est» del superlativo relativo (sin artículo) con sentido absoluto. A veces una gran superioridad se expresa por «far», «lejos», antepuesto al comparativo, o con «by far» pospuesto a él.

Grados del adjetivo

He is a most clever and most celebrated painter.	Es un pintor de muchísimo talento y muy célebre.
(My) dearest *djə:rist* mother...	Queridísima madre...
He is far younger *'jʌngə** than his brother.	Es mucho más joven que su hermano.
He is younger than his brother by far.	
He is the 'idlest by far.	Es con mucho el más perezoso.

Observación. En inglés se usa la forma de superlativo sólo cuando se trata de *más de dos* términos; tratándose de *dos* sólo, se emplea la forma de comparativo.

Amy *'eimi* is the politest of all these girls.	Amy es la más cortés de todas estas señoritas.
Amy is the politer of the two sisters.	Amy es la más cortés de las dos hermanas.

Varios adjetivos (y adverbios) tienen comparativo y superlativo relativo irregulares o derivados de otras raíces. Son los siguientes:

Positivo		*Compar.*	*Superl. relat.*
good	bueno	better *'betə**	the best *ðə* best
well	bien		
bad *bæd*	malo	worse *wɔːs*	the worst *wəːst*
badly, ill	mal		
little	poco, pequeño	less	the least *liːst*
much *mʌtʃ*	mucho	more *mɔː**	the most *moust*
many *'meni*	muchos		
far *fɑː**	lejano, lejos	farther *fɑːðə**	the farthest *fɑːðist*
forth *fɔːθ*	adelante	further *'fəːðə**	the furthest *fəːðist*
old *ould*	viejo	older *'ouldə**	the oldest *ouldist*
		elder *'eldə**	the eldest *eldist*
late *leit*	tardío	later *'leitə**	the latest
	tarde	the latter *'lætə**	the last *lɑːst*

Words

almost *'ɔlmoust*	casi	copper *'kɔpə**	cobre
because *bi'kɔz*	porque	enough *i'nʌf*	suficiente, bastante
bread *bred*	pan		
capital *'kæpitəl*	capital	Europe *'juərəp*	Europa
city *siti*	ciudad	fact *fækt*	hecho
comparison *kəm'pærizən*	comparación	in --	de hecho, en efecto

feast *fi:st*	fiesta, festín	other *ʌðə**	otros
feather *'feðə**	pluma	Paris *'pæris*	París
fine *fain*	hermoso	part *pa:t*	parte
friend *frend*	amigo	population	población
Germany *'dʒə:-məni*	Alemania	*pɔpju'leiʃən*	
		saying *'seiiŋ*	dicho, proverbio
gold *gould*	oro	silver *'silvə**	plata
haste *heist*	prisa	speed *spi:d*	velocidad
important	importante	strong *strɔŋ*	fuerte, resistente
im'pɔ:tənt		street *stri:t*	calle
inhabitant	habitante	thought *θɔ:t*	pensamiento, pensado (pas. y part. del v. «to think», «pensar, creer»)
in'hæbitənt			
iron *aiən*	hierro		
kind *kaind*	amable		
late *leit*	tarde		
lead *led*	plomo		
light *lait*	ligero	too *tu:*	también
a little *ə 'litl*	un poco, algo	United States	Estados Unidos
loaf *louf*	pan (hogaza)	*ju'naitid 'steits*	
metal *'metəl*	metal	valuable *'væljuəbl*	valioso, de valor
mountain	montaña		
'mauntin		way *wei*	camino, modo, manera
New York *'nju: 'jɔ:k*	Nueva York	world *wə:ld*	mundo

Exercise

My brother is older and taller than I (am). I am two years younger than he (is), and not so tall as he. He is the biggest and strongest boy in his class, but he is neither the cleverest nor the most diligent; in fact, he is one of the stupidest and idlest. In Spring the days are longer and warmer than in Winter. July and August are the hottest months of the year. Lead is heavier than iron, but iron is more useful; it is the most useful of all metals. Gold is more precious than silver, and silver is more valuable than copper. Which is heavier, a pound of lead or a pound of feathers? One is as heavy as the other. Feathers are lighter than lead, of course; but a pound is always a pound. London is one of the largest, richest, and most populous city in the world. It has more than eight million inhabitants. But Paris is more beautiful; it is one of the gayest cities in Europe. New York is the most important city of the United States of America; it is almost (nearly), as large as London; its population is a little less than eight millions.

Proverbs.

> Enough is as good as a feast.
> Half a loaf is better than no bread.
> Two heads are better than one.
> Better late than never.
> Second thoughts are best.
> The best of friends must part.
> More haste, less speed.
> Strike the iron while it is hot.
> Last, but not least.
> Fine feathers make fine birds.

Conversation

Who is the tallest in the class? Are you older or younger than Donald? Which is the coldest season? the hottest? Which is the shortest month? What is heavier than a feather? What metal is heavier than iron? more precious? Is a cat as useful as a dog? Which is the largest city in Germany? How many inhabitants has Berlin? Is it as populous as New York? When are the nights longest? shortest? Which of the four rules of arithmetic is the most difficult?

Reading exercise

Peter *'pi:tə** is as tall as John but not so tall as Henry. Henry is older than his brother, but younger than I. What is heavier, a pound of lead or a pound of iron? A pound of lead is as heavy as pound of iron. The strongest men are not always the wisest. A dog is more useful than a cat. My pencil is longer than Mary's. Which is the tallest of the girls? Mary is. This book is the most interesting that I have read. The highest mountains in the world are in the Himalaya. We all love a polite boy. This little child is the most beautiful I have seen in a long time. John is far more diligent than his brother. His brother is the laziest by far. I have many books but Robert has more than I. Mary is very good and very nice, too. My parents love me very much. Robert is very happy because he is going to England next year. Mary is not so happy as Robert because she is not going. Are you as tall as your brother? No, he is taller than I. You are the laziest of my pupils; your brother is the most diligent, and your cousin the nicest. You are not so strong as he, but you are much cleverer by far. Robert is much loved by all his friends because he is a very nice and polite fellow. This book is much more interesting than that.

Ejercicio

Pedro es más alto que Juan, pero no es tan alto como su hermano. Los perros son más inteligentes que los gatos. El caballo es mucho más noble que el gato. Los meses más fríos del año son enero y febrero; marzo ya no es tan frío, y los meses de abril y mayo son más agradables. Nada hay tan blanco y hermoso como la nieve. Después de nevar, el aire es más claro que antes y más seco. Tengo mucho trabajo, pero tú tienes más, porque aún no has hecho tu ejercicio de inglés. La mejor de las chicas es María. También es la mayor. Mi casa está más lejos que la tuya, pero no está tan lejos como la de tus primos. Está mucho más lejos que las nuestras. ¿Quién es mejor, Juan o María? María es mejor, pero Juan es más inteligente. El hierro es más pesado que el plomo y mucho más útil. El oro es un metal precioso y muy resistente. Es más resistente y valioso que la plata. Londres es mayor que París, y mucho más grande que Madrid. Tiene muchos más habitantes que otras ciudades. Mi hermano es el mayor de todos. Ayer no estaba muy bien; pero ahora ya estoy mejor. Este libro es muy malo; es peor que el otro.

To learn by heart

To be polite is to do and say
The kindest[1] thing in the kindest way.

1. Kindest *kindist* más amable, afectuoso.

EIGHTEENTH LESSON   LECCIÓN DECIMOCTAVA

Los tiempos de perfecto

El pretérito perfecto (present perfect) se forma, como en castellano, con el auxiliar «to have» y el verbo correspondiente en participio pasado.

Pretérito perfecto del verbo TO WALK
Yo he andado, etc.
I, you have walked   we, you, they have walked   he has walked

La forma interrogativa se hace alternando el orden de sujeto y auxiliar: «Have I walked?», y la forma negativa intercalando el adverbio de negación entre el auxiliar y el participio: «I have not walked.»

Uso del pretérito perfecto: El pretérito perfecto expresa *a)* una acción ya terminada en el momento de hablar, pero relacionada en alguna forma con el tiempo presente; *b)* una acción que continúa en el momento de hablar, pero relacionada, expresa o tácitamente, con una forma adverbial de duración anterior; *c)* una acción que pertenece al pasado en general, sin referencia a un tiempo determinado.

a) I have seen your sister on my way here. — He visto a tu hermana cuando venía hacia aquí.
b) I have had this pen for a month. — Tengo (he tenido) esta pluma desde hace un mes.
I have been in England since last Monday. — Desde el lunes estoy (he estado) en Inglaterra.
c) Every time I have seen him he has said the same. — Cada vez (siempre) que le he visto ha dicho lo mismo.
I have read this book. — He leído este libro.

Por el contrario, el pasado o pretérito (en inglés hay una sola forma para traducir el indefinido y el imperfecto españoles) indica una acción que ocurrió en el pasado y que excluye toda referencia con el tiempo actual: «I went to England last Summer.»

El futuro y el condicional perfectos se construyen como en castellano, con el auxiliar en futuro o condicional respectivamente y el verbo en participio pasado. Se emplean respectivamente para expresar una acción ya terminada antes de un momento futuro, y para repetirla en estilo indirecto.

I shall have finished my lesson by seven o'clock.	Habré terminado mi lección a las siete.
I said that I should have finished my lesson by seven o'clock.	Dije que habría terminado mi lección a las siete.

La forma continua del perfecto expresa una acción que empezó en un momento determinado y continuó durante todo aquel tiempo hasta el momento actual:

I have been reading all the evening (since six).	He estado leyendo toda la tarde (desde las seis).

El pretérito pluscuamperfecto o pasado perfecto (past perfect) en inglés expresa una acción empezada en el pasado y terminada antes de un momento determinado del mismo pasado:

I had already finished my lesson when you came.	Ya había terminado mi lección cuando viniste.

Words

accept æk-, ɔk'-	aceptar	chilly tʃili	frío
sept		curtain 'kɔːtɔn	cortina
aeroplane crash	catástrofe de	dark daːk	oscuro
'ɛəroplein kræʃ	aviación	dear diə*	querido
alright 'ɔːl'rait	bien	dinner 'dinə*	comida
at last æt laːst	por fin	draw drɔː	
a while ə wail	un rato	drew druː	correr, arrastrar
basking baːskiŋ	tostándose al sol	drawn drɔːn	
bathe beið	bañado	drive draiv	
begin biˈgin		drove drouv	conducir
began biˈgæn	empezar	driven 'drivən	
begun biˈgʌn		electric iˈlektrik	eléctrico
bring briŋ		employ imˈplɔi	emplear
brought brɔːt	traer	fire faiə*	fuego
brought brɔːt		fishing 'fiʃiŋ	pesca

Los tiempos de perfecto

flying *flaiiŋ*	volando	rise *raiz*	
full *ful*	lleno, completo	rose *rouz*	levantarse
glad *glæd*	contento	risen *'rizən*	
gladly *'glædli*	alegremente, con alegría	sea-side *si: said*	playa
		sunshine *'sʌnʃain*	sol
go to rest *'goutə'rest*	ir a descansar	silence *'sailəns*	silencio
		silent *'sailənt*	silencioso
hearth *ha:θ*	hogar	something *'sʌmθiŋ*	algo
invitation *'invi'teiʃən*	invitación	spend, spent, spent	pasar (el tiempo, dinero)
invite *in'vait*	invitar	splendid	espléndido
is over *is 'ouvə**	ha terminado	star	estrella
light *lait*	luz, ligero	though *ðou*	aunque
moon *mu:n*	luna	turn *tə:n*	volver, vuelta
motor-car *'moutəka:**	automóvil	— on	encender la luz
never *'nevə**	nunca	undisturbed *ʌndis'tə:bd*	tranquilo
out of doors *aut əv'dɔ:z*	el exterior	visit *vizit*	visita
over *'ouvə**	sobre	pay a —	visitar
picture *'piktʃə**	grabado, cuadro, retrato, película	want *wɔnt*	querer
		week-end *wi:k'end*	fin de semana
promise *'prɔmis*	promesa		

Reading exercise

It is half past five. The day is over. I have finished my work. I have studied my Spanish lessons for the day. I have had my dinner and I can now go to rest. It has grown rather cold and chilly; I have lit the fire in the hearth and I am sitting by it. All the windows have been shut already and I have turned on the electric light. I know that out of doors the stars have begun to shine the moon is out and everything is silent. I have always wanted to sit by the fire like this, with the curtains drawn, and read for a while undisturbed. But I am always so busy that I never have the time to do it. To-day, at last, I have been able to do it, and I have been sitting here for one hour. I have been thinking what I would like to do next Summer. I think that I would like to go to see a friend who lives at the sea-side and who has invited me. It has been very nice of her to send me an invitation and I have accepted gladly. It will be a very nice Summer; we shall go sailing and fishing; we shall bathe in the sea and we shall go for long rides in the motor-car. I shall also do another thing that I have always wanted to do: I shall bask in the sunshine and drive a car in the country. It will be splendid, for I like very much the sun and it will be very nice to be able to spend most of the time out of doors in a warm country. On my way back home I shall spend a week-end in Paris and I hope I shall also enjoy that very much.

Conversation

When is the day over? What do you do when the day is over? Have you been out to-day or have you stayed all day at home? Was it a nice warm day, to-day, or was it cold and chilly? Is there a moon now? Is the sun shining now? Have you received an invitation to go to England? Do you sometimes go for a ride in a motor-car? Can your sister ride a bycicle? Have you had many English lessons? How many English lessons do you have a week? Have you drive to the University this morning or have you walked? Have you written to your English friend this week? Why have you not written to him? Have you read to-day's paper? Has the moon risen already? Have you gone to spend a week-end with your friends this Spring? Can you drive a car? Can you ride a bycicle? Do you like to go for a walk in the country when the weather is nice and warm?

Conjugate:

    a) I have not studied my English lesson to-day.
    b) Have I read this book?
    c) I have not seen this picture.

Ejercicio

He llegado a casa a las 5 y media, he hecho mi ejercicio de inglés y después he escrito a mi amigo que está en Inglaterra. Mi amigo Enrique vive en Inglaterra; me ha invitado a pasar las vacaciones de verano con él, y le contesto aceptando su amable invitación e invitándole a que venga a pasar las Navidades con nosotros, aquí. Le he dicho que aquí el tiempo está ahora muy bueno, aunque ha estado nevando.

Esta noche, la luna ha salido temprano y las estrellas han empezado a brillar muy temprano también. He ido a la ventana, he corrido las cortinas y las he mirado un rato. El cielo estaba lleno de estrellas y la luna estaba muy bonita, porque era luna llena. Mis hermanos se han ido a dar un paseo; pero yo me he quedado junto a la chimenea leyendo.

Tenía un libro muy interesante que mi hermana me regaló (dio) por Navidad y aún no lo había leído. He estado leyendo hasta las 9, y mis hermanos han estado paseando hasta las nueve y media; cuando han venido hemos cenado (we had dinner) y nos hemos ido a descansar.

¿Me has traído el libro que te pedí? Sí, te lo traje ayer y lo puse encima de la mesa.

Words

accident *'æksidənt*	accidente	news *njuːz*	noticias
admire *əd'maiə**	admirar	nice, -ly *nais, -li*	bonito, agradable
after *'aːftə**	después	notice *'noutis*	notar
afternoon *'aːftə'nuːn*	tarde (la)	oh dear! *'ou'diə**	¡Dios mío!
any *eni*	algún	passenger *'pæsindʒə**	pasajero
arrange *ə'reindʒ*	arreglar	picture *'piktʃə**	cuadro, cine
at once *ət'wʌns*	al momento, de una vez	produce *prə'djuːs*	producir
bath *baːθ*	baño	sad	triste
—s *-ðz* (pl.)		seem *siːm*	parecer
breakfast *'brekfəst*	desayuno	serious *'siəriəs*	serio, importante
British *'britiʃ*	británico	sight *sait*	vista
charming *'tʃaːmiŋ*	encantador	since *sins*	desde
daisy *'deizi*	margarita	sleep, slept, slept	dormir
downstairs	abajo	sorry *'sɔri*	sentir (lamentar)
else *els*	además, más	I am —	lo siento
flower-bed *'flauəbed*	parterre	soundly *'saundli*	profundamente
gallery *'gæləri*	galería	special *'speʃəl*	especial
gardener *'gaːd(ə)nə**	jardinero	stroll *stroul*	una vuelta
keep *kiːp*		terribly *'terəbli*	muchísimo
kept *kept*	conservar	thank *θæŋk*	dar las gracias
kept *kept*		thanks, thank you	gracias
kill	matar	then *ðen*	entonces, luego
last *laːst*	últimamente	think *θiŋk*	
museum *mjuː'ziəm*	museo	thought *θɔːt*	pensar
national *næʃənəl*	nacional	thought *θɔːt*	
		unfortunately *ʌn'fɔːtʃənitli*	desgraciadamente
		wake up *weik ʌp*	despertarse
		well	bien

Reading exercise

Good morning, Jack. How are you this morning? — Very well, thank you. — Excuse me for not having breakfast with you, but I had to go out very early and I did not want to wake you up. Have you had a good night's rest? — Yes; I have, thank you. I slept so soundly that the church bells did not wake me up. I only woke up when Peter came into my room and called me. Then I got up at once, had a nice hot bath, had my breakfast and now I feel as fresh as a daisy. — And what have you been doing since you came downstairs? — Many things. First, I have been taking a stroll in your garden which is very nice and well kept. — Did your notice the new flower-beds? — Yes, they are very nicely arranged. Much nicer than when I was here last. You seem to have a very clever gardener to produce this charming picture. I shall call him to arrange my garden. — What else have you been doing? I have been reading the morning papers. — I have not read it yet. Is there any special news? — Yes; there has been a serious aeroplane crash and a bad railway accident. — Oh, dear! I am terribly sorry to hear that. Were they really serious? — It seems so. Unfortunatelly all the passengers were killed in the aeroplane crash and several in the railway accident. It is terribly sad. — And what are you going to do this afternoon? — I am going to visit the British Museum and the National Picture Gallery and then I shall have a walk in Hyde Park with Mr. Jones. That will be all for to-day. I think it is enough for one day, and I don't like to see too many sights all at once.

Ejercicio

Esta mañana he visto a tu hermana en la Universidad (University). No la había visto desde hace mucho tiempo (for a long time) y me ha gustado verla. También ella se ha alegrado porque somos muy buenas amigas. El señor Brown no pudo desayunar con su amigo porque tuvo que salir temprano. Su amigo se levantó, tomó un baño, desayunó y dio una vuelta por el jardín. Luego leyó los periódicos, que traían la noticia de un accidente de aviación y un accidente de tren en los que murieron muchas personas.

¿Has llegado de Londres esta mañana? No, llegué anoche, pero me fui a descansar en seguida y no me he despertado hasta que me han llamado esta mañana. ¿Qué has estado haciendo? He estado visitando los museos, he dado una vuelta por el parque, luego he cogido un coche (car) y he ido a comer a un restaurante de Soho. Por la tarde he ido a la Galería Nacional de Pintura y esta noche iré al cine. Creo que son muchas cosas para un solo día. ¿Qué piensas hacer mañana? No sé. Desgraciadamente, está empezando a llover (to rain) y los jardines, cuando llueve, no son una vista muy encantadora; por lo tanto, quizá vaya al cine otra vez.

NINETEENTH LESSON
LECCIÓN DECIMONOVENA

El participio pasado

Los verbos débiles forman el participio igual al pasado, esto es, añadiendo el sufijo «ed» al infinitivo: «to walk, walked, walked; to live, lived, lived».

Los verbos fuertes lo forman por un cambio de la vocal radical y la adición, en algunos, del sufijo «n», «en», o «ne»: «speak, spoke, spoken; write, wrote, written; come, came, come; go went gone». En algunos verbos el participio es igual al infinitivo.

Los verbos fuertes pueden dividirse en siete grupos según los cambios que afectan:

1.º Participio igual al infinitivo: «to come, came, come», «venir».

2.º Participio igual al infinitivo más «n»: «to see, saw, seen», «ver».

3.º Participio igual al infinitivo más «en»: «to fall, fell, fallen», «caer».

4.º Participio igual al pasado: «to hold, held, held», «agarrar, sujetar».

5.º Participio igual al pasado más «n»: «to freeze, froze, frozen», «helar».

6.º Participio igual al pasado más «en»: «to bite, bit, bitten», «morder».

7.º Infinitivo, pasado y participio distintos: «sing, sang, sung», «cantar».

To learn by heart

Infinitivo		Pasado	Participio
to cost kɔːst	costar	cost	cost
to laugh at laːf æt	reírse de	laughed at	laughed at
to hear hiə*	oir	heard həːd	heard
to pay pei	pagar	paid peid	paid
to save seiv	salvar, ahorrar	saved seivd	saved
to weep wiːp	llorar	wept wept	wept
to think θiŋk	pensar	thought θɔːt	thought
to sell sel	vender	sold sould	sold
to spoil spɔil	estropear	spoilt spɔilt	spoilt
to blow blou	soplar	blew bluː	blown bloun
to burn bəːn	quemar	burnt bəːnt	burnt
to lend lend	prestar	lent lent	lent

Words

afterwards 'aːftəwədz	después	please	por favor
all the house	por toda la casa	—d with himself	satisfecho
another ə'nʌðə*	otro	proud of praud əv	orgulloso de
as æz	como, a medida que	purchase 'pəːtʃəs	comprar
as much æs mʌtʃ	tanto	rage reidʒ	rabia, coraje
bargain 'baːgin	ganga, trato	rest rest	restante, resto
built bilt	construido	set out	partir
copper 'kɔpə*	cobre, calderilla, caldera	so much sou mʌtʃ	tanto
cry krai	llorar	sound saund	sonido
— out	gritar	tale	cuento
dread dred	temer	tempt	tentar
experience ik'spiəriəns	experiencia	thankful θæŋkful	contento, agradecido
famous 'feiməs	famoso	things θiŋz	cosas
field	campo	too much tuː mʌtʃ	demasiado
fill	llenar	toy tɔi	juguete
immediately i'miːdjətli	inmediatamente	unnecessary ʌn'nesisəri	innecesario
joy dʒɔi	goce, alegría	use juːs	uso
joyfully 'dʒɔifuli	alegremente	useful 'juːsful	útil
lesson 'lesən	lección	whenever wen-'evə*	siempre que
lost lɔːst	perdido	whistle 'wisəl	pito, silbato
money 'mʌni	dinero	worth wəːθ	valor
offer	oferta		
on the way ɔn ðə wei	en el camino		
one day	un día		

Reading exercise

Benjamin Franklin was only seven years old when he learnt a very important lesson. One day a friend gave him some coppers. Joyfully he set out for a toy shop to buy something with his money. On the way he met a friend who had a whistle. After listening to the whistle for a few minutes he offered the other boy all his money for it, and went home very pleased with himself and very proud of his bargain. When his brothers learned (supieron) how much he had paid for the whistle, they told him he had given several times its real value and they laughed at his foolishness. In a rage, he went to his room and cried for hours as he thought of the other toys that he could have bought with the rest of his money if he had not foolishly spent it. This experience taught him a lesson for which he was thankful the rest of his life. Whenever he was tempted to make an unnecessary purchase, he said to himself: «Do not give too much for your whistle», and he was thankful that he had learnt to save his money.

Ejercicio

¿Cuánto te ha costado este libro? No sé. No lo he comprado yo. Mi hermano me lo regaló el mes pasado. Le ofrecí darle los libros que necesitaba, pero parece que ya (se) los había regalado su hermana por su cumpleaños. Cuando Franklin era pequeño, un día salió a comprar unos juguetes. Pero encontró a un amigo que soplaba un silbato y lo compró. El silbato valía menos de lo que dio por él, y sus hermanos se rieron mucho de él al saberlo. La lección le fue muy útil, pues le enseñó a ahorrar su dinero. He encendido el fuego en la chimenea porque hace mucho frío. Ayer no lo encendimos porque no hacía tanto frío como hoy. No pierdas el tiempo, porque el tiempo perdido no se recupera (encuentra) nunca. No te rías del niño, porque empezará a llorar. ¿Cuánto te costaron las flores que compraste ayer? Las compró mi madre cuando salió por la tarde y no me lo ha dicho.

Conversation

Who told this story about himself? How old was Franklin when it happened? Why was he full of joy? What did he buy? Who sold it to him? What did he pay for it? Why did he feel proud of himself? Who spoilt his joy? Why did they laugh at him? What tempted him to pay so much for the whistle? Why was he afterwards thankful? What had he learnt from this experience?

Proverbs.

> A burnt child dreads the fire.
> Money lent is money spent.
> Lost time is never found again.
> Bought friends are no friends.
> Rome was not built in a day.

Ejercicio

Pedro compró un libro de cuentos y lo mandó a su hermano; lo ha perdido. El granjero dio de comer a las gallinas y cerdos. Piensa venderlos cuando estén gordos. Pagan mucho dinero por ellos. Me he herido el dedo.

Un día, un niño llevaba unas monedas para comprar juguetes. En la calle encontró a otro muchacho que tocaba un pito, su sonido le gustó y se sintió tentado a hacer un trato. Le ofreció por él todo el dinero que llevaba. Sus hermanos se rieron de lo que había hecho, pues le había costado más de su verdadero valor. Lloró de rabia.

La casa se quemó. Ellos estuvieron unos días en el campo. Lo dije así. Contaron un cuento. Los alumnos aprendieron su lección. El profesor enseñó ayer otra lección.

TWENTIETH LESSON   LECCIÓN VIGÉSIMA

Verbos débiles irregulares

Hay algunos verbos débiles que son irregulares y forman el pasado y el participio añadiendo una «t» o cambiando la «d» del infinitivo en «t», con cambio de la vocal de la raíz, o sin él. Generalmente, si dicha vocal es larga se cambia por una breve:

smell *smel*	oler	smelt *smelt*	smelt
kneel *ni:l*	arrodillarse	knelt *nelt*	knelt
lend *lend*	prestar	lent *lent*	lent
send *send*	mandar, enviar	sent *sent*	sent
build *bild*	construir	built *bilt*	built
bend *bend*	doblar	bent *bent*	bent

Algunos verbos débiles sufren un cambio en la vocal interna, sin que por ello puedan considerarse como si fueran fuertes, pues conservan el sufijo «t» o «d»:

fight *fait*	luchar	fought *fɔ:t*	fought
bring *briŋ*	traer	brought *brɔ:t*	brought
buy *bai*	comprar	bought *bɔ:t*	bought
seek *si:k*	buscar	sought *sɔ:t*	sought

Un grupo de verbos terminados en «t» y en «d» no toman terminación alguna:

let *let*	permitir	let	let
shut *ʃʌt*	cerrar	shut	shut
hurt *hə:t*	dañar	hurt	hurt
hit *hit*	golpear	hit	hit

Cierto número de verbos de esta clase acortan tan sólo la vocal interna para formar el pasado y el participio:

meet *mi:t*	encontrar	met *met*	met
feed *fi:d*	alimentar	fed *fed*	fed
bleed *bli:d*	sangrar	bled *bled*	bled

Words

admiral ˈædmərəl	almirante	remain riˈmein	permanecer
await əˈweit	esperar	ship ʃip	barco, buque
ably ˈeibli	hábilmente	shout ʃaut	grito
aware əˈwɛə*	enterado	shore ʃɔə*	costa, ribera
branch braːntʃ	rama	shot	tiro
bravely ˈbreivli	valientemente	skilfully ˈskilfuli	hábilmente
coat kout	casaca, levita	struck strʌk	golpeó, dio (en el blanco)
combined ˈkɔmbaind	combinados, unidos	struggle ˈstrʌgl	lucha, pelea
complete kəmˈpliːt	total	though ðou	aunque, a pesar de
deck	cubierta	to charge tʃaːdʒ	acometer
die dai	morir	to do one's duty ˈdjuːti	cumplir con su deber
enough iˈnʌf	suficiente	to execute ˈeksikjuːt	ejecutar
fleet fliːt	flota	to hoist hɔist	alzar, izar
gaily ˈgeili	alegremente	to pierce piəs	romper, forzar
hero ˈhiərou	héroe	to sail seil	hacer(se) a la vela
inferior inˈfiəriə*	inferior	to wound wuːnd	herir
line lain	línea	unhappily ʌnˈhæpili	desgraciadamente
medal ˈmedl	medalla, condecoración	wholly ˈhoulli	completamente
mortally ˈmɔːtəli	mortalmente	wore wɔː*	usar, llevar
off	a la altura de	wounded ˈwuːndid	herido
plan plæn	plan		
raged reidʒd	rugió		

Reading exercise

In the month of September 1805, Nelson, the most celebrated naval [neivl] hero of England, sailed gaily away from the English shore. Arriving at Cádiz, he did not remain there idly to await the combined fleets of France and Spain; but he soon put to sea again (se hizo de nuevo a la mar) when he heard that the enemies were lying off Cape Trafalgar, though his force was greatly inferior to theirs. Before he bravely and skilfully charged the enemy's ships, he hoisted, on board his own ship, the celebrated signal: «England expects every man to do his duty.» Nelson's plan [plæn] was to pierce the enemy's line at two points, and well and ably he executed it. For several hours the struggle raged terribly. Unhappily the admiral wore the coat in which he had so often fought before, with medals and stars. This made him easily seen by the enemy, and a shot very soon struck the deck of the admiral's ship.

A short time after Nelson was mortally wounded. The hero, fully aware that he must die, lived just long enough to hear the shouts of complete victory.

Conversation

Who was Lord Nelson? Where did he sail from? Did he remain at Cádiz? What did he hear about the enemy? Where is Cape Trafalgar? What did he hoist on board his ship? What was Nelson's plan? How long did the struggle go on? What coat did the Admiral wear? Why was he easily seen? Was Nelson wounded in the struggle? What did Nelson tell his men before the struggle began? Did Nelson live long enough to hear the shouts of victory?

Words

tried *traid*	juzgado	die *dai*	morir
noblemen *'noublmen*	nobles	amid *ə'mid*	entre
while *wail*	mientras	countrymen *'kʌntrimen*	compatriotas
ruled *ru:ld*	gobernó	fun *fʌn*	diversión
bring up *briŋ ʌp*	educar	merry *'meri*	alegre
spent *spent*	pasar	fled *fled*	huyó
lead, led, led	conducir	beg *beg*	rogar
beaten *bi:tn*	derrotado	mercy *'mə:si*	misericordia
castle *'ka:sl*	castillo		

Reading exercise

Mary, Queen of Scots, became Queen when she was still a baby. Her mother, who was French, sent her to France to be brought up there while Scotland was ruled in her name by one of the great noblemen.

Mary was brought up amid all the pleasures of the French Court and, first as a little girl, and later as a young girl, she was very happy in France. When she was old enough she married the son of the French King.

Most of Mary's time was spent in dancing and playing and singing and in many other pleasant ways, but, unfortunately for her, when she had been married two years, more or less, her husband died. The Queen Mother did not want her in France and she had to go back to Scotland to rule over her countrymen.

It was a great change for the young Queen used to all the fun of the gay French Court, and the Scottish nobles did not like their Queen to sing and dance and be merry. She had many friends, but she had many enemies, too, and soon she was shut up in a strong castle, built on an island in the middle of a lake.

One night, her page helped her to escape and led her ashore. Mary gathered together a little army and fought the nobles, but she was beaten; so, she fled to England to ask help from her cousin Elizabeth. But she did not get it. Mary was shut up once more in a strong castle, and later moved from one castle to another for nearly nineteen years. Finaly, she was tried and condemned to death. It is said that Elizabeth expected that Mary would beg for mercy, but Mary did not. She was fair and she was brave, and bravely did she die.

Conversation

Where did Mary spend her childhood? Was Mary a beautiful woman? Was the French Court a gay one? Whom did Mary marry? Did her husband die soon? What did she do when her husband died? Did she like life in Scotland? Did the nobles like Mary to be gay and happy? Where was she sent to prison? Who helped her to escape? Whom did she fight? Did she get help from Elizabeth? Was Mary's end a sad one?

Ejercicio

Compré un libro para mi sobrina y lo trajeron ayer por la tarde. Me ha pedido que le traiga un libro cuando salga. ¿Sabes dónde puedo comprarlo? Sí; esta mañana he comprado varios en la librería de la calle de Trafalgar. Permíteme que te los traiga yo; voy a salir y pasaré por allí. Tu hermano me ha prestado un libro muy interesante. Yo quería comprarlo, pero él me dijo que no lo hiciera, pues él me lo dejaría. El pequeño se ha hecho daño jugando con sus hermanos en el jardín. ¿Se ha hecho mucho daño? No; mucho, no. Pero los he encerrado en casa y no los dejaré salir al jardín hasta mañana. ¿Cómo se hizo daño? Se dio un golpe (se golpeó) con una rama de un árbol.

TWENTY-FIRST LESSON
LECCIÓN VIGÉSIMA PRIMERA

La voz pasiva

En la oración pasiva, la persona o cosa que recibe la acción del verbo pasa a ser sujeto del mismo, en tanto que el sujeto de la voz activa pasa a ser «prepositional object».

En inglés, la voz pasiva se forma, como en castellano, con el auxiliar «to be», en el tiempo correspondiente, y el participio pasado del verbo que se conjuga:

Activa: The children love their mother. — Los niños aman a su madre.
Pasiva: The mother is loved by her children. — La madre es amada por sus hijos.

Verbo TO BE LOVED

Present soy amado I am loved.	*Pres. perfect* he sido amado I have been loved.
Past (preterite) era, fui amado I was loved.	*Past perfect* había sido amado I had been loved.
Future seré amado I shall be loved.	*Future perfect* habré sido amado I shall have been loved.
Conditional sería amado I should be loved.	*Conditional perfect* habría sido amado I should have been loved.

Imperative sea amado	
Let me be loved. Let him be loved.	Let us be loved. Let them be loved.

En inglés, la voz pasiva se emplea también cuando en español se usa la forma impersonal con «se»:

It is said...	Se dice...
He is often *'ɔːfn* seen with *siːn wið* your sister.	Se le ve a menudo con tu hermana.
English spoken *'spoukən*.	Se habla inglés.

En inglés, el complemento indirecto también puede ser sujeto de la voz pasiva:

Activa: I gave a book to the boy for his birthday.
Pasiva: The boy was given a book for his birthday.
A book was given to the boy and a doll (muñeca) to the girl.

La forma continua del presente pasivo se usa mucho en inglés para expresar una acción que está teniendo lugar en el momento en que se habla o inmediatamente después. En español no hay equivalente literal:

Just now, I am being questioned.	En este momento me están interrogando.
I am being sent for in a few minutes.	Me vendrán a buscar dentro de unos momentos.

Exercise

The girl sees the flowers. The flowers are seen by the girl. I see the trees in the garden. The trees in the garden can be seen from the window. The books have been sent to your brother already (ya). I was told the news, but I was asked not to tell you. The children will not be given the books if they are not good. Tom is called at six, every morning. They were seen in London last week. We shall not be seen in Paris next Winter, because we are going to London, instead. Peter was told to go home. Mary and Pat are given a book each (cada una). Have you been given a book, too? No, I have not been given a book. I have been given a pen, an exercise book and some pencils.

Words

bake *beik*	cocer al horno	butter *'bʌtə**	mantequilla
baker *'beikə**	panadero	corn *kɔːn*	grano, cereal, maíz, callo
bread *bred*	pan		

customer 'kʌstəmə*	cliente	reaping-machine, reaper	segadora
cut, cut, cut kʌt	cortar	roll *roul*	panecillo
deliver di'livə*	entregar	rye *rai*	centeno
dough *dou*	masa	sack *sæk*	saco
dry *drai*	seco, secar	scythe *saið*	guadaña
farmer 'fɑːmə*	campesino	sell, sold, sold, *sel, sould*	vender
flail *fleil*	mayal	send, sent, sent	enviar
flour *flauə* *	harina	shape *ʃeip*	forma
grain *grein*	grano	sheaf *ʃiːf*	gavilla
grind, ground, ground *ai,a u, au*	moler	sickle 'sikəl	hoz
		sufficient, -ly sə'fiʃənt, -li	suficiente, -mente
into *intu*	en, dentro de	sun *sʌn*	sol
knead *niːd*	amasar	take, took, taken *ei, u, ei*	tomar
machine mə'ʃiːn	máquina	thresh *θreʃ*	trillar
make into	convertir en	threshing-machine, thresher	trilladora
mill *mil*	molino		
miller 'milə*	molinero	thus *ðʌs*	así, de esta manera
mix *miks*	mezclar		
oven *ʌvən*	horno	well *wel*	bien
pile up 'pail 'ʌp	amontonar	wheat *(h)wiːt*	trigo
put, put, put *put*	poner		
reap *riːp*	segar		

Reading exercise

Bread is made of flour, and flour is made of corn (wheat or rye). When the corn is ripe, it is reaped (cut) by the farmer with a scythe or a sickle or with a reaping-machine (reaper), and piled up in sheaves to be dried in the sun. When it is sufficiently dry, it is threshed with a flail or in a threshing-machine (thresher), and the grain is sent to the miller and ground into flour by him in his mill. The flour is put into sacks, and the sacks, are carried (brought) to the baker. The flour is mixed with water and thus made into dough, which is then kneaded and shaped into loaves and rolls. These are baked in the oven. When they are well baked, they are taken out of the oven and delivered (sent) by the baker to his customers.

Conversation

What is white bread made of? brown bread? Who reaps the corn? With what does he reap it? What dries the sheaves?

What does the farmer thrash the grain with? To whom is it then sent? Where is the grain ground? By whom? What is sent to the baker? What is the flour mixed with? What is it then called? Who kneads the dough? Where are the loaves put to be baked? When are they taken out of the oven? To whom does the baker sell them?

Ejercicio

Los campesinos siegan el trigo con las hoces. Cuando el trigo está cortado se hacen gavillas con él y se lleva al molino. En el molino, el grano se seca al sol, se muele y se convierte en harina. Con la harina se hace pan y el pan se come y es un gran alimento (food). ¿Te gusta el pan de centeno? No; a mí me gusta el pan de trigo. A mi hermana le gusta el pan de maíz. Muchos campesinos comen pan de maíz y dicen que es muy bueno. ¿Dónde se cuece el pan? El pan se cuece en el horno. Los panaderos lo amasan y le dan forma. Algunas veces le dan forma de panecillos y están muy buenos con un poco de mantequilla.

Ayer te vieron en el cine. Veo al hombre que está en el jardín. El hombre es visto por mí. Los niños fueron invitados a comer a casa de sus amigos. La puerta de la casa ha sido abierta. No será dicho que no quise venir, pues he venido la primera.

Poner en voz pasiva:

> The pupils write their lessons.
> The farmers reap the corn.
> The baker kneads the dough.
> The bakers make rolls.
> They put the corn in the sacks.

Words

allow ə'lau	permitir	contents 'kɔntents	contenido
bore bɔː*	taladrar	devise di'vaiz	planear, idear
box bɔks	caja	discover dis'kʌvə*	descubrir
careless 'kɛəlis	descuidados	escape is'keip	escapar
cease siːs	cesar, dejar de	examine ig'zæmin	examinar
change tʃeindʒ	cambiar(se)	famous feiməs	famoso
chest tʃest	cajón	find, found, found, ai, au·	encontrar
clever 'klevə*	inteligente		
close klouz	cerrar		

guard *ga:d*	guardia
the —s	los guardianes
hole	agujero
life; for —	vida; perpetuamente
on the charge *ɔn ðə tʃa:dʒ*	acusado de
plan *plæn*	plan
prison *'prizən*	prisión
prisoner *'prizənə**	prisionero
search *sə:tʃ*	registrar
treason *'tri:zən*	traición
usual *'ju:ʒuəl*	de costumbre
visit *vizit*	visitar
writer *'raitə**	escritor
wrong *rɔŋ*	mal, malo, equivocado

Reading exercise

Once a famous writer was sent to prison for life on the charge of high treason. He was permitted to study and he was also permitted to see his wife, who used to come and visit him every day. Every week, a large chest of books and clothes was allowed to enter in and out of the prison, so that he could have books to read and clothes to change. At first the contents of the chest were carefully examined; but after a time the guards grew careless for nothing was found wrong, and they ceased to search the box. Then having seen this, the writer and his wife devised a clever plan for his escape. Holes were bored in the chest and so the air allowed into it; then the prisoner went into the box and the box was closed and carried out as usual. In this way he was able to escape, and could leave the country before his escape was discovered.

Words

actor *'æktə**	actor
admit *əd'mit*	admitir
admittance *əd'mitəns*	admisión
amuse *ə'mju:z*	divertir
argument *'a:gjumənt*	discusión
attract *ə'trækt*	atraer
audience *'ɔ:diəns*	audiencia
Cerberus *sə:bərəs*	cancerbero
clear up	aclarar
decide *di'said*	decidir
delight *di'lait*	encantar
disappoint *disə'pɔint*	desilusionar
doorkeeper *'dɔə'ki:pə**	portero
entrance *'entrəns*	entrada
explanations *'eksplə'neiʃəns*	explicaciones
gain entrance *gein 'entrəns*	lograr acceso
lecture *'lektʃə**	conferencia
performance *pə'fɔ:məns*	representación
performer *pə'fɔ:mə**	actor
pinnacle *'pinəkl*	cumbre
manager *'mænidʒə**	gerente
matter *'mætə**	asunto

readings *'ri:diŋz*	lecturas		to play *plei*	representar
refuse *ri'fju:s*	negar		trick *trik*	truco
resolute *'rezəlu:t*	decidido		turn away	echar, hacer mar-
scene *si:n*	escena		*'tə:n ə'wei*	char
severe *sə'viə**	severo		writer *'raitə**	escritor
side-door	puerta lateral			

Reading exercise

When Charles Dickens, the great English writer was at the pinnacle of his fame, he undertook to give a series of readings and explanations of his own works to public audiences. One evening as he was approaching the hall in which he was to perform his lecture, he was met by a crowd of people who had been turned away because no seats were left. One disappointed man told Dickens that he might save himself the trouble of going any further as he would certainly not be admitted. The writer, delighted at the thought that he had attracted such a large audience, went resolutely to the side-door through which performers usually gained entrance to the stage. He was, however refused admittance by the doorkeeper. It was no use telling the man that he was Charles Dickens; for the severe doorkeeper said that it was an old trick that had already been tried by half a dozen people already that evening. The long argument attracted the manager to the scene, and the matter was soon cleared up. But Charles Dickens always remembered with amusement the time Cerberus turned him away from his own performance.

Ejercicio

No se permite la entrada en la sala durante la representación. Le ha sido ofrecida una buena colocación en París. Se cuentan malas noticias. Esta misma tarde ha sido enviada la carta por el criado. Al escritor no le fue permitido al principio entrar, a pesar de que dijo que era el conferenciante. Al hombre le fue ofrecido un vaso de vino por el dueño. Se divirtió muchísimo. En Australia se habla inglés. Ha sido comprado por María un regalo para sus padres. La obra fue representada varias veces por los mismos actores.

El fútbol es un juego que se juega en invierno por los estudiantes ingleses. Se llama así porque la pelota es movida con los pies en vez de con las manos. Se juega siempre con dos equipos, y en cada uno de ellos hay el mismo número de jugadores, once. Cada equipo intenta entrar la pelota en la portería del otro; cuando lo consigue, se dice que ha ganado un gol. Al portero se le permite coger la pelota con las manos para parar el gol. El equipo que consigue hacer más goles gana el partido.

MODELOS DE CONJUGACIÓN

Modelo del verbo auxiliar

TO BE, ser o estar

Present soy, estoy	*Present perfect* he sido, he estado
I am. You are. He is. We are. You are. They are.	I have been. You have been. He has been. We have been. You have been. They have been.
Past era, estaba, fui, estuve	*Past perfect* había sido, había estado
I was. You were. He was. We were. You were. They were.	I had been. You had been. He had been. We had been. You had been. They had been.
Future seré, estaré	*Future perfect* habré sido, habré estado
I shall be. You will be. He will be. We shall be. You will be. They will be.	I shall have been. You will have been. He will have been. We shall have been. You will have been. They will have been.

Conditional sería, estaría	*Conditional perfect* había sido, estado
I should be. You would be. He would be. We should be. You would be. They would be.	I should have been You would have been. He would have been. We should have been. You would have been. They would have been.

Imperative
sea yo, esté yo

Let me be. Be. Let him be.	Let us be. Be. Let them be.

Pres. subjunctive sea, esté	*Past subjunctive* fuera, estuviera, fuese, estuviese
I be. You be. He be. We be. You be. They be.	I were. You were. He were. We were. You were. They were.

Infinitive, Gerund, Pres. Part. ser, estar, siendo, estando	*Perfect* haber sido, estado, habiendo sido, estado, sido
Pres. inf. To be. *Pres. part.* Being. *Gerund* Being.	*Perf. inf.* To have been. *Perf. part.* Having been. *Past part.* Been.

Modelo del verbo auxiliar

TO HAVE, haber o tener

Present he, tengo	*Present perfect* he habido, tenido
I have. You have. He has. We have. You have. They have.	I have had. You have had. He has had. We have had. You have had. They have had.
Past (preterite) había, tenía	*Past perfect* había habido, tenido
I had. You had. He had. We had. You had. They had.	I had had. You had had. He had had. We had had. You had had. They had had.
Future habré, tendré	*Future perfect* habré habido, tenido
I shall have. You will have. He will have. We shall have. You will have. They will have.	I shall have had. You will have had. He will have had. We shall have had. You will have had. They will have had.
Conditional habría, tendría	*Conditional perfect* habría habido, tenido
I should have. You would have. He would have. We should have. You would have. They would have.	I should have had. You would have had. He would have had. We should have had. You would have had. They would have had.

Imperative haya, tenga yo Let me have. Have. Let him have.	Let us have. Have. Let them have.

Pres. subjunctive haya, tenga	*Past subjunctive* hubiera, tuviera, hubiese, tuviese
I have. You have. He have. We have. You have. They have.	I had. You had. He had. We had. You had. They had.
Infinitive, Gerund, Pres. Part. haber, tener, habiendo, teniendo *Pres. inf.* To have. *Pres. part.* Having. *Gerund* Having.	*Perfect* haber habido, tenido habiendo habido, tenido habido, tenido *Perf. inf.* To have had. *Perf. part.* Having had. *Past. part.* Had.

Modelo de verbo débil
TO WALK, andar

Present ando	*Present perfect* he andado
I walk. You walk. He walks. We walk. You walk. They walk.	I have walked. You have walked. He has walked. We have walked. You have walked. They have walked.
Past (preterite) andaba, anduve	*Past perfect* había andado
I walked. You walked. He walked. We walked. You walked. They walked.	I had walked. You had walked. He had walked. We had walked. You had walked. They had walked.

Future andaré I shall walk. You will walk. He will walk. We shall walk. You will walk. They will walk.	*Future perfect* habré andado I shall have walked. You will have walked. He will have walked. We shall have walked. You will have walked. They will have walked.
Conditional andaría I should walk. You would walk. He would walk. We should walk. You would walk. They would walk.	*Conditional perfect* habría andado I should have walked. You would have walked. He would have walked. We should have walked. You would have walked. They would have walked.
Pres. subjunctive ande I walk. You walk. He walk. We walk. You walk. They walk.	*Past subjunctive* anduviera, anduviese I walked. You walked. He walked. We walked. You walked They walked.

Imperative
ande yo

Let me walk. Walk. Let him walk.	Let us walk. Walk. Let them walk.

Infinitive, Gerund, Pres. Part. andar, que anda, andando *Pres. inf.* To walk. *Pres. part.* Walking. *Gerund* Walking.	*Perfect* haber andado, habiendo andado, andado *Perf. inf.* To have walked. *Perf. part.* Having walked. *Past part.* Walked.

Modelo de verbo débil

TO WALK

Forma interrogativa (¿Ando yo?, etc.)

Present	*Present perfect*
Do I walk?	Have I walked?
Do you walk?	Have you walked?
Does he walk?	Has he walked?
Do we walk?	Have we walked?
Do you walk?	Have you walked?
Do they walk?	Have they walked?

Past (preterite)	*Past perfect*
Did I walk?	Had I walked?
Did you walk?	Had you walked?
Did he walk?	Had he walked?
Did we walk?	Had we walked?
Did you walk?	Had you walked?
Did they walk?	Had they walked?

Future	*Future perfect*
Shall I walk?	Shall I have walked?
Will you walk?	Will you have walked?
Will he walk?	Will he have walked?
Shall we walk?	Shall we have walked?
Will you walk?	Will you have walked?
Will they walk?	Will they have walked?

Conditional	*Conditional perfect*
Should I walk?	Should I have walked?
Would you walk?	Would you have walked?
Would he walk?	Would he have walked?
Should we walk?	Should we have walked?
Would you walk?	Would you have walked?
Would they walk?	Would they have walked?

Modelo de verbo débil
TO WALK

Forma negativa (Yo no ando, etc.)

Present	Present perfect
I do not walk.	I have not walked.
You do not walk.	You have not walked.
He does not walk.	He has not walked.
We do not walk.	We have not walked.
You do not walk.	You have not walked.
They do not walk.	They have not walked.

Past (preterite)	Past perfect
I did not walk.	I had not walked.
You did not walk.	You had not walked.
He did not walk.	He had not walked.
We did not walk.	We had not walked
You did not walk.	You had not walked.
They did not walk.	They had not walked.

Future	Future perfect
I shall not walk.	I shall not have walked.
You will not walk.	You will not have walked.
He will not walk.	He will not have walked.
We shall not walk.	We shall not have walked.
You will not walk.	You will not have walked.
They will not walk.	They will not have walked.

Conditional	Conditional perfect
I should not walk.	I should not have walked.
You would not walk.	You would not have walked.
He would not walk.	He would not have walked.
We should not walk.	We should not have walked.
You would not walk.	You would not have walked.
They would not walk.	They would not have walked.

Imperative

Let me not walk.	Let us not walk.
Do not walk.	Do not walk.
Let him not walk.	Let them not walk.

Modelo de verbo débil
TO WALK

Forma progresiva (Estoy andando, etc.)

Present	*Present perfect*
I am walking.	I have been walking.
You are walking.	You have been walking.
He is walking.	He has been walking.
We are walking.	We have been walking.
You are walking.	You have been walking.
They are walking.	They have been walking.

Past (preterite)	*Past perfect*
I was walking.	I had been walking.
You were walking.	You had been walking.
He was walking.	He had been walking.
We were walking.	We had been walking.
You were walking.	You had been walking.
They were walking.	They had been walking.

Future	*Future perfect*
I shall be walking.	I shall have been walking.
You will be walking.	You will have been walking.
He will be walking.	He will have been walking.
We shall be walking.	We shall have been walking.
You will be walking.	You will have been walking.
They will be walking.	They will have been walking.

Conditional	*Conditional perfect*
I should be walking.	should have been walking.
You would be walking.	You would have been walking.
He would be walking.	He would have been walking.
We should be walking.	We should have been walking.
You would be walking.	You would have been walking.
They would be walking.	They would have been walking.

En la forma interrogativa, el auxiliar precede al pronombre: «Am I walking?», «Shall I be walking?»

En la forma negativa, el adverbio «not» se coloca entre el auxiliar y el verbo: «I shall not be walking». El subjuntivo se formará con el auxiliar en subjuntivo: «If I be walking», «If I were walking».

Modelo de verbo fuerte
TO TAKE, coger, tomar

Present cojo	*Present perfect* he cogido
I take. You take. He takes. We take. You take. They take.	I have taken. You have taken. He has taken. We have taken. You have taken. They have taken.
Past (preterite) cogía, cogí	*Past perfect* había cogido
I took. You took. He took. We took. You took. They took.	I had taken. You had taken. He had taken. We had taken. You had taken. They had taken.
Future cogeré	*Future perfect* habré cogido
I shall take. You will take. He will take. We shall take. You will take. They will take.	I shall have taken. You will have taken. He will have taken. We shall have taken. You will have taken. They will have taken.
Conditional cogería	*Conditional perfect* habría cogido
I should take. You would take. He would take. We should take. You would take. They would take.	I should have taken. You would have taken. He would have taken. We should have taken. You would have taken. They would have taken.
Pres. subjunctive coja	*Past subjunctive* cogiera, cogiese
I take. You take. He take. We take. You take. They take.	I took. You took. He took. We took. You took. They took.

Imperative coja yo Let me take.　　Let us take. Take.　　　　　Take. Let him take.　Let them take.	
Infinitive, Gerund, Pres. Part. coger, que coge, cogiendo *Pres. inf.* To take. *Pres. part.* Taking. *Gerund* Taking.	*Perfect* haber cogido, habiendo cogido, cogido *Perf. inf.* To have taken. *Perf. part.* Having taken. *Past part.* Taken.

Modelo de verbo fuerte

TO TAKE

Forma interrogativa (¿Cojo yo?, etc.)

Present	*Present perfect*
Do I take?	Have I taken?
Do you take?	Have you taken?
Does he take?	Has he taken?
Do we take?	Have we taken?
Do you take?	Have you taken?
Do they take?	Have they taken?

Past (preterite)	*Past perfect*
Did I take?	Had I taken?
Did you take?	Had you taken?
Did he take?	Had he taken?
Did we take?	Had we taken?
Did you take?	Had you taken?
Did they take?	Had they taken?

Future	*Future perfect*
Shall I take?	Shall I have taken?
Will you take?	Will you have taken?
Will he take?	Will he have taken?
Shall we take?	Shall we have taken?
Will you take?	Will you have taken?
Will they take?	Will they have taken?

Conditional	Conditional perfect
Should I take?	Should I have taken?
Would you take?	Would you have taken?
Would he take?	Would he have taken?
Should we take?	Should we have taken?
Would you take?	Would you have taken?
Would they take?	Would they have taken?

Modelo de verbo fuerte
TO TAKE

Forma negativa (Yo no cojo, etc.)

Present	Present perfect
I do not take.	I have not taken.
You do not take.	You have not taken.
He does not take.	He has not taken.
We do not take.	We have not taken.
You do not take.	You have not taken.
They do not take.	They have not taken.

Past (preterite)	Past perfect
I did not take.	I had not taken.
You did not take.	You had not taken.
He did not take.	He had not taken.
We did not take.	We had not taken.
You did not take.	You had not taken.
They did not take.	They had not taken.

Future	Future perfect
I shall not take.	I shall not have taken.
You will not take.	You will not have taken.
He will not take.	He will not have taken.
We shall not take.	We shall not have taken.
You will not take.	You will not have taken.
They will not take.	They will not have taken.

Conditional	Conditional perfect
I should not take.	I should not have taken.
You would not take.	You would not have taken.
He would not take.	He would not have taken.
We should not take.	We should not haven taken.
You would not take.	You would not have taken.
They would not take.	They would not have taken.

Modelo de verbo en voz pasiva
TO BE SEEN, ser visto

Present soy visto I am seen. You are seen. He is seen. We are seen. You are seen. They are seen.	*Pres. perfect* he sido visto I have been seen. You have been seen. He has been seen. We have been seen. You have been seen. They have been seen.
Past (preterite) era, fui visto I was seen. You were seen. He was seen. We were seen. You were seen. They were seen.	*Past perfect* había sido visto I had been seen. You had been seen. He had been seen. We had been seen. You had been seen. They had been seen.
Future seré visto I shall be seen. You will be seen. He will be seen. We shall be seen. You will be seen. They will be seen.	*Future perfect* habré sido visto I shall have been seen. You will have been seen. He will have been seen. We shall have been seen. You will have been seen. They will have been seen.
Conditional sería visto I should be seen. You would be seen. He would be seen. We should be seen. You would be seen. They would be seen.	*Conditional perfect* habría sido visto I should have been seen. You would have been seen. He would have been seen. We should have been seen. You would have been seen. They would have been seen.

Imperative
sea visto

Let me be seen.	Let us be seen.
Be seen.	Be seen.
Let him be seen.	Let them be seen.

TO BE impersonal, hay

	Afirm.	Interrogative	Negative
Present hay	There is (sing.). There are (plur.).	Is there? (sing.). Are there? (plur.).	There is not (sing.). There are not (plur.).
Past había, hubo	There was. There were.	Was there? Were there?	There was not. There were not.
Pres. perf. ha habido	There has been. There have been.	Has there been? Have there been?	There has not been. There have not been.
Past perf. había habido	There had been. There had been.	Had there been? Had there been?	There had not been. There had not been.
Future habrá	There will be. There will be.	Will there be? Will there be?	There will not be. There will not be.
Fut. perf. habrá habido	There will have been. There will have been.	Will there have been? Will there have been?	There will not have been. There will not have been.
Condit. habría	There would be. There would be.	Would there be? Would there be?	There would not be. There would not be.
Cond. perf. habría habido	There would have been. There would have been.	Would there have been? Would there have been?	There would not have been. There would not have been.
Subjunctive haya	If there be. If there be.		If there be not. If there be not.
Past subjunctive hubiera, hubiese	If there were. If there were.		If there were not. If there were not.
Imperat. haya	Let there be. Let there be.		Let there not be. Let there not be.

LISTA DE VERBOS FUERTES Y DÉBILES IRREGULARES

Present		*Past*	*Past participle*
abide ə'baid	habitar	abode ə'boud	abode
be biː	ser	was wɔz	been biːn
bear bɛə*	soportar, llevar	bore bɔː*	borne bɔːn
»	producir	»	born (nacido)
beat biːt	golpear	beat	beaten
become bi'kʌm	devenir	became bi'keim	become bi'kʌm
begin bi'gin	empezar	began bi'gæn	begun bi'gʌn
behold bi'hould	mirar, ver	beheld bi'held	beheld
bend bend	doblar	bent bent	bent
beseech bi'siːtʃ	rogar	besought bi'sɔːt	besought
bid bid	mandar, pedir	bade bæd	bidden bidən
bind baind	atar, amarrar	bound baund	bound
bite bait	morder	bit bit	bitten bitən
bleed bliːd	sangrar	bled bled	bled
blow blou	soplar	blew bluː	blown bloun
break breik	romper	broke brouk	broken broukən
breed briːd	criar	bred bred	bred
bring briŋ	traer	brought brɔːt	brought
build bild	construir	built bilt	built
burn bəːn	quemar	burnt bəːnt	burnt
burst bəːst	estallar, reventar	burst	burst
buy bai	comprar	bought bɔːt	bought
can kæn	puedo	could kud	—
cast kaːst	echar	cast	cast
catch kætʃ	coger	caught kɔːt	caught
choose tʃuːz	escoger	chose tʃouz	chosen tʃouzən
cleave kliːv	adherirse, rajar	clove klouv	cloven klouvən
		cleft kleft	cleft
cling kliŋ	colgar, pegarse	clung klʌŋ	clung
come kʌm	venir	came keim	come kʌm
cost kɔ(ː)st	costar	cost	cost
creep kriːp	trepar	crept krept	crept
cut kʌt	cortar	cut	cut
dare dɛə*	osar, provocar	durst dəːst	dared dɛəd
deal diːl	tratar en	dealt delt	dealt
dig dig	cavar	dug dʌg	dug
do duː	hacer	did did	done dʌn
draw drɔː	arrastrar, tirar, dibujar	drew druː	drawn drɔːn
dream driːm	soñar	dreamt dremt	dreamt
drink driŋk	beber	drank dræŋk	drunk drʌŋk
drive draiv	conducir	drove drouv	driven drivən
dwell dwel	morar	dwelt	dwelt
eat iːt	comer	ate et	eaten iːtən
fall fɔːl	caer	fell fel	fallen fɔːlən
feed fiːd	alimentar	fed fed	fed
feel fiːl	sentir	felt felt	felt

Verbos fuertes y débiles irregulares

Present		*Past*	*Past participle*
fight *fait*	luchar	fought *fɔːt*	fought
find *faind*	encontrar	found *faund*	found
flee *fliː*	escaparse, huir	fled *fled*	fled
fling *fliŋ*	arrojar, tirar	flung *flʌŋ*	flung
fly *flai*	volar	flew *fluː*	flown *floun*
forbear *fɔːˈbɛə**	cesar, detener	forbore *ˈbɔː**	forborne *ˈbɔːn*
forbid *fəˈbid*	prohibir	forbade *ˈbæd*	forbidden *ˈbidɔːn*
forget *fəˈget*	olvidar	forgot *fəˈgɔt*	forgotten *fəˈgɔtan*
forgive *fəˈgiv*	perdonar	forgave *fəˈgeiv*	forgiven *fəˈgivən*
forsake *fəˈseik*	abandonar	forsook *fəˈsuk*	forsaken *fəˈseikən*
freeze *friːz*	helar	froze *frouz*	frozen *frouzən*
get *get*	lograr, alcanzar	got *gɔt*	got
give *giv*	dar	gave *geiv*	given *givən*
go *gou*	ir	went *went*	gone *gɔ(ː)n*
grind *graind*	moler, pulverizar	ground *au*	ground
grow *grou*	crecer	grew *gruː*	grown *ou*
hang *hæŋ*	colgar	hung *hʌŋ*	hung
have *hæv*	tener	had *hæd*	had
hear *hiə**	oir	heard *həːd*	heard
hew *hjuː*	cortar, picar	hewed *hjuːd*	hewn *hjuːn*
hide *haid*	esconder, ocultar	hid *hid*	hidden *hidən*
hit *hit*	golpear	hit	hit
hold *hould*	sujetar, asir, agarrar	held *held*	held
hurt *həːt*	lastimar	hurt	hurt
keep *kiːp*	guardar	kept *kept*	kept
kneel *niːl*	arrodillarse	knelt *nelt*	knelt
know *nou*	saber	knew *njuː*	known *noun*
lay *lei*	poner, colocar	laid *leid*	laid
lead *liːd*	conducir	led *led*	led
lean *liːn*	apoyarse	leant *lent*	leant
leap *liːp*	saltar	leapt *lept*	leapt
learn *ləːn*	aprender	learnt *ləːnt*	learnt
leave *liːv*	dejar	left *left*	left
lend *lend*	prestar	lent *lent*	lent
let *let*	dejar	let	let
lie *lai*	echarse, tumbarse	lay *lei*	lain *lein*
light *lait*	encender	lit *lit*	lit
lose *luːz*	perder	lost *lɔ(ː)st*	lost
make *meik*	hacer	made *meid*	made
may *mei*	puedo	might *mait*	—
mean *miːn*	significar	meant *ment*	meant
meet *miːt*	encontrar	met *met*	met
mow *mou*	segar, guadañar	mowed *moud*	mown *moun*
must *mʌst*	debo	must	—
pay *pei*	pagar	paid *peid*	paid
put *put*	poner	put	put
read *riːd*	leer	read *red*	read
rent *rend*	alquilar	rent *rent*	rent
rid *rid*	librarse	rid	rid

Present		Past	Past participle
ride *raid*	montar	rode *roud*	ridden *ridən*
ring *riŋ*	sonar, tañer	rang *ræŋ*	rung *rʌŋ*
(a)rise *(ə)raiz*	levantarse, elevarse	(a)rose *rouz*	(a)risen *rizən*
run *rʌn*	correr	ran *ræn*	run *rʌn*
saw *sɔː*	serrar	sawed *sɔːd*	sawn *sɔːn*
say *sei*	decir	said *sed*	said
see *siː*	ver	saw *sɔː*	seen *siːn*
seek *siːk*	buscar	sought *sɔːt*	sought
sell *sel*	vender	sold *sould*	sold
send *send*	enviar	sent *sent*	sent
set *set*	colocar	set	set
sew *sou*	coser	sewed *soud*	sewn *soun*
shake *ʃeik*	agitar, temblar	shook *ʃuk*	shaken *ʃeikən*
shall *ʃæl*	debo	should *ʃud*	—
shed *ʃed*	verter	shed	shed
shine *ʃain*	brillar	shone *ʃɔ(ː)n*	shone
shoot *ʃuːt*	disparar	shot *ʃɔt*	shot
show *ʃou*	mostrar, enseñar	showed *ʃoud*	shown *ʃoun*
shrink *ʃriŋk*	encoger	shrank *ʃræŋk*	shrunk *ʃrʌŋk*
shut *ʃʌt*	cerrar	shut	shut
sing *siŋ*	cantar	sang *sæŋ*	sung *sʌŋ*
sink *siŋk*	hundir	sank *sæŋk*	sunk *sʌŋk*
sit *sit*	sentarse	sat *sæt*	sat *sæt*
slay *slei*	matar	slew *sluː*	slain *slein*
sleep *sliːp*	dormir	slept *slept*	slept *slept*
slide *slaid*	resbalar, deslizarse	slid *slid*	slid *slid*
sling *sliŋ*	tirar (con honda)	slung *slʌŋ*	slung
slink *sliŋk*	escabullirse	slunk *slʌŋk*	slunk
slit *slit*	rajar	slit	slit
smell *smel*	oler	smelt *smelt*	smelt *smelt*
smite *smait*	herir, golpear, matar	smote *smout*	smitten *smitən*
sow *sou*	sembrar	sowed *soud*	sown *soun*
speak *spiːk*	hablar	spoke *spouk*	spoken *spoukən*
speed *spiːd*	aligerar	sped *sped*	sped
spell *spel*	deletrear	spelt *spelt*	spelt
spend *spend*	pasar, gastar	spent *spend*	spent
spill *spil*	derramar	spilt *spilt*	spilt
spin *spin*	hilar	spun *ʌ*, span *æ*	spun
spit *spit*	escupir	spat *spæt*	spat
split *split*	dividir	split	split
spoil *spɔil*	estropear	spoilt *spoilt*	spoilt
spread *spred*	desparramar	spread *spred*	spread *spred*
spring *spriŋ*	brotar, saltar	sprang *spræŋ*	sprung *ʌ*
stand *stænd*	sostenerse, estar en pie	stood *stud*	stood
steal *stiːl*	robar	stole *stoul*	stolen *stoulən*
stick *stik*	pegar, juntar	stuck *stʌk*	stuck

Present		Past	Past participle
sting *stiŋ*	picar (un insecto)	stung *stʌŋ*	stung
stink *stiŋk*	heder, oler mal	stank *stæŋk*	stunk *ʌ*
strew *struː*	esparcir, salpicar	strewed *struːd*	strewn *uː*
stride *straid*	caminar a pasos largos	strode *stroud*	stridden *'stridn*
strike *straik*	golpear, dar la hora	struck *strʌk*	struck
string *striŋ*	ensartar	strung *strʌŋ*	strung
strive *straiv*	esforzarse	strove *strouv*	striven *strivən*
strow *strou*		strowed *stroud*	strown *stroun*
swear *swɛə**	jurar	swore *swɔː**	sworn *swɔːn*
sweep *swiːp*	barrer	swept *swept*	swept
swell *swel*	inflamar, hinchar	swelled *sweld*	swollen *swoulən*
swim *swim*	nadar	swam *swæm*	swum *swʌm*
swing *swiŋ*	balancear	swung *swʌŋ*	swung
take *teik*	tomar, coger	took *tuk*	taken *teikən*
teach *tiːtʃ*	enseñar	taught *tɔːt*	taught
tear *tɛə**	rasgar	tore *tɔː**	torn *tɔːn*
tell *tel*	decir	told *tould*	told
think *θiŋk*	pensar	thought *θɔːt*	thought
thrive *θraiv*	medrar	throve *θrouv*	thriven *θrivən*
throw *θrou*	arrojar, lanzar	threw *θruː*	thrown *θroun*
tread *tred*	pisar, hollar	trod *trɔd*	trodden *trɔdən*
under'stand	comprender	understood *u*	understood
(a)wake *əweik*	despertar	(a)woke *wouk*	(a)woke(n)
wear *wɛə**	usar	wore *wɔː**	worn *wɔːn*
weave *wiːv*	tejer	wove *wouv*	woven *ou*
weep *wiːp*	llorar	wept *wept*	wept
will *wil*	quiero	would *wud*	—
win *win*	ganar	won *wʌn*	won
wind *waind*	envolver, arrollar, soplar	wound *waund*	wound
wring *riŋ*	retorcer	wrung *rʌng*	wrung
write *rait*	escribir	wrote *rout*	written *ritən*

TWENTY-SECOND LESSON
LECCIÓN VIGÉSIMA SEGUNDA

El adverbio

El adverbio puede ser simple, derivado, compuesto o locución adverbial. Son simples: «too, yet» (demasiado, todavía); son derivados: «seldom, where» (raramente, donde); son compuestos los formados por dos palabras de distinto origen: «however» [hau'evə*], «sometimes» [sʌmtaimz] (sin embargo, a veces). La locución adverbial está en ocasiones unida por medio de un guión: «now-a-days» [nau ə deiz] (hoy en día).

Según su significado, los adverbios se dividen en adverbios de:

> Lugar: «here», «there», «in», «out», «near», etc.: aquí, allí, dentro, fuera, cerca.
> Tiempo: «early», «late», «before», «afterwards», etc.: temprano, tarde, antes, después.
> Modo: «so», «quickly», «certainly», «thus», etc.: así, de prisa, ciertamente, así.
> Cantidad: «only», «rather» ra:ðə*, «almost», «how», etc.: sólo, bastante, casi, cómo.
> Número, orden: «once», «firstly», etc.: una vez, primeramente.
> Etcétera.

La mayor parte de los adverbios de modo y cantidad se derivan de adjetivos calificativos y participios, añadiendo el afijo «ly». Algunos adjetivos se emplean, sin alteración, como adverbios. Los terminados en «ll» añaden tan sólo una «y», y los que terminan en «le» cambian la «e» en «y»; los que terminan en «ue» pierden la «e» antes de tomar la terminación «ly».

Por lo demás, en la formación de los adverbios se siguen las reglas generales de ortografía. Los adjetivos polisílabos terminados en «ly» no añaden otra «ly» para formar el adverbio; en tales casos se emplea una perífrasis.

Adj. o part.		Adverbio
handsome 'hænsəm	hermoso	handsomely
proud praud	soberbio	proudly
rich	rico	richly
diligent	diligente	diligently
cruel kruəl	cruel	cruelly
honest 'onist	honrado	honestly
loving	amante, cariñoso	lovingly
opposed ə'pouzd	opuesto	opposedly
monthly 'mʌnθli	mensual	monthly
yearly 'jiəli	anual	yearly
low lou	bajo	low, lowlily
early 'ə:li	temprano	early
full	lleno	fully
noble noubl	noble	nobly
true tru:	fiel, verdadero	truly
easy i:zi	fácil	easily i:zili
dry drai	seco	dryly (y drily)
gay gei	alegre	gayly (y gaily)

El adverbio

Adj. o part.		Adverbio
friendly *frendli*	amistoso	in a friendly way (*o* manner)

Los adverbios (de cualquier clase que sean) que admiten los grados de comparación los forman según las reglas que se dieron para los adjetivos. Los monosílabos y algunos bisílabos forman el comparativo añadiendo la terminación «er», y el superlativo añadiendo «est». Los polisílabos, incluyendo casi todos los terminados en «ly» forman el comparativo anteponiendo el adverbio «more» y colocando inmediatamente después del adverbio comparado la conjunción «than». El grado superlativo se consigue anteponiendo al adverbio «the most». Al añadir los sufijos «er» y «est», se siguen las reglas de ortografía usuales.

		Compar.	*Superl.*
soon	pronto	sooner	the soonest
early	temprano	earlier	the earliest
easily	fácilmente	more easily	the most easily
wisely	prudentemente	more wisely	the most wisely

Algunos adverbios forman el comparativo y el superlativo irregularmente:

		Compar.		*Superl.*	
well	bien	better	mejor	best	el mejor
badly, ill	mal	worse	peor	worst	el peor
little	poco	less	menos	least	el menos
much	mucho	more	más	most	el más

Obsérvese la construcción especial de «more», «better» y «sooner» con la negación:

I have no more.	No tengo más.
No sooner said than done.	Tan pronto dicho y hecho.
I know no better ...	No conozco mejor ...

Obsérvense las siguientes expresiones:

3 days ago *ə'gou*	the day before yesterday	yesterday *jestədi*	to-day	tomorrow	the day after tomorrow
3 months ago	the month before last	last month	this month	next month	the month after next

In the morning (afternoon, evening).	Por la mañana (tarde, noche).
This morning (afternoon, evening).	Esta mañana (tarde, noche).
Yesterday morning (afternoon, evening).	Ayer por la mañana (tarde, noche).
Tomorrow morning (afternoon, evening).	Mañana por la mañana (tarde, noche).
Last night.	Ayer noche.
A week ago.	Hace una semana.
A fortnight ago.	Hace quince días.
In the daytime, by day.	De día, durante el día.
At noon *nu:n*, at mid-day	Al mediodía.
In the night, at night, at midnight.	Por la noche.

Hay adverbios y adjetivos que tienen la misma forma, y adverbios que tienen doble forma, la del adjetivo y la adverbial con el afijo «ly», según el sentido:

adj. «near», cercano, -a	*adv.* «near», cerca
	adv. «nearly», casi
adj. «low», bajo, -a	*adv.* «low», bajo, en voz baja
	adv. «lowly», humildemente, vilmente
adj. «hard», duro, recio	*adv.* «hard», duramente, recio, -amente
	adv. «hardly», apenas

«Near» es también preposición: «The sun is near setting» (El sol va a ponerse).

El adverbio puede modificar un adjetivo u otro adverbio:

That book is very interesting.	Este libro es muy interesante.
She sings very well.	Canta muy bien.

Puede modificar un verbo:

He speaks slowly.	Habla despacio.
He could hardly speak.	Apenas podía hablar.

Puede modificar una oración:

Unfortunately, I did not see them.	Desgraciadamente, no los vi.

Los principales adverbios interrogativos son:

Where ... ?	¿Donde?	How much ... ?	¿Cuánto?
When ... ?	¿Cuándo?	How many ... ?	¿Cuántos?
How ... ?	¿Cómo?	How often ... ?	¿Cuán a menudo?
How long ... ?	¿Cuánto tiempo?		

El adverbio

Exercise

Will you be home tomorrow morning? No, I was at home yesterday, and I shall be home again the day after tomorrow, but not tomorrow. Tomorrow I am going to Chester with a friend. Have you read «Hamlet»? Yes, I have read it once or twice, but my sister has read it four times. When shall we have the pleasure of seeing you? Whenever you send me an invitation, I shall be very pleased to come. How did you break that window? Oh, it was an accident. How did you do it, and how long ago? My brother and I were playing near it yesterday, and unfortunately my ball broke it. Where is your ball now? I don't know; I have looked for it everywhere, but it is nowhere to be found (no la encuentro en parte alguna). Will you walk up and down the street with me while we wait for Tom? Yes, of course, but tell him to be quick (rápido). Have you nothing else to say before I go? Isn't there anything else I can do for you just now? No, thank you. I have just finished my work a few minutes ago, and I have nothing else to do for the present. How much did you pay for this book? Not much, only four shillings. How often do you go to the cinema? About once or twice a week.

Ejercicio

¿Dónde está mi sombrero? No está aquí; está en otra parte. ¿Adónde va usted ahora? Voy al jardín. ¿Dónde vive tu hermano? Vive en el molino, allá abajo, cerca del río. ¿Quiere usted ir allá? Hoy no, pero mañana o la semana próxima (next...) iré (I will). ¿Está su padre (de usted) en casa? Sí, señor, está arriba, en su cuarto, creo; si no está allí, estará abajo, en el patio. ¿Cuánto tiempo se queda usted en la escuela? Me quedo allí a veces tres horas, a veces hasta (even) cinco horas. ¿Cuántos son tres por tres? Tres por tres son nueve. En otro tiempo estaba frecuentemente enfermo, ahora tengo buena salud (I am in good health [$hel\theta$]). Mi hermana vendrá pronto. Me alegraré de verla aquí.

Words

abbey 'æbi	abadía	I rejoice ri-'dʒɔis	me alegro
ascended ə'sendid	subió (al trono)	later leitə*	más tarde, después
block blok	tajo		
building 'bildiŋ	edificio	navigator 'næ-vigeitə*	navegante
connected kə'nektid	relacionado	order 'ɔːdə*	orden
conqueror 'kɔnkərə*	conquistador	potato pə'teitou	patata
conveyed kən-'veid	conducido, llevado	repair ri'pɛə*	reparación
courtyard 'kɔːt'jaːd	patio	to behead bi'hed	cortar la cabeza
dead ded	muerto	to murder 'məːdə*	asesinar
events i'vents	acontecimientos	throne θroun	trono
famous 'feiməs	famoso	tobacco tə'bækou	tabaco
government 'gʌvənmənt	gobierno	tower 'tauə*	torre
introduce intrə'djːus	introducir		

Reading exercise

The Tower

One of the most remarkable buildings of London is the Tower. The oldest part of it was built by William the Conqueror. It is called the White Tower. With the Tower many of the most memorable events of English history are connected. Here, young Edward and his brother Richard were murdered by order of their uncle Richard, Duke of Gloucester ['glɔstə*], who, after their death, ascended the throne as Richard III. For long years nobody knew what had become of their dead bodies, till 200 years later some repairs being made in the Tower, they were found and conveyed to Westminster Abbey. In the Tower two of the wives of Henry VIII, Anne Boleyn, the mother of Elizabeth, and Catherine Howard, were beheaded, and here Sir Walter Raleigh [wɔːltə 'rɔːli], the famous navigator, who introduced the tobacco and the potato into England, laid his head upon the block. Today the Tower is no longer used as a prison, but as a government arsenal.

El adverbio

Conversation

Where is the Tower known as the White Tower? Are there many events connected with the history of England recorded there? What princes were murdered in the Tower? Who gave the order? Who ascended the throne of England when the young princes were beheaded? What name did he take? When were their bodies found? Were any queens beheaded in the Tower? What did Raleigh introduce into England? Have you ever seen the Tower?

Words

anxious, -ly *'æŋkʃəs, -li*	deseoso, impacientemente	nurse *nəːs*	enfermera
approach *ə'proutʃ*	acercarse	policeman *pə'liːsmən*	policía
by *bai*	cerca	rail *reil*	raíl
doctor *'dɔktə**	doctor	rapid, -ly *'ræpid, -li*	rápido, -amente
examination *igzæmi'neiʃən*	examen	regain control *rigein*	controlar
extraordinary *iks'trɔːdnri*	extraordinario	run, ran, run *rʌn, ræn, rʌn*	correr
fall, fell, fallen *'fɔːl, fel, 'fɔːlən*	caerse	—over *ouvə**	atropellar
happen *'hæpən*	ocurrir	school-boy *'skuːl bɔi*	colegial
hospital *'hɔspitl*	hospital	seriously *'siəriəsli*	gravemente
hurry *'hʌri*	de prisa	severe, -ly *si'viə*, -li*	grave, -mente
in future *in'fjuːtʃə**	en adelante	slip *slip*	resbalar
injure *'indʒə**	lesionar	slippery *'slipəri*	resbaladizo
injury *'indʒəri*	lesión	smash *smæʃ*	estrellarse
it seems *it siːmz*	parece	tram-car *træmkaː**	tranvía
lucky, -ily *'lʌki, -li*	feliz, afortunadamente		

Reading exercise

I say, Peter! Where are you going in such a hurry? Is anything the matter? — Unfortunately, yes. My cousin Tom has had a bad accident and is in hospital. — That is most unfortunate. How did it happen? — Oh, I don't know very well, yet. It seems that he was driving home from work and must have been going faster that usual because there were some people waiting for him. It was raining and the rails of the tram-line on Atlanta avenue were very slippery, so his car skidded, he was not able to regain control and it was struck by a tram-car. A policeman who was near by pulled him out and he was taken to hospital. The doctors have completed their examination and they said that Tom is not seriously injured and will be able to go home in a few days. The car, however, was badly smashed and it is really extraordinary that he was not more hurt.

Ejercicio

Ayer tarde, cuando estaba en la calle esperando el tranvía, ocurrió un accidente. Un chico iba muy de prisa en bicicleta, no vio que un tranvía venía muy cerca, patinó y cayó. La bicicleta se hizo pedazos, pues un auto que venía detrás le pasó por encima. Un policía que estaba por allí le llevó rápidamente al hospital, donde fue examinado por un médico. Yo también fui allí. Esperé impacientemente al médico para preguntarle. Afortunadamente, sus lesiones no fueron tan graves como creía la enfermera, y el chico podrá salir del hospital pronto, seguramente a primeros de la próxima semana. Ahora, el muchacho irá probablemente un poco más despacio y así no tendrá accidentes.

¿Cuánto tiempo hace que vives aquí? Hace seis años. ¿Dónde naciste? En Francia. ¿Vas a menudo a tu patria (home)? No, sólo dos o tres veces al año. Mi hermana va cada mes.

To learn by heart

There was an old man from Peru
Who dreamt[1] he was eating his shoe[2].
He awoke in the night
In a terrible[3] fright[4]:
And found it was perfectly true[5].

1. Dreamt *dremt* soñó. 2. Shoe *ʃuː* zapato. 3. Terrible *ˈterəbl* terrible. 4. Fright *frait* susto. 5. True *truː* verdad.

TWENTY-THIRD LESSON
LECCIÓN VIGÉSIMA TERCERA

El adverbio (continuación)

Como ya se dijo en la lección anterior, algunos adverbios tienen la misma forma que el adjetivo:

El adverbio

Our daily bread.	El pan de cada día.
He goes to work daily.	Va a trabajar diariamente.
This is hard work.	Es un trabajo difícil.
He works hard.	Trabaja mucho (duramente).
We heard a loud noise *laud nɔiz*.	Oímos un ruido fuerte.
He spoke loud.	Habló en alta voz (fuerte).

Obsérvese especialmente el adverbio «very», que puede usarse como si fuera un adjetivo:

She was very happy (adv.).	Era muy feliz.
This is the very book I wanted (adj.).	Es el mismísimo libro que quería.

Colocación del adverbio

Si el verbo no tiene complemento, el adverbio sigue inmediatamente al verbo:

He reads well.	Lee bien.
She came out.	Ella salió.

Si tiene complemento y éste es corto, puede intercalarse entre el verbo y el adverbio:

I shall read your letter now.	Leeré su carta ahora.
Put your hat on, please.	Póngase el sombrero, por favor.

Los adverbios de tiempo indefinido y algunos de modo preceden generalmente al verbo:

I always read the paper.	Siempre leo el periódico.
He briefly told the news *briːfli tould ðə njuːs*.	Dijo las noticias brevemente.
I often go to the pictures.	Voy al cine con frecuencia.
He frequently came here.	Venía aquí con frecuencia.

Pero sigue al verbo «ser» y a los verbos anómalos:

He is never in time.	Nunca llega a tiempo.
I could hardly read it *haːdli riːd it*.	Apenas pude leerlo.

En los tiempos compuestos estos adverbios se colocan entre el auxiliar y el participio:

I shall never take it.	Nunca lo tomaré.

El adverbio, con escasas excepciones, precede al adjetivo y al adverbio:

That school is very far.	Este colegio está muy lejos.
This book is very small.	Este libro es muy pequeño.

Pero el adverbio «enough» suele seguir al adverbio o adjetivo:

> This is not good enough. Esto no es bastante bueno.
> He did not write soon enough. No escribió bastante aprisa (pronto).

Algunos adverbios pueden colocarse en distinto lugar de la oración sin alterar el sentido general de la misma:

> Perhaps *pə'hæps* he did not know it.
> He did not know it, perhaps.
> He, perhaps, did not know it.

El adverbio no debe separar el verbo de la preposición «to» en el modo infinitivo:

> Tell him to come quickly.

La colocación del adverbio puede, en algunos casos, cambiar el sentido de la oración:

> He wanted the book only. Solamente quería el libro.
> He wanted only the book. Quería el libro solo.

En la oración siguiente, «only» se usa como si fuese un adjetivo:

> Only he wanted the book. Sólo él quería el libro.

Los adverbios siguientes forman el comparativo y el superlativo por medio de sufijo:

slowly	slower	slowest	despacio
quickly	quicker	quickest	de prisa
often	oftener	oftenest	a menudo

Words

abroad *ə'brɔːd*	extranjero (país)
acquisition *ækwi'ziʃən*	adquisición
cathedral *kə'θiːdrəl*	catedral
cheap *tʃiːp*	barato
cheat *tʃiːt*	engañar, estafar
coffee house *'kɔfi haus*	café
elsewhere *'els'wɛəˑ*	en otra parte
gun *gʌn*	escopeta
hunter *'hʌntəˑ*	cazador
idle *'aidl*	ocioso
knowledge *'nɔlidʒ*	conocimientos
mention *'menʃən*	mencionar
nicely *'naisli*	con esmero, bien
perfectly *'pəːfiktli*	perfectamente
shillings *'ʃiliŋs*	chelines
straightforward *streit'fɔːwəd*	derecho, recto
to be right *rait*	tener razón
to be worth *wəːθ*	valer
to be wrong *rɔŋ*	estar equivocado
try *trai*	intentar, tratar
undoubtedly *ʌn'dautidli*	indudablemente
virtue *'vəːtjuː*	virtud

Exercise

You have done badly; I hope you will do better next time. Did you know him formerly? Of course. I shall be with you presently. Let us speak boldly to them. So much the (tanto) better for you, and so much the worse for him. Never put off (diferir) till (hasta) to-morrow what can be done to-day. He rises (o «gets up», se levanta) at noon, and goes to bed long after midnight. He is more frequently at the coffee-house than at home. I never heard her sing so well. He would undoubtedly have written more nicely, if you had given him time enough. You ought to teach the child; perhaps he will then learn better. The ships arrived only the other day, and will sail again to-day a week. He was not often happy, because he was idle. It must therefore be wrong to go. We should always prefer our duty (deber) to our pleasure. Nothing is better worth [$wə:θ$] (vale más) the time and attention of young people than the acquisition of knowledge and virtue [$'və:tʃu$]. This is the easiest book I ever read; consequently, I understand it perfectly well. Shall you come back soon? Yes, as soon as I can. I have heard enough. The hunter has put down his gun. You must go straightforward; then you turn [$tə:n$] (volver) to the right, afterwards to the left, and then you will be in front of the cathedral [$kə'θi:drəl$]. This is very cheap: I paid very little for it, only a few shillings. How is it that the more you study the less you learn? How far did you go this morning? I went as far as the church, not farther. I looked everywhere for my stick, but I could find it nowhere. Never try again to cheat me. Knock hard, they are still sleeping. He walked up and down, then he sat down in the arm-chair. Can you see well, now? Not quite well, but pretty well.

Ejercicio

Él se porta (to behave) muy cortésmente (politely), más cortésmente que su hermano. El pueblo no está lejos; por consiguiente, iré a caballo hasta allí. Mi amigo llegará aquí de hoy en ocho días. Murió al (on the) día siguiente. La vi hace unos días. Estaba vestida a la moda (was fashionably). ¿Viene usted todos los días? Vengo cada dos días. ¿Ha estado usted en Inglaterra? Estuve allí hace algún tiempo. ¿Ve usted a veces a mi prima? Rara vez la veo, pero le escribo a menudo. Enviaré luego la carta. Vivo en aquella casa de allá. La casa no está muy lejos. Primero, yo tengo razón; en segundo lugar, él está equivocado; y, en tercer lugar, tú también tienes razón. Os veía con más frecuencia el año pasado. Habla de (in) un modo necio. Mi hermano está en el extranjero. Si no encontráis vuestro sombrero aquí, buscadlo en otra parte. ¿Le conoce usted? No le conozco en absoluto.

Words

cash *kæʃ*	dinero (en efect.)	together *tə-'geðə**	juntos
castle *'kɑːsl*	castillo	to go boating *'boutiŋ*	ir de excursión en barca
charabanc *'ʃærəbæŋ*	remolque (de un coche para excursión)	to go fishing *'fiʃiŋ*	ir a pescar
countryside *'kʌntrisaid*	campo (opuesto a ciudad)	to go hiking *'haikiŋ*	ir de excursión a pie
day-excursion *dei iks'kəːʃən*	excursión de un día	trip *trip*	excursión
recreation *rekri'eiʃən*	recreo, descanso	week-end *'wiːk 'end*	fin de semana
scrape (money) *skreip*	juntar, recoger (dinero)	what about ...? *wɔt e'baut*	¿qué te parece...?
steamboat *'stiːmbout*	vapor	youth hostel *'juːθ 'hostəl*	parador de estudiantes

Conversation

A. What are you going to do this week-end?
B. I really don't know, yet
A. Will you be going away somewhere?
B. I would like to. I think I deserve some recreation after a hard week's work.
A. Well, let's go together. We could go down to Brighton and spend the weekend on the beach.
B. Or even in the country. There is a lovely river about ten miles from Brighton and we could spend a day fishing or boating.
A. There are day-excursions by charabanc round the Sussex countryside, and there are some fine old castles at Beeding and Hastings that I have never seen.
B. We could also spend the weekend hiking round Sussex.

We might even take the steam-boat trip to France if we could scrape together the necessary cash.
A. Well, I would prefer to take things a little easier. Anyway, there is also plenty of night-life in Brighton, too, and I would rather take my outings from there.
B. Also, it could be done quite cheaply. Cheaper than France. Now I come to think of it, what about the youth hostels in the town?
A. They are quite good. We can try them if you like.
B. I'd like to. I have never been to one.

Ejercicio

Aunque solamente tiene 19 años, conduce muy bien, pero corre demasiado; supongo que solamente aprenderá a conducir con precaución, por experiencia, cuando le haya sucedido algún accidente. Llegará allí pasado mañana por la tarde. Me lo entregarán tan pronto como terminen. Esto está bien así. Nunca toma café después de comer. Antes de empezar su trabajo aquí, pase por mi oficina. Estoy realmente de acuerdo con usted.

To learn by heart

I would have you be
as a fire[1] well kindled[2]
that at everything catches[3]
and turns[4] it into light and flame[5].

1. Fire *'faiə* fuego. 2. Kindle *kindl* encender. 3. Catch *kætʃ* prender. 4. Turn *təːn* convertir. 5. Flame *fleim* llama.

LISTA DE ADVERBIOS DE USO MÁS FRECUENTE

Adverbios de lugar:

above *ə'bʌv* arriba
abroad *ə'brɔːd* en el extranjero, ultramar, fuera de casa
ahead *ə'hed* más allá, delante de todos
away *ə'wei* fuera, lejos
back *bæk* atrás, detrás
backwards *bækwədz* hacia atrás
below *bi'lou* abajo

beneath *bi'niːθ* debajo
behind *bi'haind* atrás, detrás
before *bi'fɔə** delante (de)
down *daun* abajo
downwards *'daunwədz* hacia abajo
far, lejos
forth, en adelante, fuera
forward(s), adelante, más allá

hence *hens* de aquí
here *hiə** aquí
herein *hiə'rin* en esto, aquí dentro
herewith *hiə'wiθ* con esto
home *houm* a casa
at home, en casa, en la patria
homeward(s), hacia la casa (el domicilio, la patria)
indoors *'indɔəz* en casa
inside *'insaid* en el interior
inwardly, al interior, dentro
near *niə** cerca
off, lejos
onward, adelante
out, fuera, afuera
outside, al exterior, afuera
outward(ly), exteriormente
outdoors *'autdɔəz* fuera de casa
over *ouvə** arriba, acabado
overhead, en alto, sobre la cabeza
thence *ðens* de allí
there *ðɛə** allí, allá

underneath *ʌndə'ni:θ* debajo
up *ʌp* arriba
up and down, arriba y abajo
to and fro } por acá y por
frou } allá, de una parte a otra
upward(s), hacia arriba
whence *wens* de donde
where *hwɛə** donde, en donde
elsewhere *'els'wɛə** en (a) otra parte
everywhere, en (por) todas partes
nowhere *'nouwɛə** en (a) ninguna parte.
anywhere, dondequiera, en cualquier parte
somewhere, en (a) alguna parte
within *wi'ðin* dentro, en el interior
without *wi'ðaut* fuera, exteriormente
yonder, allá, allí (a lo lejos)

Adverbios de tiempo:

after *a:ftə**,
afterwards } después, en seguida
-*wədz*
again *ə'gein* otra vez, de nuevo
ago *ə'gou* hace, ha
already *ɔ:l'redi* ya
always *'ɔ:lwiz* siempre
anon *ə'nɔn* pronto, al instante
at first, primeramente, al principio
at last, at } al fin, finalmente
length *leŋθ*
at present *preznt* actualmente, hoy día
at once *wʌns* de seguida
all at once, de una vez
as yet, hasta ahora
before *bi'fɔə** antes (de)
by and by, pronto, luego
early *ə:li* temprano
ever *evə** siempre, alguna vez
for ever, para siempre
ever and anon *ə'nɔn* muy a menudo
formerly, en otro tiempo, antes
generally, en general
hence *hens* desde entonces
henceforth —*'fɔ:θ* de aquí en adelante

hereafter *hiə'ra:ftə** en adelante, en lo sucesivo
immediately
i'mi:djatly } luego, al momento
directly *direktly*
instantly, al instante, instantáneamente
in time, a su tiempo, en tiempo
just *dʒʌst* hace poco, ahora, en punto
late *leit* tarde
lately, of } poco ha, de poco acá,
late } recientemente
long, largo tiempo
how long, cuanto tiempo
meanwhile *mi:n'wail* entretanto
never, nunca, jamás
now *nau* ahora
nowadays *nauə'deiz* hoy día
now and then, de vez en cuando
often *ɔfn* a menudo, frecuentemente
how often, cuantas veces
once *wʌns* una vez, en una ocasión
once more, una vez más, otra vez

El adverbio

presently, pronto, luego, ahora
rarely *rεəli*, sel- ⎫ raramente,
  dom *'seldəm* ⎭ rara vez
since *sins* desde entonces
sometimes *'sʌmtaimz* a veces
soon, *su:n* pronto, prontamente
shortly, in ⎫ en breve, dentro
  a short ⎬ de poco tiempo,
  time ⎭ al corto rato
still, todavía, aún
suddenly *'sʌdnli* de repente, de pronto

till then, hasta entonces
then, entonces, luego, después
till now, hasta ahora
since then, desde entonces
when, cuando
whenever, cada vez que, siempre que
yet, todavía, aún
not yet, aún no, todavía no
to-day, hoy
yesterday, ayer
to-morrow -*'mɔrou* mañana

Nota: La terminación «wards», «hacia», se añade a veces a algunos adverbios para indicar dirección: «downwards», «southwards».

Adverbios de modo:

(a)loud *ə'laud* en voz alta
else *els* de otra manera, más, además
fast, velozmente, de prisa
headlong, de cabeza, precipitadamente
how, cómo
ill, badly, mal
like *laik*, ali- ⎫ igualmente, como,
  ke *əlaik* ⎭ a la par de
likely *'laikli* probablemente
likewise *'laikwaiz* también, asimismo
low *lou* en voz baja
nearly *niəli* casi

otherwise *'ʌðəwaiz* de otro modo
on purpose *'pə:pəs*, ⎫ adrede
  purposely *'pə:pəsli* ⎭
readily *'redili*, ⎫ de buena gana
  willingly ⎭
so *sou*, thus *ðʌs* así, así pues
together *tu'geðə** juntos, a la vez
well, bien
in short, ⎫ en breve
  shortly ⎭
by degrees *di'gri:z* gradualmente
at once, de golpe, de una vez, al momento
all right, muy bien, perfectamente, etc.

Adverbios de cantidad y orden:

as *æz* tan
about *ə'baut* poco más o menos, cerca de
almost *'ɔ:lmoust*, ⎫ casi
  nearly *niəli* ⎭
also *'ɔ:lsou* también, aun
at all, del todo, de todo punto
at least *li:st* a lo menos, siquiera
besides *bi'saidz* además, por otra parte
enough *i'nʌf* bastante, asaz
even *i:vn* hasta, aun
little, poco
much, mucho, muy

more, más
moreover *mɔ'rouvə** además
not even, ni aun, ni ... tampoco
only *ounli* (tan) sólo, solamente
pretty *priti* pasablemente, bastante, medianamente
rather *ra:ðə** más bien, antes, bastante, algo
scarcely *skεəsli* apenas
so *sou* así, tan(to)
very, muy
something, so- ⎫ algo, un tanto
  mewhat ⎭

thoroughly 'θʌ- ⎫ enteramente,
  rəli, quite   ⎬ del todo,
  kwait, entire- ⎭ completa-
  ly in'taiəli   mente
too, demasiado, aun, también
how much, cuanto
so much, tanto

as much, otro tanto
too much, demasiado
how little, cuan poco
so little, as ⎱ tan poco
  little   ⎰
too little, demasiado poco

the more ... the more
the less ... the less
the more ... the less
the less ... the more

cuanto más ... tanto más
cuanto menos ... tanto menos
cuanto más ... tanto menos
cuanto menos ... tanto más

more and more
less and less
however (much)

más y más, cada vez más
cada vez menos
por más que, por mucho que

Cuando «más» se refiere a tiempo, se traduce por «longer»; cuando a espacio, por «farther» *[fa:ðə*]*. Obsérvese el uso de «however» delante de «much» y «many».

I can't wait any longer.
I shall not walk any farther,

No puedo esperar más.
No andaré más (lejos).

however much bread he may have...
however many horses he may have...
however much that flour may be...

por mucho pan que tenga ...
por muchos caballos ...
por mucha que sea esa harina ...

however many of them may come...   por muchos que vengan ...

Adverbios afirmativos, negativos, dubitativos, etc.:

certainly *sə:tnli* ciertamente
truly *tru:li* seguramente
indeed *in'di:d* de veras, en efecto
really *'riəli* verdaderamente
undoubtedly *ʌn'dautədli* sin duda
of course *kɔ:s* naturalmente, por supuesto
not at all, en absoluto no, de ningún modo
no more, ya no, no más
yes, sí; o yes, ¡oh! sí

not, no
no *nou* no
why *(h)wai* por qué
wherefore *hwɛə'fɔə** por lo que, por lo cual, porque
because *bi'kɔ:z* porque, pues
therefore *ðɛə'fɔ:** por eso, por lo tanto
consequently *'kɔnsikwəntly* por consiguiente
perhaps *pə'hæps* tal vez, acaso
probably, li- ⎱ probablemente
  kely *laikli* ⎰

Algunas locuciones adverbiales:

at noon, al mediodía
at midnight, a la medianoche

at random *'rændəm* a la ventura, al azar

El artículo (ampliación)

one day, un día, una vez
to-night *tə'nait* esta noche
yesterday night, } anoche
last night
the other day, el otro día, pocos días ha
next day, al día siguiente
every day, todos los días, cada día
the day before yesterday, anteayer
the day after to-morrow, pasado mañana
every other (*o* second) day, un día sí y otro no, cada dos días
this morning (evening), esta mañana (noche)
to-morrow evening, mañana por la noche
yesterday morning, ayer por la mañana
about dusk *dʌsk* al anochecer
at daybreak } al amanecer,
'deibreik } al despuntar
at dawn *dɔːn* } el día
from time to time, } de vez en
now and then } cuando
long ago *ə'gou*, } hace largo
long since } tiempo

ever since, desde entonces
all day (night, the week...) long, todo el día (noche, semana...)
to-day week (fortnight), dentro de (de hoy en) 8 (15) días
three months from yesterday, de ayer en tres meses
the week before last, la penúltima semana
a year (two years...) ago, hace un año (dos años...)
by heart *haːt* de memoria
by degrees, gradualmente
by the by, } de paso, a propósito,
by the way } entre paréntesis
by much, con (de) mucho
by all means *miːnz* de todas maneras, cueste lo que cueste
by day, de día
by night, de noche
downstairs, (escaleras) abajo
above *ə'bʌv* all, principalmente, sobre (*o* ante) todo
upstairs, (escaleras) arriba
to the right, a la derecha
to the left, a la izquierda
in vain, en vano, inútilmente
on foot, a pie
on horseback, a caballo

TWENTY-FOURTH LESSON
LECCIÓN VIGÉSIMA CUARTA

El artículo (ampliación)

El artículo determinado se emplea, en términos generales, como en español, pero no puede contraerse con ninguna preposición:

Of the girl.	De la niña.
Of the boy.	Del niño.

El artículo determinado se omite en los casos siguientes:

a) Delante de nombres en plural tomados en sentido general:

I love books.	Me gustan mucho los libros.
Trees are green.	Los árboles son verdes.
Men are mortal.	Los hombres son mortales.

pero si el plural tiene un sentido determinativo toma el artículo:

The trees of that garden are very well looked after.	Los árboles de ese jardín están muy bien cuidados.

b) Delante de nombres abstractos en sentido genérico:

Kindness is always rewarded.	La bondad es siempre recompensada.
We admire courage.	Admiramos el valor.

El nombre abstracto se convierte en común cuando le precede el artículo:

The kindness of that man is well known to all his friends.	La bondad de ese hombre es bien conocida por todos sus amigos.

c) Delante de nombres de materia en singular y en plural cuando tienen sentido genérico:

I like bread.	Me gusta el pan.
Gold is a metal.	El oro es un metal.
Glass is transparent.	El cristal es transparente.

d) Delante de los títulos seguidos del nombre propio o apellido y de los apellidos en plural (se exceptúa: «the Reverend»):

King Edward the VII.	Mr. Knowles.
Captain Smith.	Aunt Jane.
Miss Williams.	Lord Anthony Howard.

Pero diremos: «the Prince of Wales» [*weilz*], «the Duke of Gloucester» [*'glɔstə**], porque no les sigue el nombre propio.

e) Delante de los nombres que indiquen las estaciones, meses y días; fiestas señaladas, comidas e idiomas, en sentido general; plazas, calles y las palabras «mount» [*maunt*] «monte» y «lake» [*leik*] «lago»:

I love Spring.	Me gusta mucho la primavera.
In May the weather is usually fine.	En mayo el tiempo es generalmente bueno.

El artículo (ampliación)

Friday is a holiday.	El viernes es fiesta.
I spent Christmas in England.	Pasé la Navidad en Inglaterra.
We have breakfast at 8,30	Desayunamos (tomamos el desayuno) a las 8,30.
Trafalgar Square is in London.	La Plaza de Trafalgar está en Londres.
They climbed Mount Snowdon.	Escalaron el monte Snowdon.
Lake Lugano is beautiful.	El lago Lugano es precioso.
Oxford Street is not very long.	La calle de Oxford no es muy larga.

f) Delante de las palabras «home», «casa», «church», «iglesia», «school», «colegio», «College» [′kɔlidʒ] «Colegio Mayor Universitario», «market» [′maːkit] «mercado», «hospital» [′hɔspitl] «hospital», «prison» [′prizn] «prisión», «bed» [bed] «cama»:

I am going home now.	Me voy a casa ahora.
I went to church yesterday.	Fui a la iglesia ayer.
I am going to bed.	Me voy a la cama.

g) Delante de las palabras «Heaven, Paradise, hell» y «earth» en la expresión «en la tierra» (on earth):

Thy will be done on earth as it is in Heaven.	Hágase tu voluntad así en la tierra como en el cielo.

h) «Next» y «last», con el significado de «próximo» y «pasado», no llevan artículo:

Next week.	La semana que viene.
Last Summer.	El verano pasado.

En general, los sustantivos tomados en sentido determinado toman siempre el artículo:

The church near the school is very nice.
The children have learnt their lessons already.

Delante de palabras que indican partes del cuerpo y los objetos de uso personal se emplea el adjetivo posesivo en lugar del artículo:

I have cut my finger *fiŋgə**.	Me he cortado en el dedo.
I have lost my pen.	He perdido mi pluma.

El artículo indefinido, además de su uso normal como en castellano, se emplea en inglés delante de los nombres en singular que indican: nacionalidad, partido político, profesión, religión, estado civil y modo de ser, precedidos del verbo ser o de verbos de estado:

> He is a Spaniard.
> He became a Conservative.
> He was a doctor.
> He was made a Baron.
>
> He is a Catholic.
> He is a bachelor.
> He is a fool.

Con ciertas expresiones de medida y tiempo:

> Four shillings a *filiŋz ə* yard.
> Three times a day.
>
> Cuatro chelines la yarda.
> Tres veces al día.

Delante de «hundred», «thousand», «million» (cien, mil, millón) cuando no van precedidos de numeral:

> There were a hundred people there.
> One in a million *miljən*.

Con «what» exclamatorio y «such» seguidos de un nombre en singular:

> What a beautiful rose!
> What a pity!
> She was such a nice girl!
>
> ¡Qué rosa tan bonita!
> ¡Qué lástima!
> ¡Era una chica tan simpática!

Words

additional *ə'diʃənl*	adicional
bacon *'beikən*	tocino
biscuit *'biskit*	bizcocho
boil *bɔil*	hervir
brandy *'brændi*	coñac
bread and butter	pan y mantequilla
cake *keik*	pastel
cards *kaːdz*	naipes, cartas
carve *kaːv*	trinchar
cigar *si'gaːr* *	puro
chat *tʃæt*	charlar
cheese *tʃiːz*	queso
chosen *'tʃouzn*	seleccionados
class *klaːs*	clase
coffee *'kɔfi*	café
consist *kən'sist*	consistir en
conversation *kɔnvə'seiʃən*	conversación
course *kɔːs*	curso, platos (servidos en una comida)
cup *kʌp*	taza
dessert *di:'zəːt*	postre
dining-room	comedor
dish	plato (de comida)
drawing room *'drɔiŋrum*	salón
especial, -ly *is'peʃəli*	especial, -mente
fish *fiʃ*	pescado
following *'folouiŋ*	siguiente
fried *fraid* egg	huevo frito
fruit *fruːt*	fruta
fry *frai*	freir
full dinner *'dinə* *	gran comida
games *geimz*	juegos
ham *hæm*	jamón
including *in'kluːdiŋ*	incluyendo
in general *'dʒenərəl*	en general
jam *dʒæːm*	mermelada
join *dʒɔin*	unir, reunirse
lunch, -eon	almuerzo
marmalade *'maːməleid*	mermelada de naranja
music *'mjuːzik*	música

occasions *oˈkeiʒenz*	ocasiones	serve *səːv*	servir
pass	pasar	soup *suːp*	sopa
porridge *ˈpɔridʒ*	gachas	substantial *səbˈstænʃəl*	sustancial
port wine	vino de oporto	sweet *swiːt*	dulce
poultry *ˈpoultri*	aves, caza	tea *tiː*	té
principal *ˈprinsipəl*	principal	toast *toust*	tostada
pudding *ˈpudiŋ*	budín	usually *ˈjuːʒuəli*	corrientemente
remain *riˈmein*	permanecer	smoke *smouk*	fumar
retire *riˈtaiə**	retirarse	start *staːt*	empezar
roast-beef *roust biːf*	asado	upper *ʌpə**	alta
		vegetables *ˈvedʒitəblz*	vegetales

Reading exercise

Meals   Comidas

English people have at least three meals *miːlz* a day: breakfast, lunch, and dinner. Many people take an additional meal known as tea. Breakfast is usually between 7,30 and 8,30 in the morning. It is a more substantial meal than the Spanish breakfast. Usually, several of the following are chosen: fruit, porridge, eggs, either boiled or fried, bacon, ham, fish, bread and butter or toast with jam or marmalade, and coffee, tea or milk. The second meal of the day, called lunch or luncheon is eaten between 12 and 1,30. This is a light meal consisting of a simple dish of hot or cold meat, a vegetable, bread and butter and pudding. Sometimes, fruit and cheese may be had now. Bread and butter, toast, biscuits, cake and tea may be served in the afternoon at about 4 o'clock. The last meal of the day is dinner. This is the principal meal. In the upper classes and in other families where the men are working away from home during the day, the dinner is usually taken between 6 and 8 o'clock in the evening. Sometimes, on special occasions, a full dinner is served. This consists of several courses, including soup, fish, meat or poultry with potatoes and vegetables, pudding or some other sweet dish, cheese and dessert. When dinner is finished, the ladies sometimes retire to the drawing-room or the lounge, while the gentlemen remain for a while in the dining-room to drink port wine or brandy, smoke a cigar and chat. Later, they join the ladies for an evening of conversation, music, cards or other games.

Conversation

How many meals a day do you usually have? At what time do English people usually have their breakfast? Do Spaniards have breakfast at the same time? What do you have for lunch? Do you have a big lunch? Do you drink tea or coffee with your breakfast? What do you like best? Do you like to start your day with a cup of tea, or do you prefer a cup of coffee? What did you have for dinner yesterday? Do you eat the same every day? Do you like fish? What do you like better, cake or toast? Which is the most substantial meal of the day? Do you eat anything in the afternoon? At what time do you usually have dinner? Is that earlier or later than in England?

A. What did you have for dinner?
B. We had soup, boiled fish and vegetables.
A. Did you have the same yesterday?
B. No, yesterday we had roast-beef and potatoes.
A. Who carved the meet?
B. Mother always carves the meat, at home.
A. Do you usually have tea in the dining-room or do you have it in the lounge (sala de estar)?
B. We usually have it in the lounge.
A. What would you like for your breakfast, to-morrow?
B. I think, I would like a boiled egg, some bread and butter and a cup of coffee.
A. Do you like to smoke a cigarette (cigarrillo) after dinner?
B. O yes; I like it and I usually have one.
A. Will you kindly (¿quiere hacer el favor de...) pass me the toast?
B. With pleasure (con mucho gusto). Can I get you anything else?
A. Yes, please. Could you pass the jam as well?
B. Certainly. There you are (tenga).
A. Thank you.
B. Not at all (de nada). It's all right.

Ejercicio

¿Qué has tomado para desayunar? He tomado huevos fritos, pescado, pan y mantequilla, postre y un café. El café

El artículo (ampliación) 141

lo prefiero con azúcar. El primo de María es sastre (tailor ['teilə*]), es el mejor de la ciudad; su hermano está estudiando para ser médico. Los perros son animales muy útiles al hombre. La música es un arte. Ayer, a las 4, fui a ver al doctor; la enfermera (nurse [nə:s]) me dijo que volviera más tarde.

Los árboles de aquel campo dan una fruta deliciosa. Durante la cena tuvimos una larga conversación: hablamos de comidas. ¿Quiere un cigarrillo? Sí, gracias, me gusta fumar, especialmente después de la comida. Él se ha hecho católico en la India. La primavera es la estación más bonita. En el invierno vivimos en la ciudad; en el verano, en el campo.

To learn by heart

What is wrong with you?	¿Qué le ocurre a usted?
There is nothing wrong with me.	No me ocurre nada.
Never mind!	¡Qué más da! No se preocupe.
To keep one's head.	Mantenerse sereno.

Letter-writing

At the top (arriba) of the page, a little to the right, you first put your address, and then the date (fecha), for instance (por ejemplo): 26, Russell Square, London W., May 6th, 1928. If you write to a gentleman, you address him as «Sir», and you write the heading (['hediŋ] encabezamiento), not in the middle of the page, but a little to the left. If you know him intimately, you address him as «Dear Sir», or «My dear friend», while a lady is addressed as «Madam», or «Dear Madam». Business ([biznis] negocios) letters end with «Yours truly», or, if you write to a superior [sə'pi:riə*], «Yours respectfully», while in familiar letters the ending is: «Yours sincerely» [sin'siəli], or «Yours affectionately (afectuosamente)», etc. Below your signature (['signətʃə*] firma), you put the name of the sender which, however, is omitted in familiar letters.

The address of a business letter is, for instance: «Mr. George [dʒɔ:dʒ] Bramble»; that of most other letters: «George Bramble, Esq.» If you write to several gentlemen together in one letter, you use [ju:z] the word: «Messrs.»

['mesəz]. Married ladies are addressed as «Mrs.» [misiz], unmarried ladies as «Miss».

In writing to a doctor, professor, and so on (etc.), you simply put that title followed by the name of the addressee (destinatario), without «Mr.» or «Esq.», as, for instance: «Dr. George Bramble.» A boy is addressed by the word «Master»; several young ladies are addressed as «Misses», after which the name is put.

Sometimes you write in a corner on the envelope: «Please forward» (['fɔːwəd] se ruega se haga seguir), or: «Care of...» (al cuidado de ...) under the name.

Conversation

Tell me how an English letter must be arranged. What is at the top, on the right, on the left, at the bottom, and in the middle of the page? How do you address a friend? What do you put after the heading? How do you express «Señor» or «Señores»? How do you address a married lady? When do you write: «Care of»? Where do you put these words? What day of what month is Christmas-Day? What day of the month is to-day (was yesterday)? When did Columbus discover the West Indies? What are the names of the four seasons, and when do they begin? In what part of the world is the Cape [keip] of Good Hope ([houp] Esperanza)? It is in Southern ['sʌðən] Africa.

TWENTY-FIFTH LESSON
LECCIÓN VIGÉSIMA QUINTA

Los nombres geográficos

Los nombres de países, regiones, ciudades, aldeas, islas, etc., salvo algunas excepciones, nunca toman artículo en inglés, ni aun cuando vayan acompañados de adjetivos.

Sin embargo, toman el artículo cuando van seguidos de un complemento:

Old Castile *kæ'sti:l.*
The Emperor of Germany.
Asia *eiʃə* was the cradle *kreidl* of mankind *'mænkaind.*
Ancient *'einʃənt* Florence.
The corrupt Rome of the times of ...

Castilla la Vieja.
El emperador de Alemania.
Asia fue la cuna del género humano.
La antigua Florencia.
La corrupta Roma de los tiempos de ...

He aquí los nombres de las partes del mundo y los de algunos países, con los nombres de sus habitantes:

Países

		Habitantes	
Europe *'ju:rəp*	Europa	European *ju:rə'piən*	europeo
Asia *eiʃə*	Asia	Asiatic *ei'ʃ(i)ætik*	asiático
Africa *'æfrikə*	África	African *'æfrikən*	africano
America *ə'merikə*	América	American *ə'merikən*	americano
Australia *ɔ:s'treiljə*	Australia	Australian *ɔ:s'treiljən*	australiano
Arabia *ə'reibiə*	Arabia	Arabian *ə'reibiən,* Arab *'ærəb*	árabe
Austria *'ɔ:striə*	Austria	Austrian *'ɔ:striən*	austríaco
Bavaria *bə'vɛəriə*	Baviera	Bavarian *bə'vɛəriən*	bávaro
Belgium *'beldʒəm*	Bélgica	Belgian *'beldʒən*	belga
China *'tʃainə*	China	Chinese *tʃai'ni:z*	chino
Denmark *'denma:k*	Dinamarca	Dane *dein*	danés
Egypt *'i:dʒipt*	Egipto	Egyptian *i'dʒipʃən*	egipcio
England *'iŋglənd*	Inglaterra	Englishman *'iŋgliʃmən*	inglés
France *fra:ns*	Francia	Frenchman *'frentʃmən*	francés
Germany *'dʒə:məni*	Alemania	German *'dʒə:mən*	alemán
Greece *gri:s*	Grecia	Greek *gri:k*	griego
Holland *'hɔlənd*	Holanda	Dutchman *dʌtʃmən*	holandés
Iceland *'aislənd*	Islandia	Icelander *'aislændə**	islandés
India *'indjə*	India	Indian *indjan*	indio
Ireland *'aiələnd*	Irlanda	Irishman *'airiʃmən*	irlandés
Italy *'itəli*	Italia	Italian *'itæljən*	italiano
Japan *dʒə'pæn*	Japón	Japanese *dʒæpə'ni:z*	japonés
Mexico *'meksikou*	Méjico	Mexican *'meksikən*	mejicano
Norway *'nɔ:wei*	Noruega	Norwegian *nɔ'wi:dʒən*	noruego
Portugal *'pɔ:tjəgəl*	Portugal	Portuguese *pɔ:tjə'gi:z*	portugués
Prussia *'prʌʃə*	Prusia	Prussian *'prʌʃən*	prusiano
Russia *'rʌʃə*	Rusia	Russian *'rʌʃən*	ruso
Saxony *'sæksəni*	Sajonia	Saxon *'sæksən*	sajón
Scotland *'skɔtlənd*	Escocia	Scotchman *'skɔtʃmən*	escocés
Sicili *'sisili*	Sicilia	Sicilian *si'siljən*	siciliano
Spain *spein*	España	Spaniard *'spæniəd*	español
Sweden *'swi:dn*	Suecia	Swede *'swi:d*	sueco
Switzerland *'switsələnd*	Suiza	Swiss *swis*	suizo
Turkey *'tə:ki*	Turquía	Turk *tə:k*	turco

Como ya se dijo antes, los nombres de nacionalidad forman su plural regularmente:

Indian, indio
Italian, italiano
Russian ˈrʌʃən ruso

Indians, indios
Italians, italianos
Russians, rusos

Sin embargo: *a)* Cuando su terminación es «sh», «ch», «ss», «ese», son invariables:

the French, los franceses
the English, los ingleses
the Dutch, los holandeses

the Swiss, los suizos
the Chinese, los chinos

b) Cuando son compuestos del adjetivo y el sustantivo «man, woman», su plural se forma con «men, women»:

a Frenchman, un francés
a Frenchwoman, una francesa
an Englishman, un inglés

ten Frenchmen, diez franceses
ten Frenchwomen, diez franceses
two Englishmen, dos ingleses

Esta forma compuesta con «man» (pl. «men»), etc., se emplea para los individuos. Así pues: «the French», etc., indica la nación o el adjetivo; «a Frenchman» (o «woman»), «ten Frenchmen» (o «women») se refieren al individuo particularmente.

Hay varios nombres de naciones (y sus naturales) acabados en «man», que no son compuestos con «man»; hacen su plural regularmente:

German ˈdʒəːmən alemán
Norman ˈnɔːmən normando
Roman ˈroumən romano

Germans
Normans
Romans

El femenino de los nombres de habitantes se forma añadiendo «woman, lady, girl», etc., al adjetivo:

an Englishwoman
a French lady
a German girl (*o* young lady)
two Italian women

una inglesa
una (señora) francesa
una (muchacha o señorita) alemana
dos italianas

Los adjetivos correspondientes a nombres de habitantes tienen, en general, la forma de estos nombres, observándose que los compuestos con «man» («woman») pierden estas voces cuando se emplean adjetivadamente. Se exceptúan los siguientes:

sust. Dane	danés	*adj.*	Danish *'deiniʃ*
sust. Spaniard	español	*adj.*	Spanish *'spæniʃ*
sust. Swede	sueco	*adj.*	Swedish *'swiːdiʃ*
sust. Turk	turco	*adj.*	Turkish *'təːkiʃ*
sust. Pole	polaco	*adj.*	Polish *'pouliʃ*

Los mismos adjetivos, sin artículo, sirven para indicar el idioma del país respectivo:

Do you speak English?	¿Habla usted (el) inglés?
I speak English, French, Italian, Japanese and Arabic.	Hablo (el) inglés, (el) francés, (el) italiano, (el) japonés y (el) árabe.

NB. Los nombres de habitantes, y los adjetivos correspondientes, se escriben siempre en inglés con letra inicial mayúscula.

Antes de los nombres de países y grandes ciudades, la preposición «en» se traduce por «in»; antes de los de lugar menor, por «at»; la preposición «a» se traduce siempre por «to» (excepto después de unos pocos verbos, con los que se emplea «at»); la preposición «de», por «from».

I live in Italy.	Vivo en Italia.
She was in Madrid.	Estaba en Madrid.
They are at Denbigh.	Están en Denbigh.
I go to France.	Voy a Francia.
My mother went to Lisbon last month.	Mi madre fue a Lisboa el mes pasado.
He comes from Africa, from Cairo.	Viene de África, de El Cairo.
They arrived at Chester.	Llegaron a Chester.

Los nombres de montañas, ríos, islas (en el plural), etcétera, se usan como nombres comunes y toman artículo.

The Thames *temz* is in England, and the Alps *ælps* are between *bi'twiːn* Italy and...	El Támesis está en Inglaterra, y los Alpes están entre Italia y...
The banks *bæŋks* of the Rhine *rain* are beautiful.	Las orillas del Rhin son hermosas.
The Canaries are in the Atlantic ocean *'ouʃən*.	Las Canarias se encuentran (están) en el océano Atlántico.

Algunas poblaciones importantes

Antwerp *'æntwəːp*	Amberes	Bruges *bruːʒ*	Brujas
Athens *'æθinz*	Atenas	Edinburgh *'edinbərə*	**Edimburgo**
Berlin *bəː'lin*	Berlín	Geneva *dʒi'niːvə*	Ginebra

Genoa *'dʒenouə*	Génova	Paris *'pæris*	París
London *'lʌudən*	Londres	Rome *roum*	Roma
Madrid *mə'drid*	Madrid	Vienna *vi'enə*	Viena
Moscow *'mɔskou*	Moscú	Warsaw *'wɔːsɔː*	Varsovia

Los puntos cardinales

North *nɔːθ*	norte	East *iːst*	este
South *sauθ*	sur	West *west*	oeste

Words

descendants *di'sendənts*	descendientes	Milanese *milə'niːs*	milaneses
easily *'iːzili*	fácilmente	of-course *ɔvkɔːs*	naturalmente
inhabitants *in'hæbitəns*	habitantes	part *paːt*	parte
island *'ailənd*	isla	proud *praud*	orgulloso
Kingdom *'kiŋdəm*	reino	Scots, Scotch *skɔts, skɔtʃ*	escocés
language *'læŋgwidʒ*	lengua	similar *similə**	semejante
Londoner *'lʌndənə**	londinense	to stop *stɔp*	pararse
Majorca *mə'dʒɔːkə*	Mallorca	where... from?	¿de dónde...?

Exercise

Europe is large, but America is much larger. What is Asia like? Asia is the largest part of the world. We live in Germany. Paris is the capital of France, and London the capital of England. India and China are parts of Asia. Denmark is smaller than Sweden. What was the name of the late ([*leit*] difunta) Queen of England? Her name was Victoria. William the First was King of Prussia and Emperor of Germany. I have seen two Prussian soldiers and four Austrian ones. Has the young Englishman arrived? No, sir, but the young Frenchman has (arrived). Do you speak French? No, but I am learning French and English. I have an uncle in America and an aunt in Brussels. The English are proud of their navy and the Milanese of their cathedral. Is London a very large city? Yes, it has over eight million inhabitants. Majorca is an island, and Spain with Portugal, as well as Italy, and Norway with Sweden, are peninsulas. Where do you come from? From Switzerland; now I am going to Austria. What is Belgium? A small kingdom in the north-west of Europe. A Spaniard and an

Italian can understand each other easily; Spanish is very similar (semejante) to Italian. Is Spanish a fine language? Yes, and Norwegian, too. Did you stop in Paris? Yes, of-course I did. Two days. Where do the Arabs live? In many countries, especially in Asia. Is Arabic a difficult language? Very. The Scotch are descendants of the ancient Scots. Those people are two Parisians and three Londoners; the ladies with them are Frenchwomen, Dutch and Scotch ladies. Did you ascend Mount Blanc? No, but I ascended a very high mountain in the Himalaya.

Words

Antarctic Ocean *ænt'a:ktik'ouʃən*	Océano Antártico
Arctic Ocean *'a:ktik*	Océano Ártico
Atlantic Ocean *ət'læntik*	Océano Atlántico
axis *'æksis*	eje
ball *bɔ:l*	bola, pelota
cardinal *'ka:dinəl*	cardinal
— points	puntos cardinales
cause *kɔ:z*	causa, origen
city *'siti*	ciudad
compass *'kʌmpəs*	brújula
dry *drai*	seco
earth *ə:θ*	tierra
fall into	desembocar
flatten	achatada
flow *flou*	fluir
geography *dʒi'ɔgrəfi*	geografía
Great Britain *'britən*	Gran Bretaña
Indian Ocean *'indjən*	Océano Índico
knowledge *'nɔlidʒ*	conocimiento
land *lænd*	tierra
leap year *li:pjə:* *	año bisiesto
motion *mouʃən*	movimiento
mountain *mauntin*	montaña
neighbouring *'neibəriŋ*	vecinos
orange *'ɔrindʒ*	naranja
Pacific Ocean *pə'sifik*	Océano Pacífico
past *pa:st*	cerca de
point	punto
pole *poul*	polo
revolution *revə'lu:ʃən*	revolución
revolve *ri'vɔlv*	girar
— around	girar alrededo
rise *raiz*	nacer (un río)
rotate *ro'teit*	girar
rotation *ro'teiʃən*	rotación
round	redondo
sea *si:*	mar
succession *sək'səʃən*	sucesión
surface *sə:fis*	superficie
world *wə:ld*	mundo
year *jə:* *	año

Reading exercise

The north, the south, the east and the west are the four cardinal points of the compass. The earth is constantly in motion revolving on its axis once in twenty-four hours. **Day and night are caused by this rotation or revolution,** and the succession of seasons is caused by the revolution of the earth round the sun. Now, this revolution round the sun takes 365 days, which is a year. Every four years there is one that has 366 days instead of 365, and this is known as leap year. The earth is round like a ball, but a little flattened, like an orange, at the poles (north pole and south pole).

The surface of the earth is partly dry land, partly water. The five large continents or parts of the world, including the neighbouring islands, are Europe, Asia, Africa, America and Australia. The large tracts (trechos) of water or oceans between them are the Atlantic Ocean, the South Sea or Pacific [pæ'sifik] Ocean, the Indian Ocean, and the Arctic and Antarctic Ocean. Rivers rise high up in the mountains and flow into the sea, and in their course they flow past some beautiful towns. Some of the most important cities in the world stand by a river; London is by the Thames, Paris on the Seine, Rome on the Tiber, and Vienna on the Danube. The chief countries in Europe are Great Britain, Germany, Spain, Italy, France, Russia, and others. In America we have New York, Washington, St. Louis, San Francisco, Los Angeles and so on.

Words

about ə'baut	cerca de	pursuit pə'sju:t	ocupación
barren 'bærən	estéril	quiet kwaiət	tranquilo
by no means mi:nz	de ninguna manera	river 'rivə*	río
		scenery 'si:nəri	escenario, vista panorámica
city 'siti	ciudad	silvery 'silvəri	de plata
coal-mine 'koulmain	mina de carbón	situated 'sitjueitid	situado
copper 'kɔpə*	cobre	special 'speʃəl	especial
county 'kaunti	condado	spin spin	hilar
crowded 'kraudid	pobladas	spining	hilatura
duchy 'dʌtʃi	ducado	stream stri:m	corriente
farm fa:m	granja	tin tin	estaño
fertile 'fə:tail	fértil	to lie lai	yacer
ironfoundry 'aiə:nfaundri	fundición de hierro	to reign rein	reinar
		to swarm swɔ:m	hormiguear, bullir
isle ail	isla		
just off dʒʌst ɔf	muy cerca	tract trækt	trecho, extensión
lofty 'lɔ:fti	elevado, alto	united ju'naitid	unido
meadow 'medou	pradera	varied 'vɛərid	variado
northern 'nɔ:ðən	norte	vast va:st	vasto
pasture 'pa:stʃə*	pasto	weaving 'wi:viŋ	tejido
pottery 'pɔtəri	alfarería		

Reading exercise

Great Britain

The kingdom of England is part of the island of Great Britain, and though by no means a large country, it has a great variety of surface. Green pastures, fertile fields, silvery streams, flowery meadows and lofty mountains form parts of its varied scenery.

The west is a thinly peopled land of barren hills and mountains. In the centre are the crowded cities of Birmingham, Manchester, Leeds, and Sheffield. The east is a quiet country of rich pastures and large farms with their fields of corn.

Each part of the country (país) has its special pursuit. The counties of Durham and Northumberland have their coalmines; Yorkshire [jɔ:kʃə*] and Lancashire their weaving and spinning. Lincoln and Norfolk, situated on the east coast, are famous for their vast farms. Stafford and Warwick ['wɔrik] swarm with collieries, potteries and ironfoundries; while the ancient duchy of Cornwall is rich in tin and copper. The isle of Wight [wait], just off the south coast of Great Britain, has often been called the Garden of England.

The northern part of the island of Great Britain is called Scotland; Ireland, which is a little larger than Scotland, lies to the west of England. Cape Lizard is in the south, Cape Wrath [ra:θ] in the north of Great Britain.

Conversation

What is the shape of the earth? Are there many Oceans? What are they called? How many continents are there and what are their names? What are the large tracts of water called? Which is the most important part of the world? Name the most important countries in the world. Can you name any important cities (ciudades) in Europe? and in America? Can you give me the name of any river in Europe? Do you know what is the capital of England? Can you tell me where is Paris? and Antwerp? and Rome? and Lisbon? How often does the earth turn round its axis? What does the rotation of the earth round its axis cause? What causes the seasons?

What is a leap year? Every how many years is there a leap year? What forms the kingdom (reino) of England? Is the east of England rich in pastures or in coalfields? Where is the isle of Wight? What is the northern part of England called? Are there many collieries and potteries in England?

Vocabulario

exportación	exportation *ekspɔː'teiʃən*	importación	importation *impɔː'teiʃən*
física	physics *'fiziks*	matemáticas	mathematics *mæθi'mætiks*
géneros, mercancías	goods *guds*	materias, súbditos	subjects *'sʌbdʒikts*
globo	globe *gloub*	mineral	mineral *'minərəl*
hierro	iron *'aiən*	porción	piece *piːs*

Ejercicio

Este periódico trae unas noticias muy interesantes sobre la importación y exportación de toda clase de mercancías a la Gran Bretaña. Me gustan mucho las matemáticas y la física; mi profesor dice que hago grandes progresos en estas materias. El príncipe y la princesa son muy amables con todos sus súbditos. ¿Tiene usted muchos conocimientos de geografía? ¿Dónde nacen los ríos? Los ríos nacen en las montañas y desembocan al mar. El mar es una extensión de agua que cubre una gran parte de la superficie del globo. La tierra gira alrededor de su eje una vez al día, originando los días y las noches. Una isla es una porción de tierra rodeada de mar por todas partes. ¿Qué clase de minerales exporta Inglaterra? Exporta principalmente carbón y hierro.

He perdido las tijeras, puedes prestarme las tuyas. La actriz hizo admirablemente su papel de heroína. Las naranjas son redondas, pero no como una pelota. El ganado fue llevado al campo.

To learn by heart

No news is good news.
A little knowledge is a dangerous thing.
Better late than never.

Vocabulario

colina	hill *hil*	vista	landscape, sight *'lænskeip, sait*
Sicilia	Sicily *'sisili*	volcán	volcano *vɔl'keinou*
visitar	to visit *tu 'visit*, to call on		

Ejercicio

En verano van a España muchos extranjeros, sobre todo franceses, ingleses y alemanes. Algunos de ellos no entienden el español y hablan su lengua madre. Hoy me han visitado unas señoras francesas que venían de Italia con unos italianos; después de unos días se irán a Escocia. El chino y el japonés son dos lenguas muy difíciles de entender. Este doctor holandés se ha casado con una suiza y vive en Bélgica. En Austria viven muchos alemanes. Suiza es el país más montañoso de Europa; en él están los Alpes. El italiano y el español son lenguas europeas. En los Estados Unidos de América se habla inglés, pero de ninguna manera es la única lengua hablada por los habitantes de esta nación. Subiremos a la colina más alta; desde allí se ve una vista magnífica. Los griegos hablan la lengua griega y viven en Grecia. Unos escoceses llegaron ayer al puerto de Londres. En Sicilia hay un gran volcán, el Etna.

TWENTY-SIXTH LESSON
LECCIÓN VIGÉSIMA SEXTA

El genitivo y la preposición «of» (ampliación)

La posesión de un objeto puede expresarse por medio de un genitivo, de un pronombre o de un adjetivo posesivo. El genitivo del nombre, esto es, lo que llamamos *genitivo sajón*, puede emplearse igual que un pronombre posesivo:

This house is his.	This house is Tom's.
That dog is hers.	That dog is Mary's.
This pen is his.	This pen is the Doctor's.
This book is theirs.	This book is the children's.

Con frecuencia, la preposición «of» se emplea reforzando el genitivo:

A friend of mine.	Un amigo mío.
A friend of my father's.	Un amigo de mi padre.
A friend of Fred's.	Un amigo de Federico.

En un sentido más indefinido, podemos también decir:

One of my friends.	Uno de mis amigos.
One of my father's friends.	Uno de los amigos de mi padre.
One of Fred's friends.	Uno de los amigos de Fred.

Obsérvese el cambio de sentido en las expresiones:

A cup of tea.	Una taza de té.
A tea cup.	Una taza de (para) té.
A glass of wine.	Un vaso de vino.
A wine glass.	Un vaso de (para) vino.

Con frecuencia se omite la cosa poseída para evitar su repetición:

I have not my book but Mary's.	No tengo mi libro, sino el de María.
I have not seen yours but Fred's.	No he visto el tuyo, sino el de Fred.

Adviértase que el artículo que precede en castellano al pronombre posesivo no se traduce al inglés:

This is mine. Éste es el mío.

Los siguientes verbos y adjetivos van seguidos de la preposición «of», «de», como en castellano:

accuse of ə'kju:z	acusar de	glad of glæd	contento de
boast of boust	alardear de	guilty of 'gilti	culpable de
be ashamed of ə'ʃeimd	avergonzarse de	jealous of 'dʒeləs	celoso de
die of dai	morir de	proud of praud	orgulloso de
full of ful	lleno de	tired of 'taiəd	cansado de
		worthy of 'wə:ði	merecedor de

La preposición «of» se traduce también por otras equivalencias:

be afraid of bi: ə'freid	temer	remind of ri'maind	recordar que
consist of kən'sist	consistir en	taste of teist	saber a
dream of dri:m	soñar con.	think of θiŋk	pensar en, recordar

Words

basket 'ba:skit	cesto	call at kɔ:læt	ir a (tienda, casa)
bookseller 'buk'selə*	librería	chat tʃæt	charla
butcher's 'butʃə*z	carnicería	chops tʃɔps	chuletas (de carne)

El genitivo y la preposición «of» (ampliación)

collect kə'lect	recoger	insisted in'sistid	insistió
come round kʌm raund	pasar(se) por un sitio	parcel 'pɑːsl	paquete
dressmaker 'dresmeikə*	modista	purchases 'pəːtʃəsiz	compras
fond of 'fɔnd ɔv	apreciar, ser aficionado a...	shoermaker 'ʃueː meikə*	zapatería
get, got, got get gɔt	obtener, comprar	shopping ʃɔːpiŋ	ir de tiendas
greengrocer 'griːngrousə*	verdulería	stationer's 'steiʃnə*z	tienda de objetos de escritorio
hold hould	caber	thirsty θ'əːsti	sediento
		walk back wɔːk bæk	volver andando

Reading exercise

Shopping

Yesterday I went shopping. I left for town at about half past two and as it is about half an hour's walk there, I got into Chester at 3. First, I called on a friend of mine and asked her to come with me and help me with my shopping, which she did. I wanted to get some boots for Fred, so we went to the shoemaker's and bougth them. Mary had asked me to call at the dressmaker's and collect a dress she was having made. Next to Smith's, the bookseller's, to buy a book for mother. Near Smith's there is the butcher's; so we went in and got some chops for dinner. A few minutes' walk from the butcher's there lives an aunt of mine, whom I am very fond of. We went in a minute to see her, for Pat is also a friend of hers, and she loves coming round to aunt Jane's when I go see her. Aunt Jane is very nice; she insisted that we stayed for tea, and as we really were very thirsty we did. After half an hour's chat we said good-bye, as I still had to call at the stationer's for a bottle of ink, and at the greengrocer's to get some fruit and vegetables. I had so many parcels to take home that I couldn't dream of walking back, so I had to wait for the bus. Fortunately, I had brought with me Mary's basket, which is bigger than mine; but even so, it would not hold all my purchases. We went round to Pat's and she let me have another one, which I sent back to her this morning.

Conversation

What did you do yesterday? At what time did you leave home? At what did you arrive at Chester? Do you often go to Chester? What did Fred want from the town? Did your sister ask you to collect something for her? Whom did you see while you were at Chester? Did you go to see your aunt? Did you have tea with her? Who came with you to see aunt Jane? Could you walk back home? Why couldn't you walk back?

Words

angel 'eindʒəl	ángel	Order of Merit	Orden del Mérito (condecoración)
around ə'raund	alrededor, cerca	present pri'zent	regalar
brave breiv	valiente	proper 'prɔpə*	adecuado
care kɛə*	cuidado	scarce skɛəs	escaso
clothing 'klouðiŋ	ropas	sick sik	enfermo
comfort 'kʌmfət	comodidades	sight sait	vista
danger 'deindʒə*	peligro	soldiers 'souldʒə*	soldados
died daid	morían	suffer 'sʌfə*	sufrir
distress dis'tres	desgracia	to grow bright	animarse
due dju	debido	to have the feeling fi:liŋ	tener la sensación
dying 'daiiŋ	moribundo	training 'treiniŋ	entrenamiento
food fu:d	alimentos, comida	used ju:st	solía
hard ha:d time	pasarlo mal	volunteer vɔlən'tiə*	prestarse, ofrecerse
honour 'ɔnə*	honrar	want of	falta de
hospitals 'hɔspitlz	hospitales	war wɔ:*	guerra
look after	cuidar	ward wɔ:d	sala de hospital
nurse nə:s	enfermera	went back	regresó
nursing	cuidados	wounded wu:ndid	herido
order 'ɔ:də*	orden, organización		

Reading exercise

During the Crimean war the soldiers had a hard time. Men's lives were in great danger but they suffered more from cold and hunger than from anything else (más). There were very few doctors to look after them and food was scarce. Also, the hospitals were very bad and the men died for want of comfort and nursing.

People in England had the feeling that so much distress was due mostly to want of the necessary care before the war started. Then, a brave lady whose name was Florence Nightingale — and whom we all were to honour later on — full of pity for the dying soldiers volunteered to go and nurse the poor men. She had learnt to nurse when she was a girl, she liked the work and used to nurse the poor sick people around her home. She had now a proper nurse's training

El genitivo y la preposición «of» (ampliación)

and went out to Crimea to save men's lives. She soon got the hospitals in better order and sent to England for better food and clothing for the sick and the wounded. As she used to pass through the wards, every poor fellow's face grew bright at the sight of her. She was the soldier's good angel and they all loved her. When the war was over and she went back home the people presented her with a large sum of money which she gave to found a Home (residencia) for the training of nurses.

This was Florence Nightingale to whom King Edward sent the Order of Merit in 1906.

Words

between *bi'twi:n*	entre	to dirty *'də:ti*	ensuciar
dean *di:n*	deán, decano	to prepare *pri-'peə**	preparar(se)
eccentricities *eksen'trisitiz*	excentricidades	to put on	poner(se)
it was not worth while *wə:θ hwail*	no valía la pena (de)	wet *wet*	húmedo
		why?	¿por qué?
key *ki:*	llave	without *wið'aut*	sin
replied *ri'plaid*	replicó	wittier *'witiə**	más ingenioso, más chistoso
thereupon *ðɛə-rə'pɔn*	después de esto	writings *'raitiŋz*	escritos, obras

Jonathan Swift

Swift, the author of *Gulliver's* ['gʌlivəz*] *Travels*, was distinguished [dis'iŋgwiʃt] for his eccentricities as much as for his writings. He was, on a wet day, preparing to go out. His servant brought him his boots without having cleaned them. «Why did you not clean them?» said the dean. «Because I thought it was not worth while, as (pues) you will soon dirty them again.» He put them on as they were. A few moments after his servant asked him for the key of the pantry. «What for?» said Swift. «To get my breakfast.» «O!» replied the doctor, «it is not worth while eating now, as you will be hungry again in two hours.» Thereupon he went out (salió).

To learn by heart

Love many, trust[1] a few,
And always paddle[2] your own canoe[3].

1. Trust *trʌst* confiar en. 2. Paddle *pædl* remar. 3. Canoe *kə'nu:* canoa.

Vocabulario

bautizado	christened *'krisnd*	estilográfica	fountain-pen *'fauntin pen*
deportes	sports *spɔːts*	médico	physician *fi'ziʃən*
escaparate	shop-window *tʃɔp'windou*	sastre	tailor *'teilə**

Ejercicio

El hermano de Pedro se compró un traje en casa del sastre. En el mes de junio iremos a Alemania, donde viven algunos de mis amigos muy aficionados al deporte. María pasó el fin de semana en la granja de mi tía. Mi estilográfica está llena de tinta pero no escribe. Mi hermano mayor fue bautizado en la iglesia de San Pablo, y se le dio el nombre de Tomás. El hombre está muy orgulloso de su hijo; estudia en la Universidad y es muy buen estudiante. Estoy cansado de este paseo de tres horas. El padre de este hombre es médico. Tienes que hacer este trabajo ahora. Las ventanas del comedor de mi casa son pequeñas. En el escaparate de la librería hay unos libros muy interesantes.

TWENTY-SEVENTH LESSON
LECCIÓN VIGÉSIMA SÉPTIMA

El adjetivo calificativo (ampliación)

El adjetivo calificativo, que es invariable y precede al nombre que califica, sigue al verbo «ser» cuando es predicado:

> This book is good.
> This is a good book.

El adjetivo calificativo debe ir siempre seguido del nombre que califica o, para evitar su repetición, del pronombre indefinido «one»:

> Good wine is dear.
> I bought a red dress and a grey one.

El adjetivo calificativo (ampliación)

El adjetivo demostrativo y el adverbio preceden siempre al adjetivo calificativo:

>That old lady is my mother.
>She is a very nice girl.

El participio de presente y el de pasado pueden emplearse como adjetivos:

Who has brought that broken glass here?	¿Quién ha traído aquí ese vaso roto?
I have heard the barking dog.	He oído al perro que ladraba (ladrador)

El sustantivo puede emplearse adjetivadamente, especialmente cuando se quiere indicar que algo pertenece o conviene a determinado tiempo, lugar u objeto, o sirve para un uso determinado. En este último caso los dos sustantivos se unen con un guión:

A *country* gentleman.	Un caballero lugareño.
This *morning* dress suits *sju:ts* you very well.	Esta bata le está muy bien a usted.
A *milk*-jug.	Un jarro para leche.
Six *tea*-cups.	Seis tazas para té.
The *milk*-maid.	La lechera.
A *dog*-house (a kennel).	Una perrera.
Two *house* dogs.	Dos perros de guardia.
The *Town* Hall.	La Casa Consistorial, Ayuntamiento.

Los adjetivos empleados *sustantivadamente*, es decir, *solos*, tienen en inglés sentido colectivo general y valor de plurales; son invariables, y deben ir acompañados del artículo determinado:

the poor *puə**	los pobres	
the rich *rits*	los ricos	(todos los pobres, ricos, buenos, en general)
the good	los buenos	

The unfortunate ˌʌn'fɔ:tʃənit are distrustful *dis'trʌstfl*.	Los desdichados son desconfiados.

Cuando, ya sea en singular ya en plural, se le quiera dar un valor individual, hay que añadir después del adjetivo un sustantivo adecuado o el pronombre indefinido «one», como se ha dicho ya:

The unfortunate woman is much to be pitied *'pitid*.	La desdichada merece mucha compasión.
After that, the poor fellows *'felouz* went away.	Después de eso los pobres (muchachos) se marcharon.

The roguish 'rougiʃ girl laughed la:ft in my face.	La picarilla se me rió en la cara.
I have bought a red pen and two black ones.	He comprado una pluma roja y dos negras.
Who are those ladies? — The tall tɔ:l one is Mrs. B., and the stout staut one is my cousin.	¿Quiénes son esas señoras? — La alta es la Sra. B., y la gruesa es mi prima.

Varios adjetivos, por el uso, se han convertido en verdaderos nombres y se emplean como tales en singular y en plural, además de servir también como adjetivos: «male» [meil] «macho», «noble» [noubl] «noble», «black», «negro», etc.; algunos, en calidad de sustantivos, se usan sólo en el plural: «the ancients» ['einʃənts] «los antiguos», «the solids», «los sólidos», «the eatables» ['i:təblz] «los comestibles», etc.

Asimismo pueden emplearse solos los adjetivos que expresan una idea abstracta: «the beautiful» ['bju:təful] «lo bello», «the green», «lo verde».

Vocabulario

abundancia	plenty 'plenti of	mundo	world wə:ld
admirador	admirer əd'maiə*	musulmán	Mussulman 'mʌslmən
alcanzar	to obtain obtein		
bebidas	drinkables 'driŋkəblz	oprimido	oppressed əprest
		paciente	patient 'peiʃənt
brincar	to jump jʌmp	protestante	Protestant 'prɔtistənt
color	colour 'kʌlə*		
cristiano	Christian 'kristjən	reir	to laugh la:ʃ
deber	owe ou	sabiduría	knowledge 'nɔlidʒ
débil	weak wi:k		
derrotar	to defeat di'fi:t	sanar	to cure kjue*
enfrente de	opposite 'ɔpəzit	sentir, estar apesadumbrado	to be sorry bi sɔri
feliz	happy 'hæpi		
igualmente	equally 'i:kwəli		
lección	lesson 'lesn	sublime	sublime sə'blaim
lo bajo	base beis, contemtible	valiente	brave breiv
		victoria	victory 'viktəri
los modernos	the moderns 'mɔdənz	virtud	virtue 'və:tju:

Ejercicio

Esa muchacha ha sido siempre fiel a sus amigos ¿Dónde vive el señor Ferrer? Vive justamente enfrente de nuestra casa, cerca del palacio. Los buenos no son siempre dichosos sobre la (on) tierra. Los valerosos no alcanzan siempre la

El adjetivo calificativo (ampliación)

victoria, ni los débiles están siempre oprimidos. Los modernos deben a los antiguos muchas lecciones de sabiduría y virtud. En aquel dichoso país había abundancia de víveres y bebidas. Vimos a una buena anciana que pedía limosna, y mi tía me dijo: «Da algo a esa pobre.» Lord Byron [bairən] era (un) admirador de lo bello y de lo sublime; despreciaba lo bajo. El color que prefiero es (el) azul. El azul de ese mar es muy hermoso. Blancos y negros, católicos y protestantes, cristianos y musulmanes, todos son igualmente hombres. Los griegos fueron derrotados en la guerra contra los turcos en 1897. El pobre perro brincaba de alegría al ver a su amo, y el chiquillo reía y era feliz jugando con él. El buen médico atiende a un enfermo a cualquier hora. El enfermo sanó muy de prisa, pero el pobre está aún muy débil. Aquella pobre anciana es feliz cuando sus nietos están con ella. ¿Quién ha roto el jarro de la leche? Lo rompió Mary, pero no le digas nada, porque la pobre está muy apesadumbrada.

Words

address ə'dres	dirigir(se) a	handkerchief 'hæŋkətʃif	pañuelo
anything 'eniθiŋ	algo	hope houp	esperar
as well æs wel	también	hosiery 'houʒəri	calcetería
bill bil	cuenta, nota	how much? hau mʌtʃ	¿cuánto?
bit bit	un poco	hurry 'hʌri	prisa
certainly 'seː-tənli	ciertamente	latest 'leitist	última
collars 'kɔləːz	cuellos	light lait	claro, luz
counter 'kauntə*	mostrador	line lain	clase, calidad
customer 'kʌstəmə*	cliente	lot lɔt	lote, todo
dark daːk	oscuro	need niːd	necesitar
department di-'paːtmənt	departamento	parcel 'paːsl	paquete
		pay pei	pagar
desk desk	caja	perfect 'pəːfikt	perfecto
do duː	hacer	price prais	precio
else els	más, además	rather 'raːðə*	bastante
fashion 'fæʃən	moda	recommend rəkə'mend	recomendar
fine fain	estupendo	salesgirl 'seilzgəːl	dependienta
fit fit	sentar		
be a good —	sentar bien (una prenda de vestir)	salesman 'seilzmən	dependiente
		satisfied 'sætisfaid	satisfecho
glove glʌv	guante	shade ʃeid	tonalidad
grey grei	gris	shirt ʃəːt	camisa

size *saiz*	tamaño, medida	thank you *'θæŋkju*	gracias
soft	blando	the look of *ðə luk əv*	por el aspecto
socks *sɔks*	calcetines		
step this way *step*por aquí *ðis wei*		try on *trai on*	probar
		underwear *ʌndəwɛə**	ropa interior
stockings *'stɔkiŋs*	medias		
stretch *stretʃ*	estirar	wear well *wɛə**	durar
sure *ʃuə**	seguro		

Conversation

(Customer enters shop and addresses salesgirl:)
A. Good morning!
B. Good morning, madam! What can I do for you?
A. I would like a pair of grey Swede leather gloves.
B. Certainly, madam. The gloves are on that counter over there. This way, please. Would you like them dark or light grey?
A. Oh, a light shade of grey would be very nice, I think.
B. Then I am sure you will like these. They are a very good line, and very good price, too.
A. Yes, they are rather nice. How much are they?
B. Only 15/11 a pair, madam.
A. I hope they will wear well?
B. O, yes! They are warranted (garantizados) to wear well!
A. Then I shall take this pair, if they fit me. May I try them on, please?
B. Certainly, madam. They are your size, I am sure. You must take a 6 1/2 by the look of your hand. I shall stretch them a bit for you before you try them.
A. Thank you. I think they will be all right. Yes. They are a perfect fit. They feel fine. I shall take them.
B. Thank you, madam. Isn't there anything else I can show you?
A. Yes, I would like some stockings and handkerchiefs.
B. Very well, madam. Step this way, please. Hosiery is another Department.
A. I really need not see them. You know what I usually take. Send me three pairs with the gloves and a dozen big size handkerchiefs.
B. Very well, madam. Anything else?
A. No, I don't think so. I shall pay for the lot now.

El adjetivo calificativo (ampliación)

B. Please pay at the desk, will you? I shall send the parcel first thing in the morning.
(Enter customer. Salesman addresses him:)
A. Can I do anything for you, sir?
B. Could you show me some collars?
A. These are the latest fashion, and I can recommend them to wear well.
B. Good. They look all right. I take size 16. Give me half a dozen of these and four soft ones.
A. Thank you, sir. I am sure you will be satisfied with them. Can I get you any shirts, socks, or any underwear?
B. Not now, thank you. I shall come some other time. Could you send them for me? I shall pay for them now.
A. Yes, sir. I can send them tomorrow morning. Will that be all right?
B. Yes. I am in no hurry. Send them tomorrow.
A. Here is your bill, sir. Will you pay at the desk, please? Thank you, sir.
B. Good morning.

Vocabulario

alto	tall *tɔːl*	faltar	lach *æk*
blanco	white *wait*	maravilloso	wonderful *'wʌndəful*
caro	expensive *iks-'pensiv*	negro	black *blæk*
corto	short *ʃɔːt*	rojo	red *red*

Ejercicio

Ciertamente, este par de guantes negros me parece barato, pero aquel pañuelo rojo y blanco demasiado caro. Tengo tres hermanos; Pedro es el mayor, yo soy la menor. Cada día llega usted más tarde; ¿está muy lejos su casa? A unos 20 minutos de aquí pasando por el camino más corto. Prefiero las rosas rojas a las blancas, pero todas son hermosas. A algunos pobres les faltan cosas muy necesarias, pero muchas veces son más felices que los ricos. Los enfermos no pueden comer tanto como los sanos. En tu última carta me explicabas tu agradable visita al más viejo castillo de la ciudad, que se alza junto al Támesis. Mi hermana es mayor que yo, pero no tan alta. Esta casa es más hermosa que la de mi abuelo. A veces, mientras duermo sueño cosas maravillosas. Es frecuente decir: sueñas despierto.

To learn by heart

The Field Daisy ðə 'fi:ld 'deizi La margarita silvestre

I'm a little pretty thing,
always coming with the spring;
in the meadows green I'm found,
peeping[1] just above the ground,
and my stalk[2] is covered flat
with a white and yellow hat.

Little lady, when you pass
lightly over the tender[3] grass,
skip about[4], but do not tread[5]
on my meek[6] and healthy head,
for I always seem to say:
«Surely, Winter's gone away.»

1. Peep *pi:p* asomarse. 2. Stalk *stɔ:k* tallo. 3. Tender *tendə* tierna. 4. Skip about *skip əbaut* salta por encima. 5. Tread *tred* pisar. 6. Meek *mi:k* humilde.

TWENTY-EIGHTH LESSON
LECCIÓN VIGÉSIMA OCTAVA

Pronombres de relativo

Nominativo	*Acus. y dat.*	*Genitivo*
who, quien	whom	whose
which, cual		
that, que	Se declinan por medio de preposiciones.	
what, que		

«Who» se refiere siempre a personas. «Which» se refiere a animales o cosas sin sexo. «That» se emplea indistintamente para personas, cosas y animales.

The man who wrote that book is a friend of mine.
The gentleman whom you sent the letter is here.
The man whose car you bought is my brother.
The man that bought that house is very rich.
The bird that sings in the garden is a nightingale (ruiseñor).
That is the tree that I planted last year.

«What», cuando es relativo, equivale a «that which», «aquello que».

I have done what you asked me.	He hecho lo que me pediste.
I don't know what you are complaining about.	No sé de qué te quejas.

No debe confundirse «whose» con «of whom» y «of which». «Whose» es un genitivo e indica siempre posesión. Significa «cuyo», y debe preceder inmediatamente al objeto poseído *sin* artículo.

The boy whose father you met yesterday is here.	El muchacho cuyo padre conociste ayer, está aquí.
These are my children, some of whom you know already.	Éstos son mis hijos, algunos de los cuales ya conoces.
The horse of which I was so fond has died.	El caballo que me gustaba tanto ha muerto.

«Which», empleado para personas, tiene valor selectivo:

Tell me which of these children is the best, and to which you would like to give the price.	Dime cuál de estos niños es el mejor y a cuál querrías dar el premio.

«Which» puede referirse a una cláusula entera expresada antes, y se traduce por «lo que»:

He died of poverty, which was to be foreseen.	Murió de pobreza, lo que era previsible.

Si el pronombre de relativo está regido por una preposición, ésta puede ponerse al final:

I bought the book about which you spoke to me.	Compré el libro del que me hablaste.
I bought the book which you told me about.	Compré el libro que me dijiste.

El pronombre de relativo puede omitirse cuando es complemento, y en conversación ordinaria suele hacerse así. En este caso, si hay preposición, se trasladará al final:

> The girl to whom we spoke
> The girl whom we spoke to } is Peter's sister.
> The girl we spoke to

Con el relativo «that», la preposición debe *siempre* ponerse al final:

That is the picture that I told you about.	Éste es el cuadro del que te hablé.

Observaciones: La interrogación introducida por «who» no precisa el auxiliar «do»: «Who came yesterday?» «Todo lo que» se traduce por «all that». «El que», «la que», por «he who», «she who». «Those who», por «aquellos que», etc.

All that you see...	Todo lo que ves...
He who comes late will have no tea.	El que venga tarde no tomará el té.
Those who come late...	Los que vengan tarde...

Words

abroad *ə'brɔːd*	el extranjero	lawyer *'lɔːjə**	abogado
abundance *ə'bʌndəns*	abundancia	manufacture *'mænju'fæktʃə**	fabricación
believe *bi'liːv*	creer	material *mə'tiːriəl*	material
belong *bi'loŋ*	pertenecer	merchant *'məːtʃənt*	comerciante
cotton *'kɔtən*	algodón		
daily *'deili*	cotidiano	mill *mil*	molino, fábrica
deal *diːl*	tratar en, comerciar	nation *'neiʃən*	nación
		necessity *ni'sesiti*	necesidad
demolish *di'mɔliʃ*	derribar	need *niːd*	necesidad
exchange *iks'tʃeindʒ*	cambio	orange *'ɔrindʒ*	naranja
export *iks'pɔːt*	exportar	oversea(s)	allende el mar
export(s) *'ekspɔːt(s)*	exportaciones	on the other hand *ɔn ði ʌðə* hænd*	por otra parte
fabrics *'fæbriks*	géneros, telas	produce *prə'djuːs*	producir
factory *'fæktəri*	fábrica	product *'prɔdəkt*	producto
famous *feiməs*	famoso		
foreigner *'fɔrinə**	extranjero (pers.)	rail *reil*	ferrocarril
foreign *'fɔrin*	extranjero (país)	raw *rɔː*	en bruto
forward *'fɔːwəd*	enviar	require *ri'kwaiə**	requerir
goods *gudz*	géneros, mercancías	road *roud*	camino, carretera
		such as	tal
go out *gou aut*	salir	surplus *'səːplʌs*	superproducción
import *im'pɔːt*	importar	survive *sə'vaiv*	sobrevivir
import(s) *'impɔːt(s)*	importaciones	therefore *'ðɛəfɔː*	por lo tanto
in turn *təːn*	a su vez	trade *treid*	comercio
instance *'instəns*	(por) ejemplo	trader *'treidə**	comerciante
kind *kaind*	clase, especie	varied *'vɛərid*	diverso, variado
lack *læk*	falta de		

Exercise

The pens which he has brought are no good. The boy you met yesterday at home is my brother. The man who wrote that novel is dead. I am writing with a pencil that I found on the table. The goods which they sent from America have arrived in a bad condition. I need the book that I lent you. Look! That is the dog you gave me last year. My eldest daughter, whom I have often told you about, has gone to Australia. Trade is an exchange of goods and materials between nations. One country exports what it has in abundance and imports those things it lacks. Look at that man. Which do you mean? The one on the left. Who is he? He is Mr. Williams. What is he? He is a famous lawyer. The house in which he lived has been demolished. Those ladies we have just met are my mother and a friend of hers. Which is your mother, the one that is wearing the black hat? No, the one that has a grey hat on. The other is her friend. England exports fabrics to foreign countries that have no cotton mills but which, like India, have various other things which England requires. India's exports are larger than her imports.

Reading exercise

Foreign trade

Countries don't usually produce all that they need for their daily life, therefore, they have to exchange those goods which they have in order to survive. This exchange of goods and materials is called trade, and by these means one country exports or sends abroad those things of which it has a surplus and imports other things which it lacks.

England, for instance, imports raw cotton which comes to England by ship, is then forwarded by rail to the cotton mills or factories and there is manufactured into the most varied kinds of fabrics. Spain has oranges in abundance; so, oranges are exported to England, France and Germany. Thus, each country in turn, imports those things it lacks and exports others in exchange. England requires a lot of tea which is an Indian product, and so, tea and coffee are among the things that England imports. On the other hand, England exports many things that other countries lack, therefore, many British manufactured goods go overseas to foreign countries and help other people to live a better life. Thus, traders all the world over trade and deal with tradesmen and merchants of other nations.

Conversation

What is trade? Do countries produce all they need for their daily life? What do the countries do with the things which they have in abundance? Does England import or export raw cotton? Which are the chief countries from which we can get tea? What countries export coffee? Does Spain export oranges? Where are Spanish oranges exported to? What does England import from abroad? Does England trade with Spain? Have you ever been abroad? Would you like to go abroad next Summer? Where would you like to go?

To learn by heart

As you go through life
Five things observe with care[1]:
To whom you speak,
Of whom you speak,
And how, and when and where.

1. Care *kɛə** cuidado.

Ejercicio

Todavía no he (I have not yet) visto a la señora de quien usted me ha hablado; la veré hoy por la tarde (esta tarde). ¿No es ésta la señora a quien habéis enviado las hermosas flores que estaban sobre vuestra mesa? Sí, es ella. No sabe lo que dice. ¿Por qué ha hecho usted esto (*o* eso)? Él es el hombre al cual dio el niño el dinero. Aquí está el caballo de que hemos hablado y que usted quería comprar. He aquí un extranjero (foreigner [*'fɔrinə**]) que desea hablar a usted. La madre, cuyo hijo ha vuelto (come back), es feliz. Lo que estás diciendo no es verdad. Por (from) lo que veo, no me crees. Dime en qué te ocupas y te diré quién eres. Lo que significa que te gustan los proverbios. Cualquiera que sea el camino que toméis, no llegaréis esta tarde. El joven con el cual habéis salido es amigo mío y de mi hermano. El señor a quien escribo es un abogado. La casa donde vivo es de (belongs to) Juan. En la mesa hay cerezas que no están maduras.

Proverbs

Tomorrow never comes.	Mañana nunca llega.
What is done cannot be undone.	A lo hecho, pecho.

TWENTY-NINTH LESSON
LECCIÓN VIGÉSIMA NOVENA

Pronombres interrogativos

Los pronombres interrogativos son:

Who...? *huː*   Whom...? *huːm*   Whose...? *huːz*
Which...? *witʃ* }
What...? *wɔt* } Se declinan por medio de preposiciones.

Tienen el mismo significado que los pronombres de relativo, pero no pueden sobrentenderse como ocurre con aquéllos. Preceden siempre al verbo.

Who is that lady?	¿Quién es esa señora?
Who came in?	¿Quién entró?
Whom did you see?	¿A quién viste?
What did you say?	¿Qué dijo usted?
What is it?	¿Qué es esto? ¿Qué ocurre?
Which pencil have you lost?	¿Qué lápiz has perdido?
What book is this?	¿Qué libro es éste?
Send me one of your dogs. — Which?	Envíame uno de tus perros. — ¿Cuál?
Catherine... —What?	Catalina... — ¿Qué?
Whose watch is this?	¿De quién es este reloj?
To whose son did you write?	¿Al hijo de quién escribió usted?
With whom did you speak? With which man?	¿Con quién hablaste? ¿Con qué (cuál) hombre?
With what pencil did you write?	¿Con qué lápiz escribiste?

«Which» sirve para distinguir entre varias personas o cosas. «What», para preguntar sobre la calidad, naturaleza etcétera, de un ser. «What», en sentido absoluto, significa también «¿qué?, ¿qué cosa?». Con el verbo «to be» sirve para preguntar la profesión, el estado, etc., de alguien. Se emplea también como exclamativo. En este caso le sigue a veces el artículo indeterminado.

Which of these boys is Robert?	¿Cuál de estos muchachos es Roberto?
Which is his cap *kæp?*	¿Cuál es su gorra?
Which cap is his?	¿Qué gorra es la suya?
Which is which?	¿Cuál es (cada uno)?
What tree is that?	¿Qué árbol es ése?

Lección vigésima novena

What is the price *prais?*	¿Cuál es el precio?
What is your father?	¿Qué es tu padre?
What! Are you mad?	¡Qué! ¿Estás loco?
What a big horse!	¡Qué caballo tan grande!

Words

airy 'ɛəri	aireada	to look for *tu lu:k fo:*	buscar
belong bi'lɔŋ	pertenecer	to punish *tu pʌniʃ*	castigar
dale *deil*	valle	top	arriba, en lo alto
dust *dʌst*	polvo	villa *vila*	villa
Paul *pɔ:l*	Pablo	wireless *waiə*-les*	radio
the former... the latter	éste... aquél		
to cry *tu krai*	llorar		

Exercise

What is your name? My name is Paul. What is yours? What does it matter (importa) to you what my name is? With whom did you travel? Alone. What trees are those yonder? Firs (abetos). Give me that book. Which? The red one. Whose villa is that at the top of the hill? My friend Paul's. And that other in the dale? My uncle's. Which of them do you like better? The former (la primera). Why? It is more airy. Who was crying just now? It was my little girl, whom I punished. What are you looking for? I am looking for my book which I have just lost. Do you see that lady? Which? What do you mean, which? That one over there. Who is she? She is the lady whom our friend told you about. To whom did you give the newspaper? I gave it to your brother, and he took it to the office. Whom are you talking to? I see no one here. I am not talking to anyone. It is the wireless. To whom did you say (that) that belongs? To my brother. What are this boy and that one doing? They are writing; the former is very diligent, the latter is always lazy. Yesterday I met your two sisters.

Words

assist ə'sist	ayudar	eye-glasses *ai-'gla:siz*	lentes
body 'bɔdi	cuerpo	eyebrows 'aibrauz	cejas
concert 'kɔnsət	concierto		
contract 'kɔntrækt	contraer(se)	eyelashes 'ailæʃis	pestañas
describe dis'kraib	describir	eyelid 'ailid	párpado
dilating dai'leitiŋ	dilatar	eyes *aiz*	ojos
dust *dʌst*	polvo	excellent 'ekslənt	excelente
ears *jə:**	oídos, orejas		

face *feis*	cara, rostro	palate *'pælit*	paladar
feel *fi:l*	sentir	power *pauə**	poder, -ío, capacidad
feeling *'fi:liŋ*	sentidos		
hearing *'hi:riŋ*	oído	protect *prə'tekt*	proteger
instrument *'instrumənt*	instrumento	pupil *'pju:pl*	pupila
		senses *sensiz*	sentidos
iris *airis*	iris	side *said*	lado
lead *li:d*	conducir, guiar	sight *sait*	vista
light *lait*	luz	smell *smel*	oler
maker *'meikə**	fabricante	spectacles *'spektəklz*	lentes
manner *'mænə**	manera		
middle *midl*	medio	tact *tækt*	tacto
neighbour *'neibə**	vecino	taste *teist*	sabor, saborear
		to consist *kən'sist*	consistir
nose *nouz*	nariz	to dilate *di'leit*	dilatar(se)
organ *'ɔ:gən*	órgano	to employ *im'plɔi*	usar, emplear
opera-glasses *'ɔpərə 'gla:siz*	gemelos de teatro		
		tongue *tʌŋ*	lengua
painter *'peintə**	pintor	touch *tʌtʃ*	tacto

Reading exercise

The senses

How many senses have you? I have five: sight, hearing, smell, taste and feeling, or touch. What do you see with? I see with my eyes, I hear with my ears, I smell with my nose, I taste with my tongue and my palate, and I feel with all parts of my body. How many eyes have you got, and where are they? I have two eyes, which are in the middle of my face on either side of my nose. Describe the eye. The eye, which is the organ of sight, consists of many different parts; those which are most important are the iris and the pupil, which has the power of contracting or dilating. In what manner is the eye protected from light and dust? By the eyelid, which is closed in sleep, by the eyelashes and the eyebrows. How is a bad sight assisted? With spectacles or eye-glasses. Persons who cannot see well often employ an opera-glass at the theatre ([*'θiətə**] teatro) or concert.

Conversation

Who is that gentleman? He is a friend of mine. Are these pictures yours? No, they belong to my uncle. Whom are you expecting (esperar) to dinner? I expect my neighbour with his son, who wrote that nice book which pleased you so much. Which is the car you have bought? I bought the car for which you would not give seven hundred (700) pounds. Where does that road lead to? It leads to York. What do you think of the instruments (that) you saw this morning? They are excellent, but not of the best makers in London. Whose child is that? It is the painter's. To whom did you tell that dreadful ['dredful] event (espantoso acontecimiento)? I told my cousin, who was much shocked ([ʃɔkt] horrorizada) at it. With whom did he work? He worked with his father. When did that statesman (['steitsmæn] hombre de estado) die? He died in the first part of the 18th century. Did you hear what that man said? Yes, but whatever he says I do not care ([kɛə] importar). Did you go with your sister to Paris? Yes, but not with her whom you spoke with last winter. With which sister then? With Mary. Which of these ladies is your cousin? She whose eyes are so bright ([brait] brillantes). To whom will you give those fine pictures? To whomsoever I find who wants them. What book are you reading? An English book; it is very interesting. Will you listen ([lisn] escuchar) to what I am about to explain to you? Oh yes, I shall try not to lose one word.

To learn by heart

Work while you work, play while you play,
   that is the way to be cheerful[1] and gay[2].
All that you do, do with your might;
   things done by halves[3] are never done right
One thing each time, and that one done well,
   is a very good rule[4], as many can tell.
Moments are useless trifled away[5]
   so work while you work, and play while you play.

1. Cheerful 'tʃiəful alegre. 2. Gay gei contento. 3. Halves haːvz mitades. 4. Rule ruːl regla. 5. Trifled away 'traifld ə'wei desperdiciados.

Vocabulario

caramelo	sweet swiːt	nacer	to be born bɔːn
césped	grass graːs	pasar	to be the matter mætə*
difícil	difficult 'difikəlt		
dinero	money 'mʌni	raqueta	racket 'rækit
gente	people 'piːpl	robar	steal stiːl
ladrón	thief θiːf	tienda	shop ʃɔp
llamar	call kɔːl	trepar	climb klaim

Ejercicio

¿A quién pertenece esto? ¿De quién es esta raqueta de tenis? ¿En qué tienda compró su traje? Quisiera saber su nombre, qué desea y de qué país viene. ¿Cuál de sus primos vendrá mañana? ¡Qué hermoso césped! ¿Con quién hablabas? ¿Cuáles son las flores que has traído de tu jardín? ¿Qué clase tenemos ahora? ¿Quién va a decirme la lección? ¿En qué año nació Cervantes? ¿A cuál de los dos niños dio el caramelo? Dime con quién jugabas. ¿Sabe usted quién escribió la carta?

¿Qué pasa? ¿Quién tiene miedo? ¿De quién te acuerdas? ¿A quién escribes? ¿Qué diré? ¿De qué hablaré? ¿Qué hora es?

Mira las flores que planté: ¿cuáles le gustan a usted más? ¿Con quién habla usted? ¿Quiénes son esa gente? ¿Qué hace su padre? Es abogado; antes era profesor. El ladrón que robó su dinero de usted ha muerto. La canción (song) [que] estudiasteis es difícil. ¿Quién es ese caballero? ¿A quién llama usted? ¿Cuál es el reloj que usted quiere vender? ¿Cuál de los muchachos trepó al (climbed up the) árbol? ¿De quién es este retrato? ¿Qué habéis cantado? ¿Qué desea usted, caballero (sir)?

THIRTIETH LESSON   LECCIÓN TRIGÉSIMA

Pronombres reflexivos y enfáticos

Los pronombres reflexivos y los enfáticos son iguales en inglés. En singular, se forman añadiendo «self» al adjetivo posesivo para la primera y la segunda persona, y al pronombre personal en acusativo para la tercera. En plural se añade «selves» a los correspondientes adjetivos y pronombres. Se emplean para indicar que la acción del verbo recae sobre el mismo sujeto o para dar énfasis al pronombre.

I wash wɔʃ myself	me lavo (a mí mismo, -a)
you wash yourself	te lavas
he washes wɔʃiz himself	él se lava
she washes herself	ella se lava
it washes itself	(ello) se lava
one washes oneself wʌn'self	se lava
we wash ourselves	nos lavamos (a nosotros mismos)
you wash yourselves	os laváis
they wash themselves	se lavan

El verbo se conjuga normalmente en todas sus formas acompañado del pronombre reflexivo. Cuando las formas reflexivas se usan como si fueran enfáticas, el pronombre podrá variar su colocación, pero siempre irá acompañado de un pronombre en nominativo que no puede omitirse:

I will come myself.	Vendré yo mismo.
Who told you? She herself.	¿Quién te lo dijo? Ella misma.

Al adjetivo posesivo se le puede acompañar del adjetivo «own», «propio», para hacer más enfática la idea de posesión:

I have my own books.	Tengo mis (propios) libros.
You have a car of your own.	Tienes un coche de tu propiedad.

Algunos verbos en castellano son reflexivos y en inglés no lo son. He aquí algunos:

to complain kem'plein quejarse	I complain, me quejo
to dress, vestirse	I dress, me visto
to endeavour ən'devə* esforzarse	I endeavour, me esfuerzo
to rejoice ri'dʒɔis alegrarse	I rejoice, me alegro
to wonder 'wʌndə* admirarse	I wonder, me admiro
to be mistaken, equivocarse	I am mistaken, me equivoco
to boast boust jactarse	I boast, me jacto
to repent ri'pent arrepentirse	I repent, me arrepiento
to get up get 'ʌp \} levantarse to rise raiz	I get up, I rise, me levanto
to remember ri'membə* \} acordarse to recollect rekə'lekt	I remember, I recollect, me acuerdo

La forma recíproca del verbo es aquella que denota reciprocidad o cambio mutuo de acción entre dos o más personas. Se expresa añadiendo al verbo uno de los pronombres recíprocos: «one another» [ə'nʌðə*] o «each [i:tʃ] other» = «el uno al otro, los unos a los otros» (o sus femeninos):

Those two boys (girls) always quarrel *'kwɔrəl* with one another (*o* one with the other). They do not love each other.	Esos (-as) dos muchachos (-as) riñen siempre el uno (la -a) con el otro (la -a) (*o* entre sí). No se quieren (el uno al otro, o la -a a la -a, los unos a los otros, etc.).

Los pronombres reflexivos y los recíprocos se declinan de la manera usual:

She always complains *kəm'pleinz* of herself.	Siempre se queja de sí misma.
They speak ill each other, they are never satisfied with one another.	Hablan mal el uno del otro; nunca están contentos el uno del otro.

Words

behave *bi'heiv*	portarse bien	to keep in touch *tʌtʃ*	estar en relación, contacto
library *'laibrəri*	biblioteca	to take back *teik bæk*	devolver
television *'teli'viʒən*	televisión		

Exercise

Mary has her own book, but Pat uses Mary's. I have a radio of my own, and my own television. I put the book on the table myself. I, myself, put it there. Did he write that letter himself? Yes, he did; the child wrote it all by himself. No one helped him. I have my own pen and he likes his own, so we never take each other's. My friend did his exercise all by himself. They themselves took back their books to the library. They did not take mine. I myself took it there yesterday morning. The children have behaved very nicely to-day. They themselves will tell you so. I don't live in my own house; I live at my sister's. I haven't a house of my own.

The children write to one another. They don't see one another during the Winter time so they write to keep in touch with one another. Did you and Pat write to each other during the Summer? Yes, we did. I myself will read the letter. She always complains about herself. I will come myself and bring you the news. Who said that she would not come? She herself said so. We all need one another.

Words

alive ə′laiv	vivo, con vida	tired taiə*d	cansado
care kɛə*	cuidado	to heal hi:l	sanar
guard ga:d	guardar	to take care	cuidar
harm ha:m	daño	watch over	vigilar
help help	ayudar	wɔtʃ ′ouvə*	
hymn him	himno	wide waid	ancho
in order that	para que	wise waiz	sabio
Lord lɔ:d	Señor	world wə:ld	mundo
praise preiz	alabanza		

Reading exercise

It is God who made us. He made you and me, and all things. He made the sun, the moon, the stars and the earth. In God we live and move. He gives us food, and takes care of us. God is wise, and just, and good. It is he who watches over us with love. His arms are about us to guard us from harm. If we are sick, he will heal us. God is the father of all. He orders that we love each other, that we do no harm to one another, that we help ourselves, in order that he also may help us. All who are alive in the wide world, are his children, if they are good and wise. All the world is the work of his hands, and all that is good comes from him. God loves us all, and is good to all. Let us also love him, and think of him day and night. Let us sing a hymn in the praise of the Lord, our God, and behave as his children.

Vocabulario

afeitar	shave ʃeiv	moverse	to move tu mu:v
asombrarse de, preguntarse	to wonder at tu ′wʌndə* æt	muchacho	fellow ′felou
		muerto	dead ded
ayudar	to help help	nido	nest nest
casarse con	to marry ′mæri	no importa	never mind maind
comer	to dine dain		
desesperarse	despair dis′pɛə*	no ... nunca	never ′nevə*
echar	throw, threw, thrown θrou, θru:, θroun	pájaro	bird bə:d
		piedra	stone stoun
		porque	because bi′kɔ:z
guisar	to cook ′kuk	tener aspecto	to look luk
malo	wicked ′wikid	trepar a, escalar	to climb ′klaim
más lejos	farther ′fa:ðə*		
morir	die dai	valor	courage ′kʌridʒ

Ejercicio

Yo mismo leeré tus cartas, y tú mismo escribirás mis respuestas. Ella misma guisó nuestros platos (dishes). Juguemos juntos. Me casaré con Mary. ¿Me has visto? Te vi con tus amigos. Los míos son mejores que los tuyos. Jugaría con el perro si fuera nuestro, pero es suyo. ¿Es vuestro ese jardín? Sí, es nuestro (de nuestra propiedad). El vuestro está más lejos. ¿Vino usted mismo? Sí, señor, vine yo mismo ayer. ¿Está muerto ese perro? Todavía no (not yet), pero morirá pronto. El pájaro está en su nido; el gato puede trepar al árbol. Uno estudia para sí mismo. ¿Se han ayudado el uno al otro? No (lo) sé. No debe uno desesperar nunca de sí mismo. Se asombra de su propio valor.

Exercise

My father and yours are dining at her house. His car is not so good as hers. He bought it with his own money. One of my friends has just arrived. Is your father well? Yes. You look very well, but my son looks very ill. Are our parents well? Yes, they are. Are they? Yes, I, myself, told you so already. Have you done your work? Yes. Ours, yours, and theirs are done. My brother and hers are good fellows, yours and his are not. One should always do one's duty. Their clothes are dirty. Never mind. I wonder if he will come. He looks very well after being ill for such a long time. The child himself threw the stone. I know because I, myself, put it there. He himself saw it. He shaves himself every morning. She lives farther down the street. We, ourselves, have seen her go into the house. Can you cook a good dinner? Yes, I can. You yourself could not do it better.

Words

accompany ə'kʌmpəni	acompañar	certainly 'sə:tn-li	ciertamente
ballet 'bælet	ballet	company 'kʌmpəni	compañía
book *buk*	reservar (un asiento)	couple kʌpl a — of	par un par de
borrow 'bɔrou	tomar prestado	curtain calls kə:tən 'kɔ:ls	salir a saludar (en el teatro)
box office bɔks 'ɔfis	taquilla		

delightful *di'laitfəl*	delicioso, a	singer *'siŋə**	cantante
distinguish *dis'tiŋgwiʃ*	distinguido, a	singing *'siŋiŋ*	canto
		splendid *'splendid*	espléndido
dress circle *dres 'sə:kl*	anfiteatro	stall *stɔ:l*	platea (butaca de)
engagement *in'geidʒmənt*	compromiso	superb *sju(:)'pə:b*	soberbio
		suppose *sə'pouz*	suponer
enjoy oneself	disfrutar	I —	supongo
free *fri:*	libre	telephone *'telifoun*	teléfono
grant *gra:nt*	conceder		
lent *lent*	presté	tenor *tenə**	tenor
opera *ɔpərə*	ópera	theatre *'θiətə**	teatro
— glasses	gemelos de teatro	ticket *'tikit*	entrada
orchestra *'ɔ:kistrə*	orquesta	to be worth while	valer la pena
order *'ɔ:də**	encargar	*we:θwail*	
performance *pə'fɔ:məns*	representación	treat *tri:t*	obsequio, -ar
		well	bien
(tele)phone *(teli)foun*	telefonear	with pleasure *'pleʒə*	con mucho gusto
prima-ballerina	primera bailarina		
production *prə'dʌkʃən*	presentación	win, won, won *win, wʌn*	ganar
ring up	telefonear	wonderful *'wʌndəful*	maravilloso
seats *si:ts*	asientos, butacas		

Conversation

Going to the Ballet and to the Opera

A. Where are you going tonight?
B. I haven't been to the Ballet for years, so I think I will go there tonight.
A. Well, I hope you enjoy yourself.
B. A friend of mine went last night and said that the production was wonderful.
A. Yes, and I was told that the prima-ballerina gave a superb performance, and was given twelve curtain-calls.
B. Would you like to come with me? I'll 'phone the box office and see if I can book a couple of tickets for the stalls or the dress-circle.
A. It is nice of you to ask, but I have already another engagement. But I could ring up my sister and ask if she will be free to accompany you this evening if you like.
B. That would be delightful. Do, please, ring her up and ask her. Is she has any opera-glasses, perharps she would

remember to bring them along with her — I lent mine to a friend and haven't seen them since.
A. You can borrow mine with pleasure: I shall not be wanting them, and I don't think hers are much good.
B. Oh thank you very much. I'll return them tomorrow. And what are you going to do with yourself (qué vas a hacer) if I may ask?
A. Certainly. I am giving my niece a treat and I am taking her to the theatre, or maybe the Opera, if I can get any good seats.
B. That will be very nice for her. I am sure she will enjoy it very much. I myself was at the Opera last night and the singers and the orchestra were just splendid.
A. Yes, I have heard they are really wonderful; that is why I thought of taking her. I want her to hear a good tenor as she is very fond of music and of singing.
B. She will enjoy it, then, and you will have your wish granted, for he is really worth while.

Vocabulario

avergonzarse	to be ashamed *əˈʃeimd* of	jabón	soap *soup*
castigar	punish *ˈpʌniʃ*	muñeca	doll *dɔl*
éxito	success *səkˈses*	obtener	obtain *əbˈtein*
extraordinario	extraordinary *iksˈtrɔːdnri*	prudente, sabio	wise *waiz*
		rato	while *wail*

Ejercicio

Este sombrero es el mío, el tuyo es el negro. Se lavó las manos con agua y jabón. No me acuerdo de su dirección, dígamela, por favor. Estoy admirado de vuestros progresos. Cuida a mi hermano personalmente (tú mismo). Hagan esto ustedes mismos. Él se avergonzó de sus propias faltas. Las peras son para nosotros; puedes comer las que (tantas como) quieras. La niña rompió su muñeca y su madre la castigó.

Esta tarde, si encontramos entradas, iremos a la ópera, ¿queréis venir con nosotros? Vendrá también otro de mis amigos, Juan; lo conocéis, ¿verdad? Me han dicho que ponen una obra excepcional: el tenor es extraordinariamente bueno y los demás cantantes son muy conocidos, así como la orquesta. Yo voy ahora a la taquilla para comprar mi entrada y la de todos vosotros. Creo que pasaremos un rato muy agradable.

To learn by heart

Once and for all.	De una vez para siempre.
Just for once.	Por una sola vez.
As a matter of fact...	A decir verdad; el caso es...
It does not matter.	No importa.
To be in the wrong.	Estar equivocado.

Wiser today

A man should never be ashamed
to say he has been in the wrong, which
is but saying in other words that he is
wiser today than he was yesterday.

ALEXANDER POPE

THIRTY-FIRST LESSON
LECCIÓN TRIGÉSIMA PRIMERA

Adjetivos y pronombres (ampliación)

1. *Adjetivos y pronombres demostrativos*

El adjetivo demostrativo precede siempre al nombre y concuerda con él en número solamente:

> this book is mine   these books are mine
> that book is ours   those books are ours

Si para evitar la repetición se omitiera el nombre que acompaña al adjetivo demostrativo, deberá sustituirse por el pronombre indefinido «one, ones»:

I have bought a blue pencil and a red one.	He comprado un lápiz azul y otro rojo.
Here are my sons; this one is Peter and that one is John.	He aquí a mis hijos; éste es Pedro y aquél es Juan.
That is a more interesting book than that one.	Este libro es más interesante que aquél.

El pronombre demostrativo puede sustituir al nombre en algunas ocasiones:

> I like this.
> This is the same book as that.
> These are my gloves and those are yours.

«That» y «those», seguidos de la preposición «of», «de», más sustantivo, se traduce por «el de, la de, los de, las de» y equivale a un posesivo:

My house is bigger than that of your sister.	Mi casa es mayor que la de tu hermana.

Es lo mismo que:

> My house is bigger than your sister's.
> I have taken your book and that of Mary.
> I have taken your book and Mary's.

Seguidos de un relativo, «that» y «those» se traducen por «el que, los que, la que, las que»:

> Those who come late will have no tea.

2. *Adjetivos y pronombres distributivos*

Los distributivos son:

> Each *i:tʃ* cada; cada uno, -a; cada cual.
> Every *'evri* cada; todo, -a.
> Either *'aiðə**, *'i:ðə** uno u otro; uno de los dos.
> Neither *'naiðə**, *'ni:ðə** ni uno ni otro, ninguno (de los dos).

Each member of the family.	Cada miembro de la familia.
Each of the four friends must ...	Cada uno de los cuatro amigos debe ...
Every boy has a ball.	Todos los niños tienen una pelota.
Either of these books is all the same to me.	Uno u otro de estos libros me resulta igual.
Neither of them is single.	Ni el uno ni el otro (ninguno) de ellos es soltero.

3. Adjetivos y pronombres indefinidos

Los indefinidos son los siguientes:

all *ɔːl* todo, -a, -os, -as
any *eni* ⎫ alguno, -a; algo
some *sʌm* ⎭ de, un poco
anything ⎫
something ⎬ algo, alguna cosa
somewhat ⎭
many *meni* muchos, -as

no *nou* ningún, -a; no... ningún, -a
nobody ⎫ nadie, no... nadie
no one ⎭
both *bouθ* ambos, -as; los, las dos
none *nʌn* (no...) ninguno, -a
another *ə'nʌðə** otro, -a
one another ⎫ uno a otro, el
each other ⎭ uno al otro, etc.

else *els* otro, -a, más
anybody *'enibɔdi* ⎫
anyone *'eniwʌn* ⎪ alguien,
somebody ⎬ alguno
some one ⎭
little, poco
a little, un poco (de)
few *fjuː* pocos, -as
a few, algunos, -as; varios, -as
much, mucho, -a
nothing *'nʌθiŋ* nada
everything *'evriθiŋ* todo, todas las cosas
one, uno, un tal
other *'ʌðə** otro, el otro, la otra
several *'sevrəl* varios, diversos, -as
such *sʌtʃ* tal, semejante

«One ... another» y «each ... other» son también pronombres recíprocos. «Some» y «any», que corresponden a «un poco de, algo de, unos, unas», se emplean como partitivos con nombres en plural. «Many» y «much» se emplean en combinación con «how», «as», «so», «too», correspondiendo al español:

how many?	¿cuántos?	as much	tanto
how much?	¿cuánto?	too many	demasiados
as many	tantos	too much	demasiado

«Some» expresa algo positivo y limitado o parcial, y se emplea en las cláusulas afirmativas, y aun en las interrogativas (positivas o negativas) en las cuales el sentido está limitado o no hay idea de duda.

I can lend you some very useful books.	Puedo prestarle algunos libros muy interesantes.
Will you have some more tea?	¿Quiere un poco más de té?
Yes, please. I'll love some more.	Sí, gracias. Me gustaría un poco más.

«Any» se emplea en frases interrogativas, negativas y dubitativas. En frases afirmativas, «any» tiene el sentido de algo general, indefinido e incierto:

I don't want anything else.	No quiero nada más.
Don't you want any tomatoes today *təˈmaːtouz tudei* madam?	¿No quiere (algunos) tomates hoy, señora?
We don't see any flowers in that garden.	No vemos ninguna flor en ese jardín.
You may come any day you like.	Puede venir cualquier día que quiera.
If she had seen any risk *risk* ...	Si hubiera visto algún riesgo...

«All», en sentido limitado, se usa como «todo» en castellano; pero en sentido general no lleva artículo.

All the brothers were there.	Todos los hermanos estaban allí.
— Of all the brothers ...	— De todos los hermanos...
All men are mortal.	Todos los hombres son mortales.

«All», con el significado de «entero», se emplea sólo en el singular, y equivale a «whole» [*houl*] «entero». El uso del artículo se demuestra en los ejemplos siguientes:

all the house
the whole house } toda la casa, la casa entera

a whole house   una casa entera

Después de «all», «nothing», «something», «everything» no se puede usar «what», sino «that» (que puede omitirse).

This is all that we know.
This is all we know. } Es todo lo que sabemos.

«No» se emplea antes de sustantivos como sinónimo de «not any», «not one» (siempre con valor de adjetivo).

Not one
No } man was seen.   No se vio a ningún hombre.

We saw no woman.
We did not see any woman. } No vimos a ninguna mujer.

«Both», antes de un pronombre personal, debe ir seguido de la preposición «of» y el pronombre en acusativo.

Both of them.   Ambos (los dos, ellos dos).

«One» tiene el plural «ones», y el posesivo «one's». Se emplea a menudo para traducir la forma impersonal con «se» (v. gr.: «se come, se ve», etc.). El verbo con «one» está siempre en singular, pues «one» es su sujeto. «One» puede tomar el artículo definido («the one... the other»).

One cannot know...	No se puede saber...
If one reads *ri:dz* aloud *ə'laud* ...	Si se (si uno) lee en voz alta...
The one you gave me first is better than the other.	El que me diste primero es mejor que el otro.

En lugar de «one» se emplean a veces «they», «people»; y con mucha frecuencia el verbo en pasiva.

«Other», empleado como sustantivo, forma el plural añadiendo «s» y el genitivo añadiendo «'s», o «'»: «others; other's, others'».

«Such», antes de un singular, va seguido del artículo indefinido: «such an old man».

«Many a» significa «más de uno, varios», y exige el singular.

Many a captain was... { Más de un capitán fue...
Varios capitanes fueron...

Añadiendo a los pronombres «who (whom)», «which», «what» el adverbio «ever» o «soever», se forman los pronombres corrrespondientes:

whoever *hu:'evə**
whosoever *hu:sou'evə** } quienquiera que, el que, cualquiera que, etc.

whichever *witʃ'evə**
whichsoever *witʃsou'evə** } cualquiera que, aquel que, etc.

whatever *wɔt'evə**
whatsoever *wɔtsou'evə** } cualquier cosa que, por más que, sea lo que fuere, etc.

Conversation

Do you believe what he says? Whatever he says is true ([*tru:*] verdad). Which of these pictures will you sell me? Whichever you please, or all, if you will buy them. Whom do you expect to see tomorrow? I expect to see nobody; but, whomsoever I may see, I shall tell you. Is this your car? Not this, the other one. How much have you given for it? I will tell you another time. What is the matter (qué sucede)? Nothing is the matter; nothing at all (absolutamente). What do you want? I want to speak to someone here. I want some pens; have you (got) any? I have some excellent ones. Can you give me some sealing-wax ([*si:liŋ-wæks*] lacre)? Yes, if you want some. Has anybody broken my glass? Nobody has (broken it); it was the cat. To whom

Adjetivos y pronombres (ampliación)   183

will you give a newspaper? To each of the men and to whomsoever asks for it. Do you know all the family? I know each member of it. Can everybody sing? Everyone can that has a good voice (= Everyone that ... can). Have you paid for everything? No, each one paid for himself. Will you eat either of these chops ([tʃɔps] chuletas)? No, they are both old and tough ([tʌf] duras). Will neither of these teapots do (servir)? No; unless it is a metal one it will not do. What will you have soup or fish? Thank you, I will have neither. Will you have white or red wine? Either; it is quite the same (to me).

Nota: Con las comidas suele emplearse el verbo «to have» en lugar de «to take» con el sentido de «tomar».

Vocabulario

asunto	matter 'mætə*	marcharse	to go away *tu gou ə'wei*
cereza	cherry 'tʃeri		
corral, patio	yard *jaːd*	probar	to taste *teist*
costar	to cost *kɔst*	quemar	to burn down
entre	among ə'mʌŋ	si las hay	if any are there
excelente	excellent 'eksələnt	tenedor	fork *fɔːk*
lavar	to wash *tu wɔʃ*	tímido, vergonzoso	shy ʃai
manzana	apple 'æpl	travieso	naughty 'nɔːti

Ejercicio

Acompañad a una o a otra de las señoras. ¿Quiere usted café? No quiero café, sino otra taza de té. ¿No hay gallinas en el corral? Sí; hay muchas. Si alguien viene le hablaré. Mis dos sobrinos están en la India; los dos muchachos que allí ves son sus amigos. Tenemos pocas plumas y poco papel. ¿Quieres darme algunos francos? De buena gana (willingly). ¿Cuántos años habéis estado en Inglaterra? Más de cuatro. ¿Cuánto cuestan estas cerezas? Tanto como las otras. Tiene mucho dinero, pero pocos amigos. Nadie os ha visto. Las manzanas de este árbol son excelentes, pero yo no he probado ninguna. Ninguno de estos señores es tu amigo. No dijo nada. ¿No tenéis otros cuchillos? Aquí hay otro. Necesito otro tenedor. Aquí hay varios lapiceros. Algunas de estas ropas no están lavadas. Alguien llama a (knocks at) la puerta. ¿Ha visto usted a alguien? No vi a nadie. Comeré algo. Y yo te daré algo bueno que (to) comer. Nunca he visto tal gente. ¿Han encontrado ustedes algunos guantes blancos entre éstos? No encontramos ninguno. Quiero comprar naranjas; dadme unas buenas. No vi a ninguno más. No digas nada más sobre (on) este asunto. ¿Quién ha dicho tal cosa? No sé, pero alguien debe de haberlo dicho, porque yo ya lo sabía. Dame unas pocas cerezas y unas cuantas manzanas. ¿Tienes mucho dinero? No, tengo muy poco. Tengo tan poco como tú. Nunca puede saberse lo que los chiquillos van a hacer. Unos son algo tímidos, juegan poco y leen mucho; otros son traviesos, juegan mucho y estudian poco. ¿Qué libro quieres? Coge uno u otro. No quiero ninguno.

Words

acquaintance ə'kweintəns	conocido, amigo	park pɑːk	parque
altogether ɔːltə'geðə*	en conjunto	planet 'plænit	planeta
		plant plɑːnt	planta
busy 'bizi	ocupado	pleasure 'pleʒə*	placer
botanist 'bɔtənist	botánico	profit 'prɔfit	provecho
chance tʃɑːns	oportunidad	question 'kwes-tʃən	pregunta
display dis'plei	despliegue		
Earth əːθ	tierra	put a —	hacer una pregunta
guide gaid	guía		
imagine i'mædʒin	imaginar	rejoice ri'dʒɔis	alegrarse
Kew kjuː	Kew, nombre propio	relative 'relətiv	pariente
		strange streindʒ	extraño
kindness 'kaindnis	amabilidad	to be acquainted ə'kweintid	conocer
lucky 'lʌki	afortunado		
lovely 'lʌvli	encantador, delicioso	together 'tə-geðə*	juntos
make up	formamos	wandered 'wɔndəd	vagamos
paradise 'pærədais	paraíso		

Reading exercise

A visit to Kew Gardens

Yesterday was Sunday, and because the sun was shining, my wife, Mary and I decided to pay a visit to Kew Gardens. Being busy people, we do not normally give much thought to the varieties of strange and exotic plants and flowers with which Nature decorates this planet Earth. But both of us were glad that we went and that we were lucky enough

Adjetivos y pronombres (ampliación)

to have a relative who is a botanist and who had the kindness to come with us as a guide, and answered all our questions. Together we wandered through the lovely parks, a paradise of beauty. There was no tree, no plant and no flower with which our cousin was not acquainted: and he had something interesting to say about every one. A display of beautiful flowers and plants such as we saw is enough to make a miserable man rejoice; and Mary and I agreed that it is not every day that a chance to combine profit and pleasure so delightfully, comes along. On our way back we met some acquaintances of ours and we made up a party and went to have a cup of tea. We were about ten people altogether, and we had a lovely time. We could never have imagined that we would have such a nice day out.

Vocabulario

desgraciado	unhappy ʌn-'hæpi	ocupación, trabajo	work wəːk
no queda nada	there is nothing left	película	film *film*
		perezoso	lazy 'leizi

Ejercicio

Cualquier ocupación es mejor que no hacer nada. Cuéntame algo nuevo, no he recibido noticias tuyas desde la primavera pasada. Se dice que los soldados llegarán de la guerra la semana próxima. ¿Puedes prestarme un lápiz? Lo siento, no llevo ninguno. Este niño es un perezoso, no ha hecho nada en toda la mañana. Se es desgraciado cuando no se está contento. Esta película no gusta a nadie. Lo he hecho todo; no he de hacer nada más. Sólo unos pocos tendrán premio. He comprado varios libros, pero necesito algunos más. Se escriben cada quince días. ¿Tienes dinero? No tengo nada de dinero. Las dos radios se han roto, no ha quedado nada de ellas. Todo el mundo cree que esto es verdad. Me gusta azúcar en el café. En esta clase hay mesas y en cada una de ellas hay varios libros.

Words

along ə'lɔŋ	adelante	behind bi'haind	detrás
as far as əz 'faːr əz	hasta	bus bʌs	autobús
		call out kɔːl	gritar

close to *klous tu*	cerca de	main road *mein roud*	calle principal
conductor *kən'dʌktə**	conductor-cobrador	miss *mis*	señorita
consulate *'kʌnsjulit*	consulado	move along *muːv 'æloŋ*	pasar adelante
crowd *kraud*	multitud	on the top	arriba
down *daun*	abajo	passengers *'pæsindʒəz*	pasajeros
fare *fɛə**	billete, importe del billete	pence *pens*	peniques
get in *get in*	entrar, subir	plenty of *plenti əv*	abundante, mucho
get off *get ɔːf*	bajar	ring the bell *riŋ ðə bel*	tocar el timbre
get out *get aut*	bajar, salir	room *ruːm*	sitio
get there *get ðɛə**	llegar	show *ʃou*	indicar, mostrar
go down *gou daun*	bajar	station *'steiʃən*	estación
hold *hould*	sujetar, agarrar	stop	parada
— tight *tait*	— fuerte	tube *tjuːb*	metro
inside *'insaid*	dentro	wait *weit*	esperar
kind *kaind*	amable	way *wei*	dirección, camino
little way *wei*	poco trecho		
madam *'mædəm*	señora		

Conversation

On an omnibus

Conductor: (To the crowd hurrying to get into the bus.) Wait a moment for the passengers to get off, please! (He calls out.) Oxford Street, Bank, London Bridge!

Old gentleman: (Speaking to the conductor.) Does this bus go to Notting Hill Gate?

Conductor: No, sir; take the number 78 just behind. Move along, please! Plenty of room on top! Hold tight, please! (Rings the bell and moves inside.) Fares, please! Where to, lady?

Lady: I want to go to the Dutch Consulate, do you stop near there, please?

Conductor: Well, if you get off at the Royal Albert Hall it is only a few minutes walk from there. It is quite close to it. Three and a half (3 1/2 d., three pence halfpenny ['θrepəns 'heipni]), please!

Gentleman: (Sitting on the same seat as the lady.) I'm going that way myself, and I shall be pleased to show you where it is, madam.

Lady: Oh thank you so much. That's very kind of you.

Young lady: I want to get to Harrod's. Is Knightsbridge tube station the best stop for me?

Conductor: Yes, miss; then take the main road to the left, and it's about 100 yards up on your left.
Young lady: Will you tell me when we get there, please?
Conductor: Knightsbridge next stop. Here you are, miss.

Vocabulario

buscar	look for	museo	museum *mju:'ziəm*
colección	collection *kə'lekʃən*	¡qué...!	what a...!
correos	Post Office *'poust ɔfis*	útil	useful *ju:'ful*

Ejercicio

Ni este sombrero que tiene en la mano, ni aquel que está colgado en la percha es el mío. Este niño es tan inteligente como el (aquel) de nuestros vecinos. Aquellos niños que están en lo alto de la torre son alumnos de este colegio que ves enfrente. Aquel famoso arquitecto que construyó esta catedral tan bella, ha muerto. Estas colecciones serán muy útiles para mis estudios. El que busca, al fin encuentra. Son felices los que se contentan con lo suyo.

Por favor, señorita, ¿este autobús que llega me conducirá al Museo Británico? Sí, señora; suba usted, si puede, pues viene completamente lleno. ¡Qué multitud! Yo voy hasta Correos. Usted debe apearse una o dos paradas después, el cobrador se lo dirá exactamente; tendrá que andar un poco. Muchas gracias, es usted muy amable.

THIRTY-SECOND LESSON
LECCIÓN TRIGÉSIMA SEGUNDA

Verbos anómalos y defectivos (ampliación)

En la lección 13 vimos los verbos defectivos «can» y «may», «puedo», y «must», «debo». Los restantes verbos defectivos y anómalos, son:

Presente		Pasado
shall ʃæl	debo	should ʃud
will wil	quiero	would wud
ought to ɔːt tu	debiera	
need niːd	necesito (en forma negativa)	
dare dɛə*	atreverse (en forma negativa)	

Estos verbos se conjugan igual en todas las personas de estos tiempos, que son los únicos. Se llaman anómalos porque sintácticamente se usan de modo peculiar, y defectivos por carecer de la mayoría de sus tiempos.

Como los que vimos anteriormente, sus características principales son las siguientes: *a)* Llevan siempre un complemento en infinitivo. *b)* No toman la «s» característica de la 3.ª persona del singular del presente. *c)* La forma interrogativa se hace alterando el orden de sujeto y verbo. *d)* La forma negativa se hace añadiendo directamente después del verbo la negación, sin el «do» característico de la negación en los demás verbos.

El complemento en infinitivo de los verbos «shall», «will», «can», «may» y «must» no está precedido de la preposición «to» característica de este modo, así como tampoco la forma negativa de «need» y «dare». Por el contrario, «ought» la toma siempre.

«Shall» tiene el sentido de mandato, promesa, y, en su forma interrogativa, de voluntad o permiso:

> *Mandato:* You shall have to take it.
> *Promesa:* Peter shall have the book he wants.
> *Voluntad:* Shall I come, too?

Cuando es auxiliar, «shall» sirve para formar las primeras personas del futuro de los verbos: «I shall go now.»

«Will» expresa resolución o voluntad. En la segunda persona en la forma interrogativa se traduce al español por: «¿quiere usted?».

Will you take the book or not?	¿Quiere usted coger el libro o no?
I will not let you go.	No quiero dejarte marchar.
Will you come in, please?	¿Quiere pasar, por favor?

Cuando «will» es auxiliar sirve para formar las restantes personas del futuro de los verbos: «they will arrive tomorrow».

«Should» expresa una obligación moral o condicional:

| You should go to see Mary. | Debieras ir a ver a María. |

«Would», además de su significado usual, expresa también costumbre y petición cortés:

They would not come.	No quisieron venir.
He would get up at six o'clock every day.	Solía levantarse...
Would you open the window for me, please?	¿Querría hacer el favor de...?

«Should» y «would», auxiliares, expresan respectivamente las primeras y las restantes personas del condicional.

«Ought to» sólo tiene esta forma y posee un sentido semejante a «should».

| You ought to go. | Deberías (debieras) ir. |
| They ought to do it... | Deberían (debieran) hacerlo. |

Las expresiones: «hubiera debido, hubiera podido» se traducen en inglés como si fueran: «debería haber, podría haber» (y así en todas las personas), diciéndose: «I should have» o «I ought to have», «I could (o «migth») have», seguidas del participio del verbo, que en castellano está en infinitivo.

| You should (o you ought to) have done it. | Habrías debido hacerlo, deberías haberlo hecho. |
| They might (o could) have brought the glass. | Hubieran podido traer el vaso, podrían haber traído el vaso. |

El verbo «need» es anómalo en forma negativa. En las demás formas se conjuga regularmente.

| They need not take it unless they want to. | No es preciso que lo cojan a menos que quieran. |
| Do you need this book any longer? | ¿Necesitas este libro por más tiempo? |

El verbo «dare» es anómalo en forma negativa cuando significa «atreverse, tener valor». Pero se conjuga regularmente en todos sus tiempos y personas en las formas interrogativa y positiva, y con el significado de «provocar» o «desafiar».

I dare not come.	No me atrevo a venir.
Would you dare to go?	¿Te atreverías a ir?
Do you dare me to fight *fait*?	¿Me provocas a luchar?

El pasado de «dare» con el sentido de «atreverse» es «durst»:

I durst not do it.   No me atreví a hacerlo.

Words

besides *bi'saidz*	además
by all means *bai ɔːl miːnz*	¡no faltaba más!
expect *iks'pekt*	esperar
give back *giv bæk*	devolver
leave *liːv*	dejar, marcharse
not a single ... *nɔt ə 'siŋgl*	ni una ...
nuisance *'njuːsns*	fastidio
post *poust*	echar al correo
rain *rein*	llover
strong *strɔŋ*	fuerte
suit *sjuːt*	ser conveniente
that will do *ðæt wil du*	eso bastará, es suficiente
to be sure *ʃuə**	estar seguro
umbrella *ʌm'brelə*	paraguas

Exercise

Do you dare me? No, I don't. You are too strong. You need not come. We can manage without you. Peter may go if he likes, but I am sure he won't because it is too late. Besides, he has all his lessons to study, and if he does not do them now he shall have to study in the evening. Will you post this letter for me? Yes, I will. Will you have some more tea? No, thanks, I will not have any more. I might have sent you a ticket for the Opera if I had known you wanted to go. Could you lend me your English grammar? Yes, but when will you be able to give it back to me? I could send it back tomorrow, if that would suit you. Yes, that will do. May I come in? By all means, do. You ought to be able to speak English by now. I know. But I could not say a single word. Joan should have gone to see her grandmother, who is ill, but she would not, and I could not make her go. You shall go to the pictures if you are good, but if you are not good you need not expect such a treat. It is very hot in this room: shall I open the window? Yes, do; but will you close the door first? May I bring my sister to tea tomorrow? Do bring her, by all means. Would you like to have your tea in the garden? It is nice outside, now. Oh yes, that will be very nice! All right. Could you be here before four o'clock? If you could, you would see Tommy before he leaves for his music lesson. You ought to take an umbrella. It is going to rain. I don't think I will; umbrellas are such a nuisance! I always leave mine behind when I take one.

Words

advertisement *əd'və:tismənt*	anuncio	proof *pru:f*	prueba
arithmetic *ə'riθmətik*	aritmética	smoke *smouk*	fumar
beat *bi:t*	pegar	story *'stɔ:ri*	historia
college *'kɔlidʒ*	colegio universitario	student *'stju:dənt*	estudiante
dear *diə**	querido	thereupon *ðɛərə'pɔn*	a lo cual, entonces
do so *du: sou*	hazlo	to deserve *di'zə:v*	merecer
during *'djuərin*	durante	to forbid *fə'bid*	prohibir
kill yourself *kil yɔ:'self*	matarse	to gain *gein*	ganar
later *'leitə**	más tarde	to reply *ri'plai*	contestar
learning *'lə:nin*	ciencia, cultura	to smack *smæk*	pegar
pigeon *'pidʒən*	paloma	young *jʌŋ*	joven

Reading exercise

A young student had came home from college during the holidays, and wished to give his parents a proof of his learning. Having one evening two pigeons for supper, he said to them: «I can prove by the rules of arithmetic that these two pigeons are three.» «Do so, my dear», said the father. Thereupon he began: «This is one, and that is two, and one and two make three.» The father replied: «As you have done it so well, your mother shall have the first pigeon, I will take the second, and the third you may have for your great learning.»

Ejercicio

¿Puedes hacer esto ahora? No, ahora no puedo, lo haré más tarde. La semana próxima no podré venir. Tienes que estudiar toda la lección. Me dijo que quería aprender música. ¿Sabe usted hablar español? No, no he podido aprenderlo en tan poco tiempo. Mi madre no podrá venir al teatro. Deberían poner un anuncio en el periódico sobre

esto. Pueden fumar, si quieren. Podía hacerlo, pero no quiso.
¿Puedes llamarme antes de venir? Tienes que estar en casa
a las 8. ¿Quieres aprender tu lección ahora o más tarde? Si
tuviera tiempo la aprendería ahora, pero como no lo tengo
la aprenderé más tarde. Iré al cine y tú me acompañarás
(come with me). No podemos salir los domingos porque no
sabemos a dónde ir. Podías darle el dinero. Se lo hubiera
dado si lo hubiese tenido; pero, como no lo tengo, no se
lo puedo dar. Debo salir porque me esperan. Si debes salir,
sal, pero no vuelvas tarde. Hubiera podido contarle esa historia, pero no quise. Hubieras podido caerte y matarte.
Podías haber venido más temprano. Lo siento, pero no
pude. Si hubiera podido habría venido. María ha pegado
a su hijo pequeño. ¿Por qué le pegó? Porque fue muy
travieso y no quería estudiar.

Words

choose *tʃuːz*	escoger	poultry *'poultri*	aves de corral, volatería
chickens *'tʃikins*	pollos	provide *prə'vaid* with	proveer, abastecer, suministrar
commented *'kɔmentid*	comentó	reply *ri'plai*	replicar
customers *'kʌstəmə*z*	clientes	request *ri'kwest*	petición, ruego
discrimination *diskrimi'neiʃən*	discernimiento, cuidado	resident *'residənt*	huésped
expose *iks'pouz*	expuestos	sale *seil*	venta
— for sale *seil*	— para vender	shopkeeper *'ʃɔp'kiːpə**	tendero
extra *'ekstrə*	extraordinaria	(shop) window *ʃɔp 'windou*	escaparate
feed *fiːd*	alimentar, dar de comer	to be fond of	gustar de, ser aficionado
hotel-keeper *hou'tel 'kipəː**	hotelero	to be surprised *sə'praizd*	sorprenderse
occasion *ə'keiʒən*	ocasión	tough *tʌf*	duro (de alimento)
pick out	coger, seleccionar	unusual *'ʌn'juː-ʒuəl*	extraño, inusitado
please *pliːz*	complacer	visit *vizit*	visita
be —d with	estar complacido		
poulterer *'poultərə**	avicultor		

Reading exercise

A hotel-keeper having occasion to provide some extra
food for six important residents, payed a personal visit to the
poulterer. Seeing a dozen chickens exposed for sale in the

window, he went into the shop and said to the poulterer: «I want you to pick me out the six toughest chickens.» «That is a most unusual request», commented the shopkeeper. «That may be», replied the hotel-keeper, «but anything will do for poor customers». So the poulterer set to work choosing the six toughest chickens with much discrimination. «Thank you very much», said the hotel-keeper, «but on this occasion I am providing for rich customers who are fond of only the best chickens and are pleased with only the very best; so I will take the other six, please».

Questions

What did the hotel-keeper want? Was he having any important residents at his hotel? What did he do to make sure he would get the best poultry? Was the shopkeeper surprised? What did he say, then? When the toughest chickens were chosen, what did the hotel-keeper say? Which chickens did he take?

To learn by heart

The man who looks after your health[1] is called a doctor.
The man who builds bridges[2] is an engineer[3].
The man who knows about legal[4] matters[5] is a lawyer.
The man who does and cuts your hair is a hairdresser[6]

1. Healt *helθ* salud. 2. Bridge *bridʒ* puente. 3. Engineer *endʒi-'niə** ingeniero. 4. Legal *'liːgəl* legal. 5. Matters *'mætə*z* asuntos. 6. Hairdresser *hɛə'dresə** peluquero.

> God, let me live each lovely day
> So I may know, that, come what may,
> I've done my best to live the way
> You'd want me to.

Words

as well *æz wel*	también	disengaged *'disin'geidʒd*	desocupado
at least *liːst*	por lo menos	engaged	ocupado
bath *baːθ*	baño	fill in *fil in*	llenar
bathroom *'baːθruːm*	cuarto de baño	floor *flɔː**	piso, suelo
clerk *klaːk*	empleado	guest *gest*	huésped
difference *'difərəns*	diferencia	I'm afraid	temo
		include *in'kluːd*	incluir

lift *lift*	ascensor	porter *'pɔːtə**	mozo
low *lou*	bajo	register *'redʒistə**	registro
—er down	más bajo	see you *siː juː*	acompañar
luggage *'lʌgidʒ*	equipaje	service *'səːvis*	servicio
make sure *meik ʃuə**	asegurarse	sign *sain*	firmar
move into *muːv intu*	cambiarse, trasladarse	to be a nuisance *tu bi ə 'njuːsns*	ser un fastidio
particular *pə'tikjulə**	detalles	top floor *tɔp 'flɔː**	piso último
passport *paːspɔːt*	pasaporte	vacant *'veikənt*	vacío, vacante

Reading

At the hotel

Guest: I want a room for tonight, please.

Hotel Clerk: Yes, sir, we have one but I'm afraid it's on the top floor.

Guest: That is a nuisance. Haven't you anything lower down?

Hotel Clerk: I'm sorry, sir; it's been a busy week. Will you want to stay long?

Guest: At least four or five days.

Hotel C.: Well, sir, a first floor room will be empty tomorrow.

Guest: That's better. Is there much difference in the price?

Hotel C.: No, sir. We charge the same price for all rooms: it is 35 shillings for bed and breakfast.

Guest: Does that include service?

Hotel C.: Yes, and baths as well. There are four bathrooms on each floor with hot and cold water.

Guest: That will be fine. Perharps you will make sure that I have the vacant first floor room tomorrow.

Hotel C.: Certainly, sir. Now, if you will just sign the register and fill in the other particulars, I will call the porter who will take your luggage up and see you to your room which is number 106. And, sir, may I have your passport, please?

Guest: Certainly. Here it is.

Hotel C.: Thank you, sir. I hope that everything here will suit you, sir. As soon as the other room is disengaged, you can move into it. This way to the lift, sir.

THIRTY-THIRD LESSON
LECCIÓN TRIGÉSIMA TERCERA

El subjuntivo

En inglés, las formas verbales del subjuntivo se emplean muy poco en la lengua hablada, usándose en su lugar equivalencias con valor de subjuntivo. Normalmente, se conserva el subjuntivo de los verbos «to be» y «to have».

If I were king...	Si yo fuera rey...
If I had time...	Si tuviera tiempo...

El presente de subjuntivo, como ya vimos anteriormente, es igual al infinitivo sin la preposición «to» que normalmente le precede. El pasado de subjuntivo es igual al de indicativo sin ninguna variante, excepto el de «to be».

Se usa el subjuntivo para expresar: *a)* deseo; *b)* condición; *c)* propósito (precedido con frecuencia de las conjunciones «lest» y «that»); *d)* duda, suposición o temor.

a) I wish (that) he were here. — Quisiera que estuviera aquí.
God save our *seiv auə** gracious queen! — ¡Dios salve a nuestra graciosa reina!
b) If I see him (if I should see him) I shall tell him. — Si le viera se lo diré.
If I had met him I should have told him. — Si le hubiese encontrado se lo hubiera dicho.
c) I give you the pen that you may write the letter now. — Te doy la pluma para que escribas la carta ahora.
I didn't give him any money lest he should lose it. — No le di dinero no fuera a perderlo.
d) Unless he come, we can't open the door. — A menos que venga, no podemos abrir la puerta.
If he should come, tell me. — Si viniera, dímelo.

Cuando la conjunción «if» precede al auxiliar, con frecuencia se omite, alterándose entonces el orden de sujeto y auxiliar:

If he should tell you that...	Si te dijera eso...
Should he tell you that...	Si te dijera eso...
If I were rich...	Si fuera rico...
Were I rich...	Si fuera rico...

El presente de subjuntivo castellano, después de ciertos verbos, suele traducirse por el infinitivo en inglés:

Mother wants you to come with me. Mi madre quiere que vengas conmigo.

Cuando el subjuntivo expresa un propósito, los auxiliares que siguen a «that» y «lest» son siempre «may», «might» y «should».

I have taken your doll lest you should break it. He cogido tu muñeca para que no la rompas.
I shall give you a fishing-rod that you may go fishing. Te daré una caña de pescar para que vayas a pescar.
They gave the children some books that they might be quiet. Dieron unos libros a los chicos para que estuvieran quietos.

Obsérvese la traducción de «should» seguido de infinitivo perfecto por un subjuntivo español:

You should have gone. Debieras haber ido (hubieras debido ir).
You should be pleased. Debieras (hubieras debido) estar satisfecho.

Words

confess kən'fes	confesar	to be bound tu biː baund	estar obligado
fetch fetʃ	ir a buscar, traer	unfortunate 'ʌnfɔːtʃnit	desdichado
fly flai	volar	unless ʌn'les	a menos que
grievously 'griːvəsli	penosamente	whether ... or 'weðə* ɔː*	tanto si ... como si ...
save seiv	ahorrar		

Exercise

If that is true, it is a strange story. If it were so, it would be most unfortunate. I am very pleased that you be (are) here. I wish he would come before tomorrow. If it were so, it was a grievous fault; and grievously has Caesar answered it. Hold that dog that it may not bite the child. Whether you allow me or not, I will go to the pictures this evening. Hold your gloves lest you should lose them. I wish you were here. My mother is very pleased that you have come. I do not want him to read that letter. If I were rich I would buy a big car. If you were a nice boy you would fetch that book for me. If I had seen him I would have told him. If I meet her I shall tell you. Unless you consent we cannot go. Come what may, we shall take it. May you always be as happy as now. When you go to London I will give you money that you may buy what you need. Should he come before you go, tell him to wait for me. If he came I should know him. Should Mr. Brown come, what would you do? I don't know. I would have to find an excuse or other. Whether he confess(es) or not they are bound to find out sooner or later. May God bless you! I am not sure that he believed me, but I said I would go, and I went. I told him to do what he could and leave the rest to Mary. He worked hard that he might save enough money to fly to New York. I wish you would come to Paris with us next Winter. I wish I could! We would be very happy that you might come.

Words

advisable $əd'vaizəbl$	aconsejable
aerodrome $'ɛərədroum$	aeródromo
aeroplane $ɛəreplə in$	aeroplano
airleners $'ɛəlainə*s$	aviones de línea
airplane $'ɛerpləin$	aeroplano
airport $'ɛəpɔ:t$	aeropuerto
air-sickness $'ɛərsiknis$	mareo
as for	en cuanto a
altitude $'æltitju:d$	altura
be afraid $ə'freid$ (of)	temer
boat $bout$	barco
book buk	reservar
breathing $'bri:ðiŋ$	respiración
cabin $'kæbin$	cabina
certainly $sə:tnli$	ciertamente
change $tʃeindʒ$	cambiar
class $kla:s$	clase
cost $kɔ:st$	costar
engine $'endʒin$	motor
experience $iks'piəriəns$	experiencia
flight $flait$	vuelo
health $helθ$	salud
impair $im'pɛə*$	perjudicar
in advance $in əd'va:ns$	por adelantado
include $in'klu:d$	incluir
journey $'dʒə:ni$	viaje
luck $lʌk$	suerte
pressurized $'preʃəraisd$	presión acondicionada
prone $proun$	predispuesto
propeller $pro-'pelə*$	hélice
provided $prə'vaidid$	siempre (que)
rail $reil$	ferrocarril
risky $'riski$	arriesgado
safe $seif$	seguro
save $seiv$	ahorrar
sleeping-car $'sli:piŋ-kɔ*$	coche-cama
sound-prove $saund-pru:v$	a prueba de ruido
tired $'taiə*d$	cansado
to risk $risk$	arriesgar
to worry $tu 'wʌri$	preocuparse
train $trein$	tren
travel $'trævl$	viajar
trip $trip$	viaje

Conversation

A. I was thinking of flying to London on my next trip. It would be a change because I'm rather tired of long distance journeys by train or boat.
B. If I were you I would fly. It is a most enjoyable experience, provided that you are not prone to air-sickness. And it is so quick! You can leave Barcelona at 2 p. m. and be in London the same afternoon, and there are no stops on the way.
A. Isn't it a bit risky? And, I am afraid, also expensive?
B. Well, it's as safe today as rail or road travel. And as for expense, it doesn't cost much more than first class rail and boat travel if you include food and sleeping-car. And you might save yourself money in the time that you save.
A. As I'm not in the best of health, perharps the noise from the propellers and the high altitude would be bad for me.
B. You need't worry too much about that. You see, most airliners today have sound-proof cabins which are also pressurized so that the passengers breathing is not impaired.
A. Well, I'm not a very good sailor, but I think I'll risk it.
B. Good. But remember to book your ticket well in advance, though. It's always advisable to do that, for I am sure the flights are all booked. I hope that you enjoy it and have a nice journey. Good luck.

Questions

Where are you going? Are you going by boat, by air or by train? Have you ever flown before? Are you a good sailor? Is flying to London expensive? Do you have to book your tickets in advance? At what time is the plane leaving the air-port? At what time must you be there? Are you in good health? Do you think altitude might be bad for you? At what time does the plane arrive in London? Is it save to fly? Is it safer to travel by boat or by plane? Do you enjoy a flight?

El subjuntivo

Words

at any rate	sea como fuere, por lo menos	old-fashioned $ould'fæʃənd$	anticuado
B. B. C. $bi: bi: si:$	B. B. C.	organization $ɔ:gənai'zeiʃən$	organización
commercial $kə'me:ʃəl$	comercial	popularity $pɔpju'læriti$	popularidad
comparatively $kəm'pærətivli$	comparativamente	private $'praivit$	particular
consider $kən'sidə*$	considerar	produce $prə'dju:s$	producir
demand $di'ma:nd$	demanda	programme $'prougræm$	programa
electrical $i'lektrikəl$	eléctrico	recently $'ri:sntli$	recientemente
electronics $i'lektrɔniks$	electrónico	soleright $soul\ rait$	monopolio
foundation $faun'deiʃən$	fundación	television set $'teli'viʒən\ set$	televisor, telerreceptor
get rid $get\ rid$	deshacerse	televisor $'televaizə*$	televisor
gradually $'grædjuəli$	gradualmente	to be fun $fʌn$	estar divertido
hitherto $'hiðə'tu:$	hasta aquí	to view $vju:$	contemplar, ver
improvement $im'pru:vmənt$	mejora	up-to-date $'ʌptudeit$	moderno
interference $intə'fiərəns$	interferencia	wireless set $'waiə:les$	aparato de radio
machine $mə'ʃi:n$	máquina		
model $mɔdl$	modelo		

Reading exercise

Nowadays, an English house is considered old-fashioned if it does not have a television. At any rate, its popularity has recently led to the foundation of several private organizations which produce programmes now, where hitherto the B. B. C. (British Broadcasting Corporation) had the sole right. Also, the demand for television sets has been so great, that for a long time, the most up-to-date models have been gradually becoming comparatively less expensive. Of course, that means that many people are getting rid of their old wireless sets and getting the new televisor.

Besides, present improvements in electronics are getting rid of the nuisance of the local interference from other electrical machines, and certainly in some years time we will be able to view any station we wish in colour.

To learn by heart

I have been wondering 'wʌndəriŋ...   Me he estado preguntando...
To ring up.   Telefonear.
To ring off.   Colgar, cortar la comunicación.
To come to the point pɔint.   Ir al asunto, ir al grano.

The daffodils   Los narcisos

I wandered [1] lonely as a cloud [2]
That floats [3] on high over vales [4] and hills,
When all at once I saw a crowd [5],
A host [6] of golden [7] daffodils,
Beside the lake, beneath the trees,
Fluttering [8] and dancing [9] in the breeze [10].

W. WORDSWORTH

1. Wander 'wɔndə* vagar. 2. Cloud klaud nube. 3. Float flout flotar. 4. Vales veilz valles. 5. Crowd kraud multitud. 6. Host houst hueste. 7. Golden 'gouldən doradas. 8. Flutter 'flʌtə* agitarse. 9. Dance daːns bailar. 10. Breeze briːz brisa.

Vocabulario

absurdo	absurd əb'səːd	ojalá, quisiera...	I wish ... ai'wiʃ
admitir	admit əd'mit	salir para	to leave for tu liːv fɔː*
aprobar (examen)	to get through		

Ejercicio

Si aún viviera, confirmaría mis palabras. Salgo de Madrid para Barcelona en avión. Pruébese el abrigo para ver si le sienta bien. Ha sido un viaje delicioso y no tan caro como creíamos. Es realmente muy agradable viajar en tren. Estudia mucho para que puedas aprobar los exámenes. Si sucediera así sería completamente feliz. ¡Ojalá no hubiera estado enfermo! Me preguntó si había pedido prestado el paraguas. Aunque fuera extranjero se le hubiera concedido el premio. Esta historia es demasiado absurda para que la crea. Que salga el que lo sepa hacer. Si tuviéramos dinero, compraríamos un coche. Habla el alemán como si hubiera nacido en Alemania. Lo admite como si fuera verdad. El que haya obtenido premio podrá tomarse unos días de fiesta. Pienso hacer el viaje en avión en vez de barco, aunque sea más caro; no me asusta volar y es mucho más rápido.

THIRTY-FOURTH LESSON
LECCIÓN TRIGÉSIMA CUARTA

El infinitivo

El infinitivo es la parte del verbo que expresa la acción sin referencia a tiempo ni a persona: «to go, to walk», «ir, andar». Va usualmente precedido de la preposición «to».

El infinitivo puede usarse como sujeto:

> To swim is good for the health.
> To eat is necessary.

Puede también usarse como complemento:

> I would like to swim well.
> John wants to learn English.
> He expects to have a price.
> Have you told him to play the piano?

El infinitivo se usa también en forma de perfecto:

| He seems to have gone already. | Parece que ya ha ido (haber ido). |
| He ought to have taken the book to Peter. | Tendría que haber llevado el libro a Pedro. |

El infinitivo puede usarse en inglés en voz pasiva, que se traduce por infinitivo simple:

| This house is to let. | Esta casa está por alquilar. |
| This picture is to be sold. | Este cuadro es para vender. |

La preposición «to» que generalmente precede al infinitivo se omite cuando el infinitivo sea complemento de uno de los verbos siguientes:

a) «Shall», «will», «may», ya sean auxiliares, ya sean verbos principales:

> He shall go now.
> I will not see him.
> You may come if you like.
> She says that she might come.

b) «Can», «must», «dare», «need», «make», «bid» (ordenar):

> I cannot do it.
> You must give it to her.
> I dare not say so.
> They need not come unless they want to.
> You make me angry æŋgri
> I bid you come.
> Rain makes flowers grow.

Pero después de «need» y «dare», en frases afirmativas e interrogativas, el infinitivo se usa precedido de «to»:

> Do you need to go out now?
> He dares to go out.

c) Después de «let», auxiliar de imperativo, también se omite «to»:

> Let me go.

d) Tampoco se usa después de ciertos verbos de percepción:

> I have *heard* her sing that song before.
> I *watched* her walk in the garden.
> I *beheld* (vi) the sun rise.
> I have *know* him do it before.

El infinitivo puede también emplearse como complemento indirecto del verbo principal. En este caso constituye la llamada oración de infinitivo:

> I don't want him to go to Paris.
> I want you to stay here.
> Mother wants you to come.

El infinitivo inglés se traduce, entonces, al español por un subjuntivo: «No quiero que vaya a París», «Quiero que te quedes aquí», «Madre quiere que vengas».

Los verbos «to have» y «to be» seguidos de infinitivo corresponden a los tiempos de obligación españoles «haber de» y «tener que»:

I have to see him before tomorrow.	He de verle antes de mañana.
I had to tell him the news.	Hube de darle la noticia.
I am to go at once	He de ir inmediatamente

Las expresiones españolas «estar para», «ir a», se traducen al inglés por «to be about» [əbaut] o «to be going»

El infinitivo

seguidos de infinitivo. «Acabar de» se traduce por «to have just» seguido de participio de pasado:

I was going to leave here.	Iba a marcharme de aquí.
I was about to tell you.	Estaba para decírtelo.
She had just told them when you arrived.	Acababa de decírselo cuando tú llegaste.

Words

declare *di'klɛə*	declarar	the day after tomorrow *ðə dei 'a:ftə* tə'mɔrou*	pasado mañana
expect *iks'pekt*	esperar		
pictures *'piktʃəz*	cine		
Post Office *poust 'ɔfis*	correo	to care *tu kɛə*	importar
		witness *'witnis*	testigo

Exercise

I don't know what is to be done with that boy, he is always ill. The witness declared this to be true. The teacher ordered the lesson to be read by Peter. There was no room for the car to go through. Is this house to let? I don't think so; I think it is to be sold. I wish it were to let, for I would like to rent it (alquilarla). Rain makes everything grow. It is necessary to live. Without it we would all die. Didn't you hear him tell you to close the door? Do you want me to come with you to the Post Office? No, I want you to take Mike to the pictures. I expect he didn't come in time. I think he wants to go to play with his friends. I have heard him come. Shall I ask him? Yes, please do. I heard him say that he could not come to-day. He will come the day after tomorrow. I like to read, but I don't like to study my lessons. Would you like to learn English? I want to see her before she goes away. We did not see the boy go; he must have gone before we arrived. Will mother let you come? Did they want you to come with us? I don't care what they think, but I don't want to go out with them.

Words

apparently *ə'pærəntli*	al parecer	at present *'prezənt*	ahora
as a matter of fact *æs ə mætə* ov fækt*	en realidad	by the way *wei*	a propósito
		collect *kə'lekt*	recoger
aspirin *əs'pirin*	aspirina	complain of *kəm'plein*	quejarse de

couple 'kʌpl	par
epidemic epi-'demik	epidemia
excepting ik-'septiŋ	exceptuando
fever 'fiːvə*	fiebre
get on get ɔn	continuar
hallo hə'lou	hola
headache 'hedeik	dolor de cabeza
hot-water-bottle hɔt 'wɔːtə* 'bɔtl	bolsa de agua caliente (para la cama)
illness ilnis	enfermedad
influenza, 'flu influ'enzə	gripe
measles 'miːzəlz	sarampión
medicine 'med(i)sin	medicina
order 'ɔːdə*	ordenar, mandar
overnight 'ouvə*nait	durante la noche
persuade pə-'sweid	persuadir
prescription pris'kripʃən	receta
recover ri'kʌvə*	restablecerse
recurrence ri-'kʌrəns	recaída
rely ri'lai on	confiar
scarlet fever 'skaːlit 'fiːvə*	escarlatina
send for	enviar a buscar
serious 'siəriəs	grave
severe si'viə*	doloroso
sore throat 'sɔː θrout	dolor de garganta
symptom 'sim(p)təm	síntoma
temperature 'tempritʃə	temperatura
to be careful tu biː 'kɛəːful	tener cuidado
to be grieved tu biː 'griːvd	estar apenado, afligido
to be off tu biː ɔːf	salir, marchar(se)
to run a temperature	tener fiebre
touch of 'tʌtʃ ov	ataque ligero (de enfermedad)
trust trʌst	confiar

Conversation

Illness

A. Hallo Mrs. Smith, how are you?
B. I am very well, thank you, but my daughter is not so well. She complained of a severe headache yesterday, so I put her to bed with a hot-water-bottle and a couple of aspirins. But she seems to have developed a high temperature overnight, so I persuaded her to stay in bed.
A. Oh, I am sorry. Perharps she has a touch of influenza; there is an epidemic going about. Have you called your Doctor?
B. Oh yes. As a matter of fact, I'm just off now to collect the prescription. I asked the Doctor if it might be a recurrence of the scarlet-fever that my daughter has just had, but apparently the symptoms are different. It is really the first illness in the family since my baby

Michael had measles. Excepting hers, last month, of course!
A. Well, I trust it will be the last for a time. I hope that your daughter recovers soon and when she does, perhaps you could take her away for a little holiday. It would do you both a world of good.

Y. By the way, did you know that Helen's boy is not very well?
Z. No, I didn't. I'm so sorry to hear that. I hope it's nothing serious?
Y. We don't know yet. We have sent for the Doctor and he only said that he must stay in bed and be kept very quiet. Which is most difficult, indeed.
Z. But what symptoms does he show?
Y. He complains of a bad headache and a sorethroat, and he runs a temperature.
Z. It must be a touch of 'flu. There is a lot of it about. It is not a bad epidemic, still, you have to be careful.
Y. Well, we can't say, just at present. We must wait and see. The Doctor has not ordered any medecine except aspirin to keep the temperature down.
Z. I hope he will recover soon. You will let me hear how he is getting on?
Y. Certainly. I will. Rely on me.

Two short stories

A lazy man who thought that he would become[1] a beggar[2] rather than find himself a job[3], stood at a street corner[4] pretending[5] to be dumb[6]. Day after day he stood there, and he got quite a lot of money. One day, a passer-by[7] who knew the beggar by sight went up to him and said: «Have you been dumb long, my good man?» The beggar, taken unawares[8], replied: «Oh, ever since an accident ten years ago.»

---

1. Become *bi'kʌm* convertirse en. 2. Beggar *'begaː** pordiosero. 3. Job *dʒɔb* empleo. 4. Corner *kɔːnə** esquina. 5. Pretend *printend* fingir. 6. Dumb *dʌm* mudo. 7. Passer-by *paːsə* bai* transeúnte. 8. Unawares *ʌnæ'wɛəːs* desprevenido.

King William the third was once upon a march[1] for some secret[2] expedition[3]. He was entreated[4] by one of his generals to tell him what he intented to do but the king would not tell him. So, instead of giving him the answer he asked him: «Can you keep a secret?» The general said he could. Then the king said: «Well, so can I when I have to.»

1. March *ma:tʃ* marcha. 2. Secret *sikrit* secreto. 3. Expedition *ekspi'diʃən* expedición. 4. Entreat *intri:t* rogar.

To learn by heart

My heart[1] leaps[2] up when I behold[3]
A rainbow[4] in the sky:
So was it when my life began,
So it is now I am a man,
So be it when I shall grow old[5]
Or let me die!

W. Wordsworth

1. Heart *ha:t* corazón. 2. Leap *li:p* saltar. 3. Behold *bi'hould* veo. 4. Rainbow *'reinbou* arco iris. 5. Grow old *grou ould* envejecer.

Said the robin[1] to the sparrow[2]:
«I should really like to know
Why these anxious[3] human beings
Rush about[4] and worry so.»
Said the sparrow to the robin:
«Friend, I think that it must be
That they have no Heavenly[5] Father
Such as cares for[6] you and me.»

1. Robin *'rɔbin* petirrojo. 2. Sparrow *'spærou* gorrión. 3. Anxious *'æŋkʃəs* inquieto. 4. Rush about *rʌʃ ə'baut* precipitarse. 5. Heavenly *'hevnli* celestial. 6. Care for *kɛə* fɔ:* preocuparse.

Ejercicio

El granjero esperaba que el niño obedeciera su orden y que no permitiera a los cazadores entrar en su campo. Sé que esto es verdad. No puedo admitir que el prisionero sea inocente. Este valiente soldado ha combatido en muchas batallas, y no ha sido vencido nunca. He tenido el placer de ver una película excepcional. El abogado necesita tomarse unas vacaciones. Pide a tus padres que te perdonen *(to forgive you)* por tu desobediencia. Los vecinos me permitieron que usara su teléfono. Déjame ver esta fotografía, por favor. Tomás pidió a Isabel que bailara. ¿Me permite que use su pluma?

THIRTY-FIFTH LESSON
LECCIÓN TRIGÉSIMA QUINTA

Participio y gerundio

El participio puede ser de presente: «having», «walking», y de pasado: «had», «walked». El de pasado se emplea:

a) para formar los tiempos de perfecto:

I have bought a book.	He comprado un libro.
I shall have gone to London.	Habré ido a Londres.

b) para formar la voz pasiva:

We are loved by our parents.	Somos amados por nuestros padres.
We shall be given a book.	Nos darán un libro.

c) como adjetivo, con las mismas funciones que éste:

A faded flower *feidid flauə**.	Una flor marchita.
A broken glass.	Un cristal roto.
The flowers are faded.	Las flores están marchitas.

El participio de presente se emplea:

a) para hacer la forma progresiva:

> I am going to London.
> I shall not be coming to the cinema.

b) como adjetivo, con igual función que éste: calificar al nombre, ser modificado por un adverbio, sustituir a un nombre y admitir grados de comparación.

The barking dog frightened me *'ba:kiŋ dɔg 'fraitnd mi*.	El perro que ladraba me asustó.
The soldier was in an almost dying state *'daiiŋ steit*.	El soldado estaba en estado casi moribundo.
He shall come to judge the living and the dead.	Vendrá a juzgar a los vivos y a los muertos.
This picture is more striking *straikiŋ* than the other one.	Este cuadro es más sorprendente que el otro.

El participio puede equivaler a una cláusula adverbial de razón, tiempo, condición, etc.

>Reading that book you will learn a lot of things.
>While you are reading that book, you will learn...
>Having met Mary, we went to the pictures.
>After I had met Mary, we went to the pictures...
>Turning to the right you will find the Post Office.
>If you turn to the right you will find the Post Office.

Obsérvense las expresiones:

| A well-read *red* man. | Un hombre culto. |
| A well-behaved boy *bi'heivd bɔi*. | Un niño bien educado. |

El gerundio ejerce la función de un nombre. Si el verbo es transitivo retiene además su función verbal y puede tener un complemento.

| He likes riding. | Le gusta montar (a caballo). |
| He loves eating pears. | Le gusta comer peras. |

El gerundio, siendo equivalente a un nombre, puede estar regido por una preposición, y puede estar precedido del artículo:

| Instead of writing a card ring them up. | En lugar de escribirles una tarjeta, telefonéales. |
| I am engaged in knitting of a jumper *dʒʌmpə**. | Estoy ocupada tejiendo un jersey. |

El gerundio puede ser sujeto y complemento del verbo:

| Killing animals is cruel. | Matar animales es cruel. |
| He enjoys swimming. | Disfruta nadando. |

A veces la preposición que rige el gerundio no se traduce al castellano.

| He scaped *skeipt* by quickly *'kwikli* jumping over a wall. | Escapó saltando de prisa por encima de un muro. |

Si un nombre de persona o de animal precede a un gerundio, dicho nombre suele ponerse en genitivo o posesivo.

| This is my brother's doing. | Esto es obra de mi hermano. |
| I am sorry at his going away. | Siento que se vaya. |

Participio y gerundio

Nótese que la misma forma puede ser participio y gerundio según el uso.

Gerundio: A walking stick.   Un bastón (para caminar).
A bathing suit.   Un traje de baño (para bañarse).
Participio: A fading flower.   Una flor que se marchita.
A floating raft *ə floutiŋ ra:ft.*   Una balsa flotante.

Words

according *ə'kɔ:diŋ*	según	pitch *pitʃ*	tono
clear *kliə*	clara	purpose *pə:pəs*	propósito
costume *'kɔstju:m*	traje	raise *reiz*	elevar
distinctly *dis'tiŋtli*	con claridad	remark *ri'ma:k*	observación
forecast *'fɔrəka:st*	previsión	run away *rʌn ə'wei*	escapar
interrupt *intə'rʌpt*	interrumpir	voice *vɔis*	voz
left *left*	dejar, marchar(se)	walking tour *'wɔ:kiŋ tuə*	excursión a pie
message *'mesidʒ*	mensaje	weather *'weðə*	tiempo

Exercise

They insisted on my going to London with them. What is that big building over there? Oh, that is the General Post Office, and that one next to it will be a bank. He interrupted his reading for the purpose of making a remark. When you have finished speaking, I shall say what I have to say. There is no need for raising your voice above the natural pitch; I can hear you quite well. After waiting a little longer we left a message and left. I, being your father, know best what is good for you. We could not help laughing at his words. He sounded so amusing! We have finished doing what we had to do, so now we shall be going home. He ran away by jumping over the fence. On arriving in London I will send a wire. Having finished lunch he began to read the paper. He came running up the garden path (sendero). We don't mind going to the pictures, only let it be a nice film. Would you mind opening that window? Speaking distinctly, in a natural clear voice, is a sign of distinction (distinción). According to the weather forecast it is going to snow. Seeing is believing. Have you got your bathing costume here? We could go for a swim before lunch. I sat for an hour waiting for your brother but he didn't come.

What are you doing now? I am finishing my home work for tomorrow. Peter and I may be going on a walking tour next Summer. Are you coming? I'm sorry, I can't just now. I am finishing a letter, but I shall be coming as soon as I have finished it.

Vocabulario

afición, diversión favorita	hobby 'hɔbi	tranvía	tramway, tram 'træmwei
poesía	poetry 'pouitri	Universidad	University ju(ː)ni'vəːsiti
siga	go on gou ɔn		
tanto tiempo	so long sou lɔŋ		

Ejercicio

Se ha ido sin decir adiós. Andar es para mí un gran placer. Al llegar al hotel llamaré por teléfono a mi amigo Juan. A mi hermano le gusta cazar, es su diversión preferida. Después de esperar el tranvía un cuarto de hora, llegó completamente lleno. Se quedó a jugar en vez de ir a la Universidad. Estaba pensando en *(about)* la película que vi ayer. Mi hermana es muy aficionada a la pintura. En casa nos gusta desayunar a las ocho. Siga escribiendo, por favor. Ver es creer. Antes de empezar el ejercicio cierre el libro. Venga cuando haya terminado de leer toda la poesía. Después de hablar tanto tiempo no dijo nada interesante.

Words

actually 'æktʃuəli	de hecho	cut off	cortar (comunicación)
automatic ɔːtə-'mætik	automático	dial 'daiəl	marcar (número)
avoid ə'vɔid	evitar	disconnect diskə'nekt	desconectar
bright brait	brillante, vívido	engaged in-'geidʒd	comunica (el teléfono)
brushes brʌʃiz	cepillos		
button bʌtn	botón	event i'vent	caso, acontecimiento
buzz bʌz	zumbido		
call kɔːl	llamada (telefónica)	exchange iks-'tʃeindʒ	central (teléfonos)
call-box	cabina	get back get bæk	devolver
characteristic kæriktə'ristik	característico	hang up hæŋ ʌp	colgar
		helpful helpful	servicial
completely kəm'pliːtli	completamente	hold hould	coger, asir
conversation 'kɔnvə'seiʃən	conversación	hold on the line	no se retire
		interrupt intə-'rʌpt	interrumpir
corner 'kɔːnə*	esquina		

lettered *letə*d*	marcado con la letra ...
lift *lift*	levantar
line *lain*	línea
microphone *'maikrəfoun*	micrófono
nail-polish *'neilpɔliʃ*	barniz de uñas
natural *'nætʃrəl*	natural
noise *nɔiz*	ruido
note *nout*	nota
obtain *əb'tein*	obtener
operator *'ɔpəreitə**	telefonista
order *'ɔːdə**	pedido
painted *'peintid*	pintada
pause *pɔːz*	pausa
phone *foun*	teléfono
place *pleis*	colocar
press *pres*	apretar
price *prais* list	lista de precios
proceed *prə'siːd*	proceder
properly *'prɔːpəli*	correctamente, bien
provided *prə'vaidid*	siempre que
public *'pʌblik*	público
receiver *ri'siːvə**	receptor
require *ri'kwaiə**	necesita
rest *rest*	soporte
rhythmic *'riθmik*	rítmico
right away *rait ə'wei*	en seguida
sample *'sampl*	muestra
situated *'sitjueitit*	situada
slot *slɔt*	ranura
sort *sɔːt*	especie
sound *saund*	sonido
state *steit*	indicar (decir)
subscriber *səb'skraibə**	abonado
talk *tɔːk*	hablar
telephone *'telifoun*	teléfono
warehouse *'wɛəhaus*	almacén
working	funcionando
you are through *ju: aː θruː*	(ya) tiene conexión

Reading exercise

The public telephone

In most large English towns the telephone is completely automatic; that means that you do not have to ask an operator to get you the number you want. The call-box is painted bright red and is usually situated at the corner of a busy street. When you want to ring up someone, you first lift the receiver from the rest, then place 4 pennies in the slot and dial the number you require. When you hear somebody answer the phone at the other end, you press the button lettered A, and proceed to talk into the microphone. If on dialling your number you do not hear the characteristic rhythmic noise (brrr-brrr-pause-brrr-brrr-pause), a sort of buzzing sound, but instead you hear a series of high pitched sounds on the same note, which means that the number you want is engaged, you press the button lettered B, and you will get back your 4 pennies. That means that the line is engaged. You may press this button and receive your money back at any time provided that you have not pressed button A; so that if you have made a mistake in dialling your number and the person answering is helpful enough to state the number you have actually dialled before you have pressed button A, you may get your money back.

Conversation

It may happen that the telephone is not working properly and you will be unable to obtain your number by dialling. It may also happen that the apparatus is not automatic. In such an event, you must dial O, that is the exchange, and speak to the operator. Your conversation will then go something like this:

Operator: Number, please?

Subscriber: 20504 (two, 0, five, 0, four) please. (Or if you are in a city like London where letters are used: BAYSWATER 0504.)

Operator: The number is engaged, I'm sorry.

Subscriber: Will you call me when it is free? My number is Kensington 2355 (two, three, double five).

Operator: I have your call to Bayswater 0504 now.

Subscriber: Thank you.

Operator: You're through.

Subscriber: Is that Messrs. Jones & Co? I want to speak to Mr. Robertson.

Mr. Robertson: Hallo, Robertson here.

Subscriber: Green and Sons speaking. Would you send a box of sample brushes to our warehouse as soon as you can. I might have a big order for you.

Mr. Robertson: Certainly, I'll do that right away.

Mr. Green: Thank you very much. Could you send us also your price list for your new nail-polish?

Mr. Robertson: Do you mean the new «Sports Girl»?

Mr Green: That's right.

Mr. Robertson: Very well. I shall enclose the list together with a sample bottle.

Mr. Green: Thank you very much. Good-bye.

Words

box *bɔks*	palco	shocking *'ʃɔkiŋ*	chocante
company *'kʌmpəni*	compañía	smile *smail*	sonrisa
enter *entə**	entrar	to address *ə'dres*	dirigirse
humour *'hju:mə**	humor	to blush *blʌʃ*	ruborizarse
inform *in'fɔ:m*	informar	to pray *prei*	rogar
Lordship *'lɔ:dʃip*	señoría	to reply *ri'plai*	replicar
monster *'mɔnstə**	monstruo	to stammer *'stæmə**	balbucear
opposite *'ɔpəzit*	opuesto (delante)	to turn *tə:n*	volver(se)
scarlet *'ska:lit*	escarlata	ugly *'ʌgli*	feo, -a

Exercise

A gentleman, sitting at the theatre in one of the boxes in company with Lord North, not knowing his Lordship, entered into conversation with him, and seeing two ladies come into an opposite box, turned to him, and addressed him with: «Pray, sir, can you inform me who is that ugly woman who has just come in?» «Oh», replied his Lordship with great good humour, «I can, that is my wife». The gentleman blushed scarlet, and replied stammering: «Sir, I ask your pardon ... I ... I don't ... I don't mean her, I mean that ... that shocking monster who is with her.» «That», replied his Lordship with a smile, «is my daugther».

To learn by heart

Happy birthday to you.	Feliz cumpleaños.
Happy feast *fi:st*.	Felicidades (por el santo).
Congratulations *kəngrætju'leiʃəns!*	¡Enhorabuena!
Have a good time!	¡Que se divierta!

Night

The sun descending in the west,
The evening star does shine;
The birds are silent in their nest,
And I must seek [1] for mine.
The moon like a flower
In heaven's high bower [2]
With silent delight.
Sits and smiles on the night.

1. Seek *si:k* buscar. 2. Bower *'bauə** cenador, glorieta.

THIRTY-SIXTH LESSON
LECCIÓN TRIGÉSIMA SEXTA

Verbos impersonales

Se llaman verbos impersonales los que se emplean solamente en la tercera persona del singular con el pronombre neutro «it» como sujeto, en infinitivo y en participio.

It annoys ə'nɔiz me very much. — Me molesta mucho.
It seems that he was right. — Parece que tenía razón.

El verbo «to be» se emplea frecuentemente con carácter impersonal, acompañado del adverbio «there» en lugar del pronombre «it», y corresponde al verbo español «haber» impersonal. Se conjuga sólo en tercera persona singular y plural. Las formas interrogativa y negativa se hacen como las de «to be»: «is there?», «¿hay?»; «there is not», «no hay». Véase la conjugación completa de esta forma en la página 115.

There is a mouse in the kitchen kitʃən. — Hay un ratón en la cocina.
Was there a doctor there? — ¿Había un médico allí?
There wil be many *meni* birds bə:ds in that cage keidʒ. — Habrá muchos pájaros en esa jaula.
There were men in those times, who... — En aquellos tiempos hubo hombres que...
Will there be a great feast in Barcelona? — ¿Habrá una gran fiesta en Barcelona?
There are two dogs in the courtyard 'kɔ:tja:d. — Hay dos perros en el patio.

Verbo «to be» impersonal

En inglés, la forma impersonal es más frecuente que en español, empleándose en oraciones que en castellano requieren una forma personal.

It was she who told me. — Ella fue la que me lo dijo.
It will be we... — Seremos nosotros...
It will be they. — Serán ellos.

El verbo «to be» con carácter impersonal se emplea en inglés para expresar el estado físico o atmosférico.

It is cold *kould*, warm *wɔːm*.   Hace frío, calor.
It was windy, foggy *'fɔgi*.   Hacía viento, había niebla.

Verbo TO RAIN, llover

INDICATIVE		INFINITIVE
Present lleve It rains.	*Pres. perfect* ha llovido It has rained.	*Present* llover To rain.
Past llovía, llovió It rained.	*Past perfect* ha llovido It had rained.	*Past* haber llovido To have rained.
Future lloverá It will rain.	*Fut. perfect* habrá llovido It will have rained.	PARTICIPLE
		Pres. part. lloviendo Raining.
Conditional llovería It would rain.	*Cond. perfect* habría llovido It would have rained.	*Past. part.* llovido Rained.

Los más comunes entre los verbos de tiempo son:

to snow *snou* nevar	it snows, nieva
to rain *rein* llover	it rains, llueve
to hail *heil* granizar	it hails, graniza
to lighten *laitn* relampaguear	it lightens, relampaguea
to freeze *friːz* helar	it freezes, hiela
to thunder *'θʌndə** tronar	it thunders, truena
to drizzle *drizl* lloviznar	it drizzles *drizlz* llovizna
to thaw *θɔː* deshelar	it thaws, deshiela
to dawn *dɔːn* alborear	it dawns, alborea
to grow dark, anochecer	it grows dark, anochece

Los verbos citados arriba, excepto «to freeze», «to lighten», «to grow dark», se emplean también, sin alteración de forma, como sustantivos («the thunder, the snow», etc.).

Nótese: «the frost», «el hielo»; «the lightning» [′laitniŋ] «el relámpago»; «the darkness», «las tinieblas». «Un relámpago», «a flash [flæʃ] of lightning»; «los relámpagos», «the flashes of lightning»; «el rayo», «the thunderbolt»; «una tronada», «a thunderclap» [′θʌndəklæp].

That house was struck by lightning.	Un rayo cayó sobre esa casa.

Para expresar el tiempo transcurrido desde un momento pasado determinado hasta el momento de hablar, se emplea «since» con el verbo «to be» en tercera persona del singular y con el pronombre impersonal «it». El verbo ha de estar siempre en afirmativo:

It is two years since I (last) saw her.	Hace dos años que no la veo.
It is three days since he went off *sins hi: went o:f.*	Hace tres días que se fue.

Para expresiones de distancia se emplea una forma semejante:

It is 360 miles from Paris to London.	Hay 360 millas de P. a L.

Las locuciones de tiempo pasado con «ha hace» se traducen por «ago» [ə′gou] pospuesto a la indicación de tiempo.

Ten years ago.	Hace diez años
I went to London three weeks ago.	Fui a Londres hace tres semanas.

Cuando se quiera hacer referencia, no al momento pasado en que empezó la acción, sino a todo el tiempo transcurrido desde entonces hasta el momento en que se habla, se usa en inglés una forma personal seguida de la preposición «for»:

I have lived here for a year.	Hace un año que vivo aquí (o he vivido aquí durante un año).
I have not played tennis for a long time.	Hace mucho tiempo que no juego al tenis.
I have not seen him for years	Hace años que no le veo (le he visto)

Verbos impersonales

Los verbos siguientes, y algunos más, pueden emplearse con carácter impersonal y personal:

to look, parecer	it looks, parece
to grow, aumentar, crecer	it grows, aumenta, crece
to happen *hæpn* acontecer	it happens, acontece
to seem *tu si:m* parecer	it seems, parece
to begin *tu bi'gin* empezar	it begins, empieza
to become *tu bi'kʌm* convenir, llegar a ser, convertirse (en)	it becomes, sienta bien, llega a ser, se convierte (en)

It looks as if it were going to rain.	Parece que va a llover.
They look guilty.	Parece que son culpables.
It is growing dark.	Está oscureciendo.
That child is growing very fast.	Este niño crece muy de prisa.
It happened to be Monday.	Sucedió que era lunes.
I happen to be present.	Aconteció que estaba presente.
It seems all right.	Parece que está bien.
They seem to be right.	Parece que ellos tienen razón.
It began to rain.	Empezó a llover.
We shall begin a new chapter.	Empezaremos un nuevo capítulo.
It is most becoming.	Es muy favorecedor (sienta muy bien).
He became a Doctor.	Se hizo médico.

Las expresiones «se dice», «se espera», «se cree», se traducen por pasiva con el pronombre neutro «it»:

It is said...	Se dice...
It is hoped...	Se espera...
It is expected...	Se espera...

La forma impersonal con «se» puede también traducirse sustituyendo «it» por «people»:

People said so.	La gente lo decía.
People talked and laughed.	La gente charlaba y reía.

Los verbos de tiempo, «to be cold», «to be hot», usados en forma personal, significan «tener frío», «tener calor»:

I am cold.	Tengo frío.
I am hot.	Tengo calor.

Obsérvense las expresiones siguientes:

I have a cold.	Tengo un enfriamiento (tengo un resfriado).
I've got a cold.	Tengo un enfriamiento.

To catch cold. Coger un enfriamiento.
I like it here. Me gusta este lugar (aquí).
Afterwards, there was Luego se bailó.
dancing.

Words

cloudy 'klaudi	nublado	thunderstorm 'θʌndəstɔːm	temporal, tormenta
draught drɑːft	corriente (de aire)	to clear up kliːr 'ʌp	serenarse
flake fleik	copo	to damage 'dæmidʒ	dañar
flood flʌd	inundación	to pour pɔə*	llover a cántaros
heat hiːt	calor	turn təːn	turno
hurricane 'hʌrikən	huracán	weather 'weðə*	tiempo (atmosférico)
lightning-rod 'laitniŋrɔd	pararrayo	wet through θruː	calados hasta los huesos
nasty 'nɑːsti	asqueroso, malo	what is the matter with...?	¿que le ocurre a...?
pane pein	cristal		
peasant 'pezənt	campesino	what is the weather like?	¿qué tiempo hace?
risk	riesgo		
shade ʃeid	sombra		
sultry 'sʌltri	sofocante		

Exercise

I am afraid it will rain, the wind is in the South. The weather is cloudy, I hope it will clear up this afternoon. Ninety-five degrees in the shade! We shall have a thunderstorm. It is lightening and thundering; this thunderstorm is not yet past. What do you think of the weather? I expect we shall have a wet day. What a rain! We are wet through. Is it raining? Yes, it is; it is pouring. Did it freeze last night? Yes, it did. It has frozen; how bitterly cold it is! The rain has fallen down in torrents. It is snowing. It is freezing as hard as it can. From where does the wind come? It is from the North. The wind has changed, it has abated (calmado); it was a hurricane. Do you think it will be bad to-morrow? No, I don't think so, the barometer has risen. What nasty weather! I got a very bad cold in this weather. Please, shut the window, it is windy; there is a draught in this room.

Is it long since you saw him? It is about six months. Whose turn is it? (¿A quién le toca?) It is mine. It is beginning to rain. Yesterday it snowed the whole day. I think it will hail tomorrow. Why do you think it will hail? Because it is so stormy and sultry to-day. It has been lightening the whole night. Did you hear thunderclaps? Yes; a thunderbolt struck a peasant's hut ([hʌt] choza) and the church. Were they damaged? The former, yes; but the latter was protected by the lightning-rod. How far is it from here to Florence? It is 400 kilometers. What is the matter with your sister (with you, with them). She is not feeling very well, to-day. It happened that a pane of glass broke, and it seemed as if a pistol were shot. What is the weather like? It is very bad, but it seems to be getting better (está mejorando). What is the weather like in your part of the country? It is always nice. It is not fine. It is windy.

Vocabulario

a eso de	about ə'baut	jaula	cage keidʒ
a menudo	often ɔfn	locos y sabios	foolish and wise waiz
diablo	devil 'devil		
dos horas seguidas	two hours consecutively	mientras	while hwail
		regañar	to scold skould
en todo caso	in any case keis	suceder	to take place
entrar en	to enter		

Ejercicio

¿Llueve? Sí, llueve a cántaros. Llovió ayer también. ¿Nieva? Creo que nieva; en todo caso, hace una hora ha nevado. Yo no lo he visto; ¿ha nevado mucho? No, [no] ha nevado sino (only) un poco. ¿Relampaguea? Sí, relampaguea y truena; hay tormenta. Hay muchas tormentas este año; ayer tronó y relampagueó dos horas. Hoy hace buen tiempo; ayer hacía demasiado calor (it was too warm). ¿Cuántos pájaros hay en la jaula? Hay cinco (en ella). Siempre ha habido en el mundo locos y sabios. No había agua en el vaso. ¿Habrá bastante vino en la botella? Creo que sí (I think so). ¿Qué hora es? Son las cuatro. A eso de las cinco me despiertas, si no llueve. ¿Crees que lloverá? No creo que llueva. Aquí graniza muy a menudo. Hoy hiela y ayer heló también. ¿Oíste tronar anoche? No, no lo oí. Parece que hará buen tiempo. No puedo ir a verte porque tengo un enfriamiento y no puedo salir. Cierra esa ventana; hay corriente en esta habitación y cogerás un enfriamiento. ¿Crees que va a llover? Me parece que sí. ¿Hay algo en casa para comer? Sí, hay pan y mantequilla, queso, fruta y leche. ¿Cuántas personas hay en esta oficina? Creo que hay cinco hombres y tres mujeres.

Words

around ə'raund	alrededor	occasional	intermitente, ocasional
as long as æz lɔŋ æz	(siempre que) en cuanto	ə'keiʒənəl	
barometer be-'rɔmətə*	barómetro	outlook 'autluk	previsión
		periods 'piəriəds	preiodos
		pond pɔnd	estanque
blow blou	soplar	pour pɔː*	llover mucho
bright brait	brillante, despejado	rapid 'ræpid	rápido
		renowned ri'naund	renombrado, conocido
changeable 'tʃeindʒəbəl	cambiable		
		shelter ʃeltə*	cobijo, guarecerse
clap of thunder	trueno	shine ʃain	brillar
dangerous 'deindʒrəs	peligroso	shower 'ʃauə*	chaparrón
		skate skeit	patinar
degree di'griː	grado	ski ski	patinar
easterly 'iːtəli	del este, de levante	surely ʃuə*li	seguramente
		sort sɔːt	especie, clase
fast faːst	rápidamente	temperature 'tempritʃə*	temperatura
fog fɔg	niebla		
foggy fɔgi	lleno de niebla	thermometer θə'mɔmətə*	termómetro
follow 'fɔlou	seguir		
forecast fɔːkaːst	previsión del tiempo	to consider kə'nsidə*	considerar
frozen frɔːzn	helado	torrent 'tɔrənt	torrente
hard haːd	mucho, duro	unbearable ʌn'bɛərəbl	insoportable
heat hiːt	calor		
ice ais	hielo	unsettled 'ʌn'setld	inseguro
interval 'intəvəl	intervalo		
just now	ahora mismo	warm wɔːm	caliente, templado
local 'loukəl	local	warmer 'wɔːmə*	más templado
mainly meinli	principalmente	what sort of	qué (clase de)
mild maild	templado	windy 'windi	hace viento
mist mist	neblina	zero 'ziːrou	cero

Conversation

A. What sort of weather have you been having in Barcelona?

B. Well, the sun has been shining everyday for as long as I can remember. The temperature has been around 75 degrees Fahrenheit, in the shade, every day. Occasionally, however, it gets cloudy, the barometer falls rapidly, and lightning flashes can be seen. That is the time to take shelter as fast as possible, for thunder claps

and a torrent of rain follow very quickly. And what is the weather like in London?
A. Well, England is renowned for its changeable weather. Just now, it is cloudy and an easterly wind is blowing hard. But the forecast says that the weather will clear up, and there will be bright periods. Yesterday it was rather foggy and there was a little drizzle.
B. Surely, the weather is quite misty at this time of the year. From the way that Spanish people talk about English weather, we would suppose that you had frost, snow and ice in the Summer.
A. Ha! Ha! Actually, we do not get enough snow to make a sport of skiing in this country; and the ponds are so seldom frozen over that most parents consider them too dangerous for their children to skate upon.

Weather forecast

Today's weather: Light westerly winds; mainly clouded; occasional rain; local morning fog; rather misty.
Further outlook: Unsettled; a little warmer.
Week-end forecast: Changeable weather, with occasional showers, but bright intervals.

The barometer is falling.	El barómetro baja.
It is pouring with rain.	Llueve a cántaros.
The thermometer is 1 degree above zero (freezing-point).	El termómetro marca 1 grado sobre cero (temperatura de congelación).
This heat is unbearable ʌn'bɛərəbl.	Este calor es insoportable.
It is raining hard.	Llueve muchísimo.
It is rainy.	(El tiempo) está lluvioso.

Words

all day long	todo el día	indoors 'in'dɔ:z	en casa (en el interior)
blow one's nose	sonarse		
brisk *brisk*	rápido	mackintosh 'mækintɔʃ	impermeable
cough kɔ(:)f	tos		
don't (never) mind	no te preocupes por (no te importe)	mind *maind*	importar
		necessary 'nesisəri	necesario
dry *drai*	seco	or o:	o
fire *faiə**	fuego	shive *ʃivə**	tiritar
goloshes gə'lɔ-ʃiz	chanclos	shoes ʃu:z	zapatos
		sneeze sni:z	estornudar

solid 'sɔlid	fuerte, sólido	wear wɛə*	usar
umbrella ʌm-'brelə	paraguas	wet	húmedo, lluvioso
waterproof 'wɔ:təpru:f	impermeable	wet through wet θru:	calado, mojado

Conversation

Don't mind the weather

A. I'm going out for a brisk walk.
B. But you can't go out in this windy rainy weather!
A. Well, I take a walk every day whether it's wet or dry. Don't you think that it will do me more good than staying indoors and shivering in front of the fire? That's the best way I know of catching a cold.
B. You had better put on your galoshes, because once you've got wet feet you may get more than just a cold.
A. No, I don't think they are neccesary, because I have a pair of solid, waterprove shoes. And I shall wear a mackintosh and take my umbrella.
B. Well, please yourself, but look at me sneezing and coughing and blowing my nose all day long. And all because I would not wear my galoshes and got wet through.
A. I will be all right. You'll see. Good-bye.
B. Good-bye. If you catch cold don't say I didn't tell you. See you later.

Ejercicio

El invierno pasado, cuando estaba en Alemania, nevaba cada día; el termómetro marcaba (was) siempre varios grados bajo cero. Me sorprende que no cogiera un resfriado; me hubiera molestado mucho tener que sonarme, estornudar, toser durante todo el viaje. Cuando llueve cojo mi paraguas, y así no me mojo. A mi abuelo no le importa que haga viento. Se acerca una tempestad; mira cómo relampaguea y truena. En Londres hay tanta niebla, que muchas veces los coches tienen que llevar las luces encendidas durante todo el día. Espero que el viernes estará el día despejado y saldrá el sol, porque quiero ir a esquiar. Hay mucha nieve en la montaña y no está helada.

Tengo frío. Lo siento, he olvidado coger el paraguas. Los niños estarán contentos. Está lloviendo. ¡Qué helada está el agua! Se espera que no llueva hoy. Se dice que hará mucho frío. Hay personas a quienes no les importa el viento.

To learn by heart

To rain cats and dogs.	Llover a cántaros
To pour with rain.	Llover a cántaros.
To be as cold as an iceberg *'aisbə:g*.	Ser (o estar) tan frío como un témpano.
As quick as lightning.	Rápido como una centella.

> Blow, blow, thou Winter wind,
> Thou art not so unkind [1]
> As man's ingratitude [2];
> Thy tooth is not so keen [3]
> Because thou art [4] not seen
> Although thy [5] breath [6] be rude [7].
>
> W. SHAKESPEARE

1. Unkind *ʌn'kaind* cruel. 2. Ingratitude *in'grætitju:d* ingratitud. 3. Keen *ki:n* penetrante. 4. Thou art *ðau a:t* tú eres (forma anticuada). 5. Thy *ðai* tu (anticuado). 6. Breath *breθ* aliento. 7. Rude *ru:d* rudo.

THIRTY-SEVENTH LESSON
LECCIÓN TRIGÉSIMA SÉPTIMA

Preposiciones

Las preposiciones inglesas más usadas son:

above *ə'bʌv* sobre (más alto de)
about *ə'baut* cerca de, alrededor de
across *ə'krɔs* por medio de, a través de
against *ə'geinst* contra
after, después de, tras, según
along *ə'lɔŋ* a lo largo de
amid *ə'mid* / amidst } en medio de, entre
among *ə'mʌŋ* / amongst } entre
at, a, en, en casa de

before *bi'fɔə** antes de, ante, delante de,
behind *bi'haind* tras, detrás de
below *bi'lou* / beneath *bi'ni:θ* } debajo de
beside *bi'said* al lado de
besides *bi'saidz* fuera de, además de
between *bi'twi:n* / betwixt *bi'twikst* } entre
beyond *bi'jɔnd* más allá de, sobre, allende
by *bai* por, de, junto a

concerning kən'sənɪŋ tocante a, as for respecto
as to de (a)
down daun abajo
during 'djuərɪŋ durante
for, por, durante, para
from, de, desde, por
in
into 'intu } en, (a)dentro
near nɪə*
nigh nai } cerca de, junto a
next to
notwithstanding 'nɔtwɪθstændɪŋ a pesar de
of ɔv de
off ɔːf separado de, lejos de, etc.
on, upon ə'pɔn sobre, en
out of, fuera de
over, sobre, más allá de
round raund
around ə- } alrededor de
since, desde (hace)
till, until ʌn'til hasta
through θruː por, por medio de
to, a, por, hacia, a la casa de
towards tə'wɔːdz hacia
under 'ʌndə* bajo
up ʌp sobre, en lo alto de
underneath ʌndə'niːθ debajo de, bajo
with wɪð con
within wɪð'in entre, en el espacio de, dentro de
without wɪð'aut sin, fuera de

Algunas preposiciones son también adverbios de tiempo o de lugar.

Preposiciones compuestas:

according to, según, conforme a
as far as, hasta
but for, sin, a no ser
by means of } por medio de,
by virtue of } en virtud de
by the side of, al lado de
close to, (muy) cerca de
contrary to, contrariamente a
far from, lejos de
for the sake seik of, a causa (por amor) de
for want of
from want of } por falta de
from under, de debajo de
from within, de adentro
in the middle of, en medio de
in the midst of, entre, por entre
in spite spait of, a pesar (despecho) de
in order to, con el fin de, a fin de, para
instead in'sted of, en lugar (vez) de
in front of } a en frente de, fren-
opposite to } te a
on (in) behalf bi'haːf of, en favor de
on account ə'kaunt of, a causa de
on this side of, por (a) este lado de
on the other side of, al otro lado de
out of, por fuera de
owing 'ouɪŋ to, a causa de, debido a
with regard rigaːd to, respecto a

Ejemplos:

According to the rule.
As far as the end of the street.
From under the bed.
In the middle of the night.
On account of the rain.
On the other side of the bridge.
Out of the town.

Según la regla.
Hasta el fin de la calle.
De debajo de la cama.
En medio de la noche.
A causa de la lluvia.
Al otro lado del puente.
Fuera de la ciudad.

Las siguientes preposiciones castellanas pueden traducirse de varias formas. A continuación damos las más usuales:

a { at (reposo)
    to (movimiento)

en { in, at
     into (cuando está expresado el lugar)

por { by (el agente)
      for (la causa)

de { of (posesión)
     from (procedencia)
     with (materia)

sobre { over (sin apoyo)
        above (más elevado, arriba, superior)
        on, upon (con apoyo)

debajo { under (debajo de)
         below   (más bajo de,
         beneath inferior a)

fuera off (lejos de, quitado de)

hasta { till, until (tiempo)
        as far as (espacio)

entre { among (varios, más de dos)
        between (dos términos)

Las preposiciones se unen a veces a verbos, modificando su significado.

To outdo *aut'du:* superar; to go in, entrar; etc.

A menudo la preposición se pone al fin de la cláusula (véase lección 36.ª).

If many men are alluded to.   Si se alude a muchos hombres.

La preposición que rige un pronombre interrogativo o relativo, en lugar de precederle, puede colocarse después del verbo en el lugar que correspondería al complemento.

Whom are you speaking about?   ¿De quién habláis?
These are the books which you   Éstos son los libros sobre los que
  asked me about.   me preguntaste.

El relativo «that» siempre lleva la preposición al final de la cláusula, y lo mismo ocurre con el adverbio «where».

This is the man that you sent the   Éste es el hombre al que mandaste
  books to.   los libros.
This is the place where we came   Éste es el lugar adonde vinimos
  to yesterday.   (al que vinimos) ayer.

Uso de algunas preposiciones

«Above»: arriba, sobre (superioridad, ya física, ya moral).

The sky above.	El firmamento (que está) en lo alto.
The captain is above the lieutenant *lef'tenent, lu'tenənt*	El capitán está por encima del teniente.
I won't give you a penny above ten shillings.	No te daré un penique más de diez chelines.

«Over»: sobre, encima (posición de un objeto encima de otro sin contacto directo), lugar, posición, repetición, exceso.

The lamp is over the table.	La lámpara está encima de la mesa.
The aeroplane flies over the fields.	El aeroplano vuela sobre los campos.
Read this over again.	Lee esto otra vez.
Are there any bisquits *biskits* left over?	¿Han quedado algunas galletas?

«On, upon»: sobre, encima de (posición de un objeto sobre otro en contacto directo), tiempo determinado, estado, relación con.

I left the book on the table.	Deje el libro en la mesa.
On New Year's day...	El día de Año Nuevo...
On fire.	Ardiendo (quemándose).

«In»: en, dentro de (situación en un lugar), movimiento hacia dentro, lapso de tiempo, modo.

I am in the room.	Estoy en la habitación.
Come in!	¡Entra!
In a minute!	¡Dentro de un minuto!
In the end.	Al fin, por fin.
In a bad temper.	De mal humor.

«Into»: dentro (movimiento de fuera adentro), división.

I walked into the shop.	Entré en la tienda.
The glass was broken into a hundred pieces.	Se rompió el vaso en cien pedazos.

«From»: de, desde (punto de partida), dirección, origen, causa, diferencia.

I come from London.	Vengo de Londres.
I received a letter from your sister.	He recibido una carta de tu hermana.
He died from a heart attack.	Murió de un ataque al corazón.

Spaniards are different from Englishmen.	Los españoles son diferentes de los ingleses.
I shall be there from 2 to 3.	Estaré allí de dos a tres.
Butter comes from milk.	La manteca sale de la leche.

«Of»: de (relación de un objeto con otro, posesión, causa).

The door of the room.	La puerta de la habitación.
The works of Shakespeare ʃeiks-piə*	Las obras de Shakespeare.
I am afraid of ghosts *gousts*.	Tengo miedo a los fantasmas.

«Below, beneath»: inferioridad en cualquier concepto o sentido.

The lieutenant is below the captain.	El teniente está por debajo del capitán.
Below the sun.	Debajo del sol.

«Under»: bajo, debajo (posición opuesta a «on»).

The dog is lying under the table.	El perro está tumbado debajo de la mesa.
The paper is under the book.	El papel está debajo del libro.

«At»: en, a (situación en reposo, tiempo, dirección).

I live at Chester.	Vivo en Chester.
I am at home.	Estoy en casa.
He came at three o'clock.	Vino a las tres.
The children threw stones at the cat.	Los niños tiraban piedras al gato.

«To»: a, para (movimiento hacia o hasta un lugar, finalidad).

I wrote to her.	Le escribí.
This train goes to London.	Este tren va a Londres.
I am going to the tailor's.	Voy al sastre.
I came to see the sports.	Vine para ver los deportes.

«Across»: a través, al otro lado (movimiento de una parte a otra).

The Post Office is just across the street.	La oficina de Correos está al otro lado de la calle.

«Through»: por, a través de, por completo (paso de una parte a otra).

He jumped through the window.	Saltó por la ventana.
Did you get through your examination?	¿Pasaste tu examen?
It is raining hard and I am wet through.	Está lloviendo mucho y estoy completamente mojado.

«By»: por (agente, instrumento, modo, proximidad).

This book is written by Bernard Shaw.	Este libro está escrito por Bernard Shaw.
I like travelling by car.	Me gusta viajar en coche.
She sat by the fire.	Estaba sentada junto al fuego.

«For»: por, para (finalidad, duración de tiempo o espacio).

This book is for you.	Este libro es para ti.
I sat there for an hour.	Estuve sentado allí una hora.
They walked for miles in the woods.	Anduvieron durante horas en el bosque.

Words

bare $b\varepsilon\vartheta$*	liso, desnudo	monk $m\Lambda\eta k$	fraile, monje
bones $bounz$	huesos	perched $p\vartheta{:}t\int t$	posado
bridge $brid_3$	puente	roof $ru{:}f$	tejado
cell sel	celda	rushed $r\Lambda\int t$	corrió, se precipitó
comprehension $k\vartheta mpri'hen\int\vartheta n$	comprensión	screen $skri{:}n$	biombo, mampara pantalla (cine)
covered $'k\Lambda v\vartheta d$	cubierto	sea level $si{:}\ levl$	nivel del mar
crucifix $'kru{:}sifiks$	crucifijo	skull $sk\Lambda l$	calavera
ditch $dit\int$	foso, hoyo	slight $slait$	ligero, delgado
huge $hju{:}d_3$	gran, enorme	soar $s\vartheta\vartheta$*	elevarse, volar
jump $d_3\Lambda mp$	saltar	sword $s\vartheta{:}d$	espada
keep out, kept out, kept out $ki{:}p\ aut,\ kept\ aut$	contener	thread θred	hilo
		tiles $tailz$	tejas
		tunnel $t\Lambda nl$	túnel
		valley $'v\ae li$	valle
knelt $knelt$	arrodillado	village $vilid_3$	pueblo
mason $'meisn$	albañil	wall $w\vartheta{:}l$	muro

Exercise

We walked as far as that village. From what village are you coming (*o:* What village are you coming from)? To whose house are you to go this evening? To my friend Anthony's. Come down, you might fall. With what is that roof covered? With tiles. He rushed into the house crying.

Can you jump over that ditch? That hill (colina) rises above all the others. A sword hung over Damocles's head. Put the stick on the table. The bird is perched on that tree; it kept soaring over us and above the other birds; then it flew over the house upon the tree. Our village is below your villa (quinta). The road passes below the mountain and across the valley; the railways passes under our house and through the mountain. The tunnel is very long. Think before you speak.

In a small cell, within four bare walls, a monk knelt by a low chair, under a huge crucifix; over his head hung a skull; all around the cell old books and bones were to be seen. And without the cell a splendid sun shone over the world.

Till when will you be staying here? Until you send me away. How far did you go? As far as Middlesex. As far as the end of the street. As far as you can see. My friend fell into a ditch. Your chair is between the door and the window. Francis is behind the screen, and the screen is before the fire. He stood before me like a hero. Before going out, let me know. When we went out of that shop, he took me by (por) the hand. Whom were you speaking to? What are you thinking of? Never mind ([*maind*] no importa) what I am thinking of. We shall meet you over (*o* beyond) the bridge. Among twenty apples there was but (no había sino) a good one. We were eight, besides the children. Do not go beyond that wall.

Vocabulario

a causa de	because of	levantarse	to rise *raiz*
aire	air *ɛə**	librero	bookseller *'bukselə**
arrojar	to fling *fliŋ*		
arroyo	rivulet *'rivjulit*, brook *bruk*	maltratado	ill-treated *'iltri:tid*
baúl	trunk *trʌnk*	molino	mill *mil*
bolsillo	pocket *'pɔkit*	morar, vivir	dwell *dwel*
circunvecinos	all around	pasar	to pass *pɑ:s*
con que	provided *prə'vaidid*	piso	floor *flɔə**, story *stɔ:ri*
chal	shawl *ʃɔ:l*	sacar	to take out
despertar	to awake *ə'weik*	saltar	spring, sprang, sprung *spriŋ, spræŋ, sprʌŋ*
empujar	to push *puʃ*		
herido	wounded *'wu:ndid*	sótano	cellar *'selə**

tanto mejor	so much the better	vista	sight *sait*
torre de iglesia	steeple *sti:pl*	volver	to come back

Ejercicio

Tuvimos que volver a causa del mal tiempo. En el segundo piso vive la anciana de que te hablé ayer. Después del almuerzo irás al correo. No empujes la silla contra la mesa. No se puede viajar sin dinero. Bajo la casa hay un sótano. Guárdese usted esto en el bolsillo. No he visto a mi amigo desde hace siete años. Los discípulos han paseado con su maestro a lo largo del río. Me quedo en casa a causa de la lluvia. El gato saltó sobre la mesa. ¿Estaba usted en casa de su sastre? No, estaba en casa del librero. Pasaremos por el molino de Pedro, ¿no es verdad? Sí, con tal que volvamos dentro de dos horas. ¿Conoces al señor C.? Le conozco de (by) vista. ¿Llueve? Está nevando desde ayer. El pájaro voló sobre la torre de la iglesia, la cual se levanta sobre todos los árboles circunvecinos. ¿Se puede vivir fuera del aire? No, por cierto (not indeed). ¿Quién ha arrojado la piedra (stone) contra la ventana? No sé, tal vez ese niño que estaba corriendo a lo largo del arroyo. Saca del baúl el chal rojo. Anduve todo el día por la ciudad sin encontrar a mis amigos. Me dejó dormir hasta las diez; luego me despertó. Llegamos hasta el arroyo y volvimos. El perro está herido. No deben maltratarse los animales. Si llega a tiempo, tanto mejor.

Words

barrow *'bærou*	carretón	fare *fɛə* *	tarifa, precio
booking-office *'bukiŋ 'ɔfis*	ventanilla	fast-train *fa:st trein*	rápido (tren)
bookstall *'bukstɔ:l*	quiosco de periódicos	flag *flæg*	bandera, estandarte
carriage *'kæridʒ*	vagón	get a move (hurry *'hʌri* up)	darse prisa
change *tʃeindʒ*	cambiar		
cheap *tʃi:p*	económico, barato	guard *ga:d*	guarda (jefe estación)
compartment *kəm'pa:tmənt*	departamento	had better *hæd betə* *	es preferible, conveniente
day-excursion *dei iks'kə:ʃən*	excursión de un día	labels *'leiblz*	etiquetas
		luggage *'lʌgidʒ*	equipaje

miss *mis*	perder (el tren, etc.)	return *ri'tə:n*	billete de ida y vuelta
nonsmokers *nɔn'smoukəz*	no fumadores	single *'siŋgl*	billete (de ida solamente)
nonstop *'nɔn'stɔp*	directo (tren)	stick *stik*	pegar
onto *ɔntu:*	en, dentro, adentro	smokers *'smoukəz*	fumadores
platform *'plætfɔ:m*	andén	third class	tercera clase
porter *'pɔ:tə**	mozo	ticket *tikit*	billete
pound-note *'paund 'nout*	billete de una libra	tip *tip*	propina
pull out *'pul aut*	arrancar, salir	to advance *əd'va:ns*	progresar
put down	depositar, entregar	to leave *li:v*	salir
rack *ræk*	red (del vagón)	undergraduate *ʌnde'grædjuit*	estudiante universitario
		underground *'ʌndəgraund*	metro, ferrocarril subterráneo
		wave *weiv*	ondear, agitar

Conversation

At the railway station   En la estación

James and Charles, two Oxford undergraduates, arrive at Paddington Station in a taxi.

Porter (taking luggage and putting it onto a barrow): Where to, sir?

Dick: Oxford. What time is the next train?

Porter: Four thirty, sir. You will have to get a move (or hurry up).

Dick: If we miss it, how long will we have to wait for the next train?

Porter: The next one is not till 5.30, sir, and it's not a fast-train and nonstop like the 4.30. You would have to change at Reading.

Charles: We had better stick labels on the trunks. Will you put the other things on a third class carriage for us, porter?

Porter: Smoker or non-smoker, sir?

Charles: Anywhere where there's room. What platform does the train leave from?

Porter: Number two, sir.

Dick: Will you get the tickets from the booking office, Charlie, while I go to buy a paper at the bookstall?

Charles: All right. (At the Booking-Office). Two to Oxford, please. What is the third class fare?

Booking-clerk: Ten-and-nine single, and twenty-one and six return. But there's a cheap day-excursion ticket for seven and nine.
Charles: Thank you. Two excursion then, please. (He puts down a pound note and receives four and six change.)
On Platform.
Porter: I have put your luggage in the rack in this compartment, sir.
Charles: Thank you. (He gives him a tip.)
James: We made it in time.
The guard waves his green flag, and the train pulls out from the platform.

Ejercicio

Sus hijos están jugando a la pelota en la plaza. Espero el autobús para ir a la Universidad. En aquella mesa hay una hoja de papel. Por este camino no llegará a ser famoso. Detrás de mi casa está la plaza del mercado. El perro está durmiendo debajo de una silla. Por la escalera podemos subir y bajar. Pasaremos por el puente y así llegaremos antes que él. Siéntese a la mesa, vamos a comer. Este alumno progresa día a día. José está hablando de su viaje en avión a Nueva York. Estaré en casa a las dos y media de la tarde. Esta catedral es la más famosa del mundo. ¿Irá hoy otra vez al campo? Sí, me gusta salir con este tiempo. Esta mañana temprano estábamos, según mi termómetro, a 5 grados bajo cero, por esto encendí el fuego. No hay ninguno entre estos libros que me interese. ¿Por qué se ríe de mí? Después de la representación iré a casa inmediatamente. Shakespeare vivió en el reinado de la reina Isabel. Cada día voy con mi hermano a pie al colegio porque el tranvía va completamente lleno a las nueve de la mañana.

To learn by heart

To be in a mood for...	Estar de humor para...
To ring off.	Colgar el teléfono.
To ring up.	Llamar por teléfono, telefonear.
What's up?	¿Qué pasa? ¿Qué hay?
Up to now...	Hasta ahora...

I was angry [1] with my friend:
I told my wrath [2], my wrath did end.
I was angry with my foe [3]:
I told it not, my wrath did grow.

WILLIAM BLAKE

1. Angry *æŋgri* irritado.   2. Wrath *rɔːθ* ira.   3. Foe *'fou* enemigo

THIRTY-EIGHTH LESSON
LECCIÓN TRIGÉSIMA OCTAVA

Conjunciones e interjecciones

1. La conjunción sirve para unir palabras y oraciones. Pueden ser coordinativas y subordinativas. Las primeras unen oraciones principales; las segundas, una oración principal a una subordinada o dependiente de aquélla.

I went home *and* you went to the pictures. (Coordinativa.)	Yo fui a casa y tú fuiste al cine.
Either you did it *or* your sister. (Coordinativa.)	Tú o tu hermana lo hicisteis.
We gave him ten pounds, *still*, he was not pleased. (Coordinativa.)	Le dimos diez libras; no obstante, no se contentó.
Tell me *whether* you will be able to come or not. (Subordinativa.)	Dime si podrás o no venir.
I am so tired *that* I cannot come. (Subordinativa.)	Estoy tan cansado, que no puedo venir.
I am not going to the pictures *because* I have to work. (Subordinativa.)	No voy al cine porque he de trabajar.

Las conjunciones más usadas son:

also *ɔːlsou* también
after *'aːftə** después que
and, y
as *æz* como, porque, cuando, pues
but, pero, mas, no — sino
else, sino (si no), o
ere *ɛə** antes que (*o* de)
except, a menos que, si no

for, pues
however, sin embargo, pero
if, si
lest, para que no
moreover *mɔː'rouvə** además
nevertheless *nevəðə'les* sin embargo
nor, tampoco, ni

notwithstanding nɔtwið'stændiŋ no obstante (que), a pesar de que, aunque
now, ahora (bien)
or, o, o bien
provided prə'vaidid con tal que
scarcely 'skɛəsli apenas
since *sins* desde que, pues (que), ya que
so *sou* así, por eso, pues
still, sin embargo, no obstante
than ðæn que
although ɔːl'ðou ⎫ aunque, si
though ðou ⎭ bien
because bi'kɔːz porque
before bi'fɔː* antes que
that ðæt que, para que
then ðen pues, entonces, con que, luego
therefore ðɛəfɔː* así que, por eso

till, until, hasta que, mientras no
too tuː también
well, bien, pues, con que
unless ʌn'les si no, a menos que
when *wen* cuando, en que
whenever wen'evə* cada vez que, siempre que
whereas wɛər'æz mientras que, a la vez que, ya que
wherefore wɛə'fɔ* por lo que (cual)
whereupon wɛərə'pɔn sobre que (lo cual), después de lo cual
whether 'weðə* si, (sea) que (dubitativo)
while *wail*, whilst *wailst* mientras, en tanto
why *wai*, hwai por qué
yet, sin embargo, con todo eso, no obstante

Conjunciones compuestas:

as — as, tan — como
not so — as, no tan — como
both — and, tanto — como, así — como, (y) — y
either — or, o — o
neither — nor, ni — ni
nor... either, ni... tampoco
not only — but, no sólo — sino
now — now, ya — ya
whether 'weðə* — or, sea — sea
as if, como si
as long as, mientras, en tanto
seeing that, pues, visto que, puesto que
on condition kən'diʃən that, a condición de que
the more mɔː* so as, tanto más cuanto que

as soon as, luego que, tan pronto como
as well as, así (...) como
as often as, siempre que, cada vez que
but that, sino que
even iːvn if, aunque, aun si
not even if, ni aun si, ni aunque
in order that, para que, a fin de que
in order to, para, con el fin de
according ə'kɔːdiŋ to ⎫ según
seeing how ⎭
not even, ni aun, tampoco
so much that, tanto que
so that, así que, de suerte que
inasmuch inæz'mʌtʃ as, en cuanto (que), puesto que
but for, si no..., a no ser (por).

Ejemplos:

I shall come although it rains.
I shall come even if it rains.
Tell me why you did not come.
I'll tell you why I did not: because I was ill.
I have neither gold nor silver.

Vendré aunque llueve.
Vendré aunque llueva.
Dime por qué no viniste.
Te diré por qué no vine: porque estuve malo.
No tengo ni oro ni plata.

Conjunciones e interjecciones

My father is tall, and not short.	Mi padre es alto, y no pequeño.
My name is not Peter, but John.	Mi nombre no es (no me llamo) Pedro, sino Juan.
That young lady is both beautiful and rich.	Esa joven es tan hermosa como rica (es hermosa y rica).
Whether he need it or not, I will not give it to him as long as I need it myself.	Tanto si lo necesita como si no, no se lo daré mientras yo lo necesite.

«That» se omite con frecuencia cuando su omisión no oscurece el sentido. «Too» se coloca después de la cláusula a que hace referencia. En curso de oración se coloca entre dos comas.

I told you (that) I couldn't do it.	Te dije que yo no podía hacerlo.
Mary is coming, too.	María viene también.

Words

assist ə'sist	ayudar	imprudent im'pru:dənt	imprudente
age eidʒ	edad	snatch snætʃ	arrebatar
approve ə'pru:v	aprobar	to drop drɔp	dejar caer
bold bould	atrevido	to improve im'pru:v	enmendarse
careless 'kɛəlis	descuidado	to knit nit	hacer punto
cross	enfadado, malhumorado	to pardon pa:dn	perdonar
despise dis'paiz	despreciar	to perform pə'fɔ:m	cumplir, realizar
discipline 'disiplin	disciplina	to promise 'prɔmis	prometer
extraordinary iks'trɔ:dnri	extraordinario	to tell a lie lai	decir una mentira
fate feit	destino, suerte	to wait weit for	esperar
feast fi:st	fiesta		
give in	ceder		

Exercise

As you study much, you will make good progress. I must go, for my brother and uncle are waiting for me. The weather was both wet and cold. Both his father and cousin are officers. It is not very interesting; however, I will learn it. He has promised to come, but I fear (temo) he is not well enough. Enough is as good as a feast. I will not drink this bad beer lest it should make me ill. She is knitting a jersey for her brother although she has never done any knitting before. Don't be cross with the boy because he has really improved a lot since last Summer. Won't you give in? It would be better for you if you did. You should never tell a lie. We shall see you at church, either on Sunday next, or on Sunday a week. Neither music nor reading pleases him. Unless we hear it again, we cannot believe it. Despise not poverty (pobreza), lest it be your own fate. If you promise, you must also perform. Assist such persons as need your assistance as long as you live. Either speak yourself, or let me speak. She is but fifteen (years old). How tall she is for her age! Although he was her friend, he could not approve what she did. Though it is very extraordinary it certainly did take place. He dropped his book before I reached him; else I should have snatched it from his hand; now, I should not have liked to come to that. I am afraid you do not know your lesson, notwithstanding you have the book in your hand. He did wrong, nevertheless I will forgive him. The soldiers were bold, yet they were conquered (vencidos), as they had no discipline. She is so careless that it would be unwise to trust her. Though often cold and hungry, still the poor boys are healthy. The officer took his sword then he walked out of the room. The boy said: wait for me!

Vocabulario

costumbre	habit *'hæbit*	miel	honey *'hʌni*
inmediatamente	immediately *i'mi:djetli*	reir	to laugh *tu la:f*
juicioso	sensible *'sensibl*	separar, quitar(se)	to take off

Ejercicio

Los niños deben ser juiciosos; si no, serán castigados. He visto al hombre, pero no le conozco. Puesto que llueve, me quedaré en casa. Creo que a usted no le gusta la miel; si no, comería usted de ella, pues es muy buena. Querría jugar, pero no tengo tiempo, pues no he terminado todavía mis ejercicios de inglés. Cuando llegué a París, hacía buen tiempo. Si usted va a Londres, iré con usted. No creo que venga el abuelo. No sabemos si está todavía aquí, o no. No le hablaré más mientras viva. Entró como si estuviera en su casa, y no sólo no se quitó el sombrero, sino que se sentó sobre la mesa. Cuando la veas, dile que iré tan pronto como haya acabado mi ejercicio. Cada vez que voy a esa iglesia, me encuentro con (to meet) ella. Ya se ríe, ya llora. Aunque mi vecino tuviese razón, yo no cedería. No tengo ni dinero ni amigos. El rey de Inglaterra ya vive en Londres, ya en Windsor. Cuando viene, siempre deja usted la puerta abierta; es una costumbre muy mala. ¡Es usted muy descuidado! En caso de que nuestro primo venga mañana, dele usted esta carta inmediatamente. Cuando hube acabado mi lección, salí. Me parece que (as if) el niño ha dicho una mentira.

2. Las interjecciones más usadas son las siguientes:

ah *a:!* oh!, ¡oh! ¡ah!
ho!, ¡eh! ¡hola!
tush *tʌʃ!* ¡bah!
oh, dear!, ¡ay! ¡oh!
fie *fai!* pish *piʃ!* ¡qué feo! ¡quita!
hurrah *hu'ra:!* ¡hurra!
hist!
hush *hʌʃ!* } ¡chito! ¡quedo!

lo *lou!* ¡mira!
alas *ə'la:s!* ¡ay de mí!
what the deuce *dju:s!* ¡qué diablos!
hallo!, ¡hola!
hail *heil!* ¡salud!, ¡salve!
woe *wou!* ¡ay! ¡guay!

Además se emplean otras clases de palabras como interjecciones; he aquí las más usadas:

well!, ¡bien!
I say!, ¡oiga! ¡eh! ¡hola!
good!, ¡bien!
behold *bi'hould!* ¡mira!
begone!, ¡fuera!
peace *pi:s!*
silence *'sailəns!* } ¡silencio!
away! begone *bi'gɔn!* ¡fuera!
courage *'kʌridʒ!* ¡ánimo! ¡valor!
forward *'fɔ:wəd!* ¡ea! ¡adelante!
beware *biwɛə*!* attention!, ¡cuidado!
help!, ¡socorro!

Thank God!, ¡gracias a Dios!
well then!, ¡vamos!
would to God!, ¡ojalá!
really *'riəli!* ¡en verdad! ¡de veras!
wonderful *'wʌndəful!* ¡estupendo!, ¡maravilloso!
hark *ha:k!* ¡oíd! ¡escuchad!
softly *sɔftli!* gently!, ¡despacio!
why!, ¡y qué! ¡y pues! ¡cómo!
welcome!, ¡bien venido!
farewell *fɛə'wel!* ¡adiós!
good-bye *-bai!* ¡adiós!

Words

axe *æks*	hacha	counters *'kauntəs*	fichas (en el juego)
bark *ba:k*	corteza	gamekeeper *'geimki:pə**	guardabosque
cards *ka:dz*	naipes	get into	entrar
case *'keiz*	caso	greet *gri:t*	saludar
cherry-tree *'tʃeri tri:*	cerezo		

guitar *gi'tɑːr**	guitarra	story *stɔri*	historia, cuento
hereafter *hie'rɑːftə**	en lo futuro	to be glad *glæd*	estar contento, satisfecho
history *'histəri*	historia	to be sorry *'sɔri*	sentir, apesadumbrarse
lier *laiə**	embustero	toy *tɔi*	juguete
pack *pek* of cards	baraja	truth *truːθ*	verdad
purse *pəːs*	monedero	witches *'witʃis*	brujas
report *ri'pɔːt*	explosión, detonación		

Exercise

Do you see the queen and the prince? Hurrah! here they are! I say! who teaches you the guitar? Oh! I learn with my music-mistress (maestra de música). Alas! what can I do? Really; you are a case! Oh, dear! where is my book? Tush! you have lost it! Hallo! gamekeeper! Where is my gun? You will find it in the car, sir. Strange! where can I have put the cards? It was a whole pack. Oh! you have put them away with the counters. They are in the desk. Fie! why have you hidden my opera-glassess? Really! it was not I! Behold! the moon is rising! What is the time? It is half past nine. Begone! or do you wish me to hurt you? No, I will go as soon as I have found my purse. Hush! do you hear nothing? Yes. I hear the report of a gun. Hark! Where is the hunting-horn (cuerno de caza)? Welcome! Have you brought the Doctor with you? Yes, of course. How is mother now? How did the witches greet Macbeth? All hail, Macbeth! that shalt be king hereafter! Welcome! Make yourselves at home! Thank you very much.

Exercise

Tell the truth

A good many (muchos) years ago there was a little boy, called George [dʒɔːdʒ]. One day someone gave him a bright new axe to play with. It was not the best toy for a little boy. Still he was much pleased with it, and went here and there, trying it on nearly everything that came in his way.

At last he got into the garden. Here he cut the bark of a young cherry-tree. When his father went that way, he saw what was done, and said: «Who has cut my nice tree?» George heard his father, ran [up] to him, and cried out: «Father, I cannot tell you a lie, I did it.»

His father was sorry the tree was cut, but he was very glad his boy had told the truth. George was a good boy not able to tell a lie. Even when a liar speaks the truth, no one believes him.

Now I must still tell you that the boy of this story became one of the greatest men that ever lived. He was George Washington ['wɔʃiŋtən], of whom you will hear in your history lessons.

Words

abbey 'æbei	abadía	gazes 'geiziz	mira
architect 'a:kitekt	arquitecto	glimpse glimps	ojeada
architecture 'a:kitektʃə	arquitectura	government 'gʌvənmənt	gobierno
artist 'a:tist	artista	heart ha:t	corazón
bank bænk	banco	idea ai'di:ə	idea
beloved bi'lʌvd	amado	immense i'mens	inmenso
build bild	construir	last la:st resting-place	última morada
building 'bildiŋ	edificio	Law Courts lɔ: kɔ:ts	Palacio de Justicia
busy 'bizi	ocupado, atareado	lie, lied, lied	mentir
catch a glimpse kætʃ ə glimps	echar una ojeada	lofty 'lɔfti	altivo
cenotaph 'senota:f	cenotafio	magnificent mæg'nifisnt	magnífico
close by klous bai	muy cerca	Mansion 'mænʃen House	residencia oficial del alcalde de Londres
Columbus kə-'lʌmbəs	Colón		
column 'kɔləm	columna	masterpiece 'ma:stəpi:s	obra maestra
coronation kɔrə'neiʃən	coronación	meet mi:t	encontrar (persona)
cross krɔ:s	cruzar		
crumble 'krʌmbl	derrumbarse	mighty 'maiti	poderoso
descend di'send	bajar	monarch 'mɔnə:k	monarca
dome doum	cúpula		
dust dʌst	polvo	monument 'mɔnjumənt	monumento
empire 'empaiə*	imperio		
end end	fin	national 'næʃnl	nacional
enter 'entə*	entrar	office 'ɔ:fis	oficina
famous 'feiməs	famoso	official ə'fiʃəl	oficial
Foreign Office	Ministerio de Asuntos Exteriores	on the left	a la izquierda
		opposite 'ɔpəzit	delante de

painting 'peintiŋ	pintura
Parliament 'pɑ:ləmənt	Parlamento
pass pɑ:s	pasar
Police pə'li:s	policía
precede pri:'si:d	preceder
residence 'rezidəns	residencia
ride raid	paseo en coche
right rait	derecha
on, to the —	a la derecha
sacred 'seikrid	sagrado
square skwɛə*	plaza
statesman 'steitsmən	hombre de estado
statue 'stætju	estatua
symbol 'simbəl	símbolo
The Lord Mayor mɛə*	el alcalde
thoroughfare 'θʌrəfɛə*	vía pública
to house haus	albergar
to tower	alzarse
tower tauə*	torre
valuable 'væljuəbl	valioso
venerable 'venərəbl	venerable
war wɔ:*	guerra
War Memorial me'mɔ:riəl	monumento a los caídos en la guerra
warrior 'wɔriə*	guerrero
witness 'witnis	ser testigo, atestiguar
world wə:ld	mundo

Reading exercise

Sight-seeing

You cannot see London in a day: but those of us who have little time to spend on sight-seeing can catch a glimpse of many of its famous buildings and monuments in a very few minutes, by taking a ride on the top of a bus.

For instance, let us take the bus running from Victoria Station to Mansion House, the official residence of the Lord Mayor.

It will pass Westminster Abbey, the last resting-place of famous kings, warriors, artist, poets and statesmen. Its walls have witnessed the coronation of our Queen and of the monarchs who preceded her for many hundreds of years. It has been called «the most sacred and venerable building in the whole Empire». Close by the Abbey stand the magnificent Houses of Parliament, dominated by the tower of «Big-Ben», the clock that can be heard on the wireless all the world over. The bus now enters Whitehall, the home of most of the great government Offices. On the left, opposite the Cenotaph, Britain's national war memorial, is the Foreign Office; and further up on the right is the War Office and the offices of the Metropolitan Police. Towering high over Trafalgar Square, at the end of Whitehall, is Nelson's Column; the world famous admiral gazes down over London as Columbus does over Barcelona; both statues are symbols of their country's greatness at sea. And on the far side of Trafalgar Square stands the National Gallery which houses a valuable collection of paintings. The bus will now turn to the right, past Charing Cross and through the Strand, at the end of which can be seen the Law Court, and two of the churches built by the great architect, Christopher Wren. The bus continues its journey down Fleet Street on to Ludgate Hill. Now we can see the dome of Wren's masterpiece of architecture, St. Paul's Cathedral: a building which stood through the long years of the second world war, while the buildings all around it crumbled into dust. And so our bus enters the famous square around which stand the Bank of England, the Royal Exchange and the Mansion House. The immensity of the traffic in this busy thoroughfare indicates that we have arrived at the very heart of this mighty city and to the end of our ride.

To learn by heart

Inside out.	Del revés.
Upside down.	Cabeza abajo.
To burst into tears *bə:rst intu tiəs*.	Romper a llorar.
Time is up.	Es la hora.
In the nick of time *nik ov 'taim*.	En el momento preciso.

> One ship drives east and another drives west
> With the selfsame [1] winds that blow.
> 'Tis the set of the sails [2]
> And not the gales [3]
> Which tells us the way to go.
>
> E. W. WILCOX

1. Selfsame *'selfseim* mismos. 2. Sails *seilz* velas. 3. Gales *geil*- galerna (viento).

THIRTY-NINTH LESSON
LECCIÓN TRIGÉSIMA NOVENA

Auxiliares repetidos

En inglés, al contestar a una pregunta, además del adverbio «yes» o «no», suele repetirse el auxiliar de la pregunta.

Have you seen my book? Yes, I have.
Did you get the newspaper? No, I didn't.
Will you post this letter for me? Yes, I will.
Am I right? Yes, you are.
Can I come? No, you can't.

Las expresiones «¿verdad?», «¿no?», «¿no es así?», «¿conque...?», es decir, las preguntas confirmativas o comentativas, se traducen al inglés repitiendo el auxiliar empleado en la oración a que hace referencia, o el auxiliar «do» y «did», respectivamente, si el tiempo del verbo es presente o pasado simple.

La pregunta confirmativa es la que exige confirmación o refutación de un hecho recién expresado. Si la oración a que hace referencia es afirmativa, la pregunta será negativa, y viceversa.

Peter is here, isn't he?	Pedro está aquí, ¿verdad?
You haven't read the paper, have you?	No has leído el periódico, ¿verdad?
You don't like wine, do you?	No te gusta el vino, ¿verdad?
You like milk, don't you?	Te gusta la leche, ¿no?
Peter went with you, didn't he?	Pedro fue contigo, ¿no?
Pat didn't go with you, did she?	Pat no fue contigo, ¿verdad?

La pregunta que llamamos comentativa es un comentario del hecho expresado por el mismo que habla o de lo dicho por otra persona. Suele indicar interés, ironía o amenaza por parte de quien la hace. Equivale en castellano a «¿no es verdad?», «¿conque...?», «¿ah, sí?», «¿no es cierto?». La pregunta comentativa es afirmativa si la oración a que se refiere es afirmativa, y es negativa cuando aquélla es negativa. Con frecuencia se anteponen a la oración «so», «now».

So, you are right, are you?	Conque tienes razón, ¿verdad?
Now, he arrived yesterday, did he?	Así que llegó ayer, ¿no? (sé que no es así)
So, you have told her, haven't you?	Conque no se lo dijiste, ¿verdad?
I am going to the pictures.	Me voy al cine.
(Com.) Oh, are you?	¿Ah, sí?
I am very tired.	Estoy muy cansado.
(Com.) Are you?	¿Sí? (¿Ah, sí?)
Peter has just arrived.	Pedro acaba de llegar.
(Com.) Oh, he has just arrived, has he?	Conque acaba de llegar, ¿no?

Las expresiones «también» y «tampoco»

«También» se traduce al inglés repitiendo el auxiliar de la oración a que hace referencia, precedido de «so» y seguido del sujeto. Si el verbo de la oración principal está en presente o pasado se emplearán los auxiliares «do» y «did» respectivamente.

Mary likes tea, and so do I.	A María le gusta el té, y a mí también.
We have read her letter. So has Mary.	Hemos leído su carta. María también.
You will write to aunt Joan. So will he.	Vosotros escribiréis a tía Juana. Él también.
We have bought a house, and so have they.	Hemos comprado una casa, y ellos también.

«Tampoco» se traduce al inglés repitiendo el auxiliar de la oración a que hace referencia, precedido de «neither» o «nor» y seguido del sujeto. Se emplearán respectivamente «do» y «did» cuando el verbo de la oración sea presente o pasado simple.

He doesn't like reading, and neither do I.	No le gusta leer, y a mí tampoco.
She didn't know her lesson, nor did you.	No supo su lección, y tú tampoco.
I had not heard the bell. Neither had Mary.	No había oído el timbre. María tampoco.
I shall not tell him. Neither shall I.	No se lo diré. Ni yo tampoco.
I am not going. Neither am I.	Yo no voy. Yo tampoco.

LISTA DE ALGUNOS VERBOS COMPUESTOS CON ADVERBIOS Y PREPOSICIONES

come along	irse	ask for	pedir
come in	entrar	call on	visitar
come out	salir	count on	contar con, esperar
get up	levantarse		
go back	volver	get over	restablecerse, superar
go in	entrar		
go out	salir	look after	cuidar
go through	examinar	look for	buscar
let out	dejar salir	look out of	mirar por, asomarse
let in	dejar entrar		
put on	ponerse	see about	considerar
put out	quitarse	see into	investigar
set out	partir	see to	atender
take off	quitarse	take after	parecerse

talk over	discutir	sit by	sentarse junto a
think over	considerar	get into	subir a
wait for	esperar	bring down	bajar (cosa)
cut down	reducir	take up	subir (cosa)
keep out	apartarse	cut off	cortar
run into	tropezar(se)	take out	sacar
run over	atropellar	write down	escribir, anotar

LOCUCIONES ESPECIALES CON LOS VERBOS «TO DO» Y «TO MAKE»

To make friends.	Hacer amigos.
To make a mistake.	Equivocarse.
To make a journey.	Hacer un viaje.
To make an effort.	Hacer un esfuerzo.
To make a noise.	Hacer ruido.
To make a speech.	Hacer un discurso.
To make enquiries.	Hacer averiguaciones.
To do an exercise.	Hacer un ejercicio.
To do a sum.	Hacer una suma.
To do business.	Hacer negocios.
To do something.	Hacer algo.
To do nothing.	No hacer nada.
To do one's duty.	Cumplir con su deber.
To do one's hair.	Peinarse.
To do one's nails.	Arreglarse las uñas.

Words

achieve *'ətʃiːv*	lograr	patronage *'pætrənidʒ*	protección, patrocinio
beach *biːtʃ*	playa	pavilion *pa'viljən*	pabellón
breeze *briːz*	brisa	province *'prɔvins*	provincia
certain *'səːtn*	cierto	popularity *pɔpju'læriti*	popularidad
compensate *'kɔmpenseit*	compensar	public holiday *'pʌblik 'hɔlədi*	fiesta oficial
cure *kjuə*	cura		
delights *di'laits*	delicias	salty *'sɔːlti*	salado
entertainment *entə'teinmənt*	entretenimiento	seaside resort *'siː'said ri'zɔːt*	lugar de veraneo en la costa
escape *is'keip*	escapar		
establish *is'tæbliʃ*	establecer, consagrar	shopping-centre *'ʃɔpiŋ 'sentə*	centro comercial
fashionable *'fæʃnəbl*	de moda	theatrical *θi'ætrikəl*	teatral
fishing village *'fiʃiŋ 'vilidʒ*	pueblo pesquero	tiny *taini*	diminuto
inconvenience *inkən'viːnjəns*	molestia	to bathe *tu beið*	bañarse
journey *dʒəːni*	viaje	to persuade *pə'sweid*	persuadir
magnificent *mæg'nifisnt*	magnífico	variety *və'raiəti*	variedad
		vitality *vai'tæliti*	vitalidad
oriental *ɔːri'entl*	oriental	watering-place *'wɔːteriŋ 'pleis*	balneario
palace *'pælis*	palacio		
patient *'peiʃənt*	paciente		

Reading exercise

Brighton

Every week-end and public holiday thousands of Londoners escape from the heavy air of the city to the sea breezes of Brighton, a seaside town just 55 minutes by train to the south of the Capital. In modern times one of the most famous seaside resorts in the world, it was, until the eighteenth century no more than a tiny fishing village. It achieved some popularity when a certain doctor made it known that the sea was unusually salty there and that he was in the habit of curing his patients by making them bathe in the sea and drink the water. However, it was the patronage of the Prince of Wales (later King George IV) which established Brighton as the most fashionable watering-place on the South Coast; and he built there a magnificent oriental palace known as the Royal Pavilion. To-day, Brighton maintains its popularity because of its variety and the vitality that young people bring to its life. The beautiful countryside lies seven minutes from the beaches by car. It has a shopping centre second to none in the Provinces. And it offers first class theatrical and sporting entertainment at all times of the year. Many thousands of men and women who work in London have their homes in Brighton; they find that the delights of the town compensate for the inconvenience of their daily journeys.

Words

ashes *'æʃiz*	cenizas	district *'distrikt*	distrito
baker's shop *'beikəːz ʃɔp*	panadería	dreadful *'dredful*	espantoso
blessing *'blesiŋ*	bendición	effect *i'fekt*	efecto
calamity *kə'læmiti*	calamidad	event *i'vent*	evento
		flames *fleimz*	llamas
clean *kliːn*	limpio	homeless *'hɔmlis*	sin hogar
consume *kən'sjuːm*	consumir	intermittently *intəː'mitəntli*	intermitente-mente
cross *krɔs*	cruz	mark *maːk*	marcar
deadly *'dedli*	mortal	once and for all *wʌns æn fɔrɔːl*	de una vez para siempre
death *deθ*	muerte		
disease *di'ziːz*	enfermedad	parched *paːtʃt*	resecas
disapear *disə'piə**	desaparecer	plague *pleig*	plaga

practically 'præktikəli	prácticamente	to signify 'signifai	significar, querer decir
purge pə:dʒ	purgar, purificar	to spread spred	extenderse
rare rɛə*	raro	to state steit	afirmar
record ri'kɔ:d	informe	to sweep swi:p, swept, swept	barrer, arrasar
render 'rendə*	volver(se), quedarse(se)	swept	
site sait	lugar, emplazamiento	visitation visi-'teiʃən	visita
timber 'timbə*	madera	waves weivz	olas, oleadas
to arrest ə'rest	detener		

The great plague and the great fire of London

Waves of plague had swept London intermittently since the reign of James I; but the plague of 1665 was the worst, and spread suddenly and with deadly effect. Over the east district of London, in particular, the air was heavy with death, and it was rare, indeed, to find a front door not marked with the cross signifying that death had visited that house. Sixty-eight and a half thousand people died of the disease.

Calamity followed calamity, for the plague had not completely disappeared when the Great Fire broke out. It started in a baker's shop near London Bridge (a site now marked by the Monument recording that dreadful event), and it was not arrested until practically the whole area of the city had been burnt out. For three days and nights the flames, fanned (aventadas) by a strong wind, swept hungrily through the narrow streets whose timbered houses had been parched by an unusually hot and dry Summer. The records state that the fire consumed eighty-nine churches, thirteen thousand houses in four hundred streets and rendered two hundred thousand people homeless.

But even this terrible visitation proved to be a blessing. For it purged the streets once and for all of disease, and from the ashes of the old city arose a new London built more carefully, more widely, more cleanly, and, so, more healthily.

Words

cottage 'kɔtidʒ	casita, choza	sternly 'stɛːnli	severamente, duramente
decades 'dekeidz	décadas	tea-set 'tiː set	juego de té
disastrous diˈzaːstrəs	desastroso	to change tʃeindʒ	cambiar
elopement 'iloupmənt	fuga	to conceal kənˈsiːl	ocultar(se)
enraged inˈreidʒ	irritado	to decorate 'dekəreit	decorar
extremely iksˈtriːmli	extraordinariamente	to elope 'iloup	fugarse
following 'fɔlouiŋ	siguiente	to fall in love fɔːl in lʌv	enamorarse
forbade fəˈbeid	prohibió	to occur əˈkəː*	suceder, aparecer
frequently 'friːkwentli	frecuentemente	to reward riˈwɔːd	recompensar
legend 'ledʒənd	leyenda	to shed ʃed	dejar caer, desprenderse
Mandarin 'mændərin	mandarín	turtle-dove 'təːtl dʌv	tórtola
match mætʃ	unión, boda	unequal 'ʌniːkwəl	desigual
orange tree 'ɔrindʒ triː	naranjo	vow vau	juramento
overheard ouvəˈhəːd	oyó, espió	whip wip	látigo
pattern 'pætən	modelo, dibujo	willow 'wilou	sauce
pursue pəˈsjuː	perseguir		
secretary 'sekrətri	secretario		

The legend of the Willow Pattern [1]

Several decades ago, China tea-sets decorated with the blue Willow Pattern were extremely popular in English houses, and may still frequently be seen. The pattern represents the following legend:

A Chinese Mandarin had an only daughter named Le-Chi, who fell in love with Chang, a young man who lived in a house on the island, and who had been her father's secretary. The father overheard them one day making vows of love under the orange tree, and sternly forbade the unequal match. However the lovers made up their minds to elope: They concealed themselves for a while in the gardener's cottage, and then made their escape in a boat to the island home of Chang. But the enraged Mandarin pursued them with a whip, and would have beaten them

---

1. «Willow Pattern», dibujo chino convencional, en azul y blanco. Se emplea en porcelanas.

to death had not the gods rewarded their fidelity by changing them into turtle-doves.

The picture is called the Willow-Pattern not only because it is a tale of disastrous love, but also because the elopement occurred «when the willow begins to shed its leaves».

Words

approached *ə'proutʃt*	se acercó, se dirigió	Oedipus *'iːdipəs*	Edipo
childhood *'tʃaildhud*	infancia	riddle *'ridl*	acertijo
crawl *krɔːl*	arrastrarse	solve *sɔlv*	resolver
devour *di'vauə*	devorar	sphynx *sfiŋks*	esfinge
heedless *'hiːdlis*	desatento, desoyendo	supports *sə'pɔːts*	aguanta
lay *lei*	yacer, estar tumbado	tail *teil*	cola
lair *lɛə*	guarida	traveller *'trævlə*	viajero
manhood *'mænhud*	virilidad, edad viril	unfortunate *ʌn'fɔːtʃnit*	incómodo
monster *'mɔnstə*	monstruo	upright *'ʌprait*	derecho
mythology *mi'θɔlədʒi*	mitología	upset *ʌp'set*	trastornado
		warning *'wɔːniŋ*	aviso, advertencia
		wings *wiŋz*	alas

The riddle of the Sphinx

According to Greek mythology, there once lived near the city of Thebes a monster called the Sphinx. It had the face of a woman, the feet, body and tail of a lion, and the wings of a bird. She would lay in wait on a rock in the mountain where she dwelt for any traveller to pass. She would ask them a riddle, and if they could not answer it, she would carry the unfortunate person to her lair and there devour him. The riddle was this: «What is it that in the morning goes on four legs, at noon on two, and in the evening on three?»

At last Oedipus, heedless of all warning, approached the terrible rock and answered the Sphinx: «Man: who in childhood crawls on all fours (hands and knees), in manhood walks upright, and in old age supports himself with a stick».

The Sphinx was so upset that the riddle had been solved, that she threw herself off the mountain rock, and died.

Words

compared kəm'pɛəd	comparado	misery 'mizəri	infortunio, desgracia
dearly 'diəli	cariñosamente	new-found 'njufaund	recién hallado
despair dis'pɛə*	desesperación	pick up pik ʌp	coger
fragrance 'freigrəns	fragancia	power 'pauə*	fuerza, poder
gift gift	don	still stil	inmóvil
gloat glout	recrearse, divertirse	to realize 'riəlaiz	darse cuenta, comprender
golden 'gəldn	de oro	to rejoice ri-'dʒɔis	regocijar(se)
grant graːnt	conceder	to resolve ri-'zɔlv	resolver, decidir
greet griːt	dar la bienvenida, saludar	to spend spend	pasar (el tiempo)
hail heil!	¡salve!	to worry 'wʌri	preocuparse
happiness 'hæpinis	felicidad	touch tʌtʃ	tacto
horrified 'hɔrifaid	horrorizado, aterrorizado	treasure 'treʒə	tesoro
magic 'mædʒik	mágico	unhappiness ʌn'hæpinis	desgracia

Midas and the golden touch

Once upon a time there lived a king who loved gold more than anything else in the world. One day, one of the gods seeing the king gloating over his golden treasures, resolved to teach him a lesson. «Hail, Midas», said the god, «I will grant you the Golden Touch, if that is what you desire most». «The Golden Touch», exclaimed Midas, hardly able to believe his ears. «Do you mean that everything I touch will turn to gold?» «Yes», answered the god, «but it will not bring you happiness». «But it must do», replied Midas, «for it will make me the richest man in the world». And so king Midas received the magic gift, and spent the day turning everything he touched into gold. He rejoiced in his new-found power. He was not worried because he could not eat; or because the roses turned to gold and lost their fragrance; for was he not the richest man in the world? Then he called his little daughter to him, and when she ran to greet her father, he bent down and picked her up. At once she became heavy and still, and the horrified king saw that he was holding a golden statue. His happiness turned to misery and despair, for he loved his little daughter dearly. However, the god saw Midas' unhappiness, and realizing that he had learnt his lesson, told the king that the water from a certain river would change back anything that Midas had touched. And so the king's happiness returned when he felt the warm kiss of his daughter once again. As for gold, he never wanted to see any more of it as long as he lived. «Compared with love», he said, «it is a very small thing».

Words

alley *'æli*	callejón, camínito	commandment *kə'ma:ndmənt*	mandamiento
brain *brein*	cerebro, inteligencia	demand *di'ma:nd*	exigencia, ruego
blow away! *blou 'əwei!*	¡salta!	desperate *'despərit*	desesperado, furioso
blow your brains	saltar la tapa de los sesos	disobeyed *'diso'beid*	desobedecieron
bother *'bɔðə**	molestarse	lane *lein*	sendero, callejón
call *kɔ:l*	llamada	look *luk*	aspecto
calm *ka:m*	tranquilo	retort *ri'tɔ:t*	replicar
come across *ə'krɔ:s*	encontrarse	return *ri'tə:n*	volver
come back *kʌm bæk*	volver	traveller *'trævlə**	viajero

Anecdotes

The teacher told the children about the Garden of Eden (el paraíso terrenal), and how Adam and Eve had disobeyed the commandment that they should not eat the fruit of the tree. «Now, children, can anyone tell me what that lesson teaches us?» «Yes, madam», replied a small boy; «eat less fruit».

A man was stopped in a dark alley by a desperate looking fellow. «Hand over your money, or I'll blow your brains out», was the demand. «Blow away», was the calm reply. «You can live in London without brains, but you must have money».

A traveller was walking along a country lane when he came across an old man. He stopped and asked the old man how long it would take him to walk to the nearest village. But he received no reply; the man went on with his work not even bothering to look up. So the traveller continued on his way. But he had not got very far when he heard a call: «Hey (oiga), mister! Come back!» The traveller returned, and the old man said: «It will take you twenty minutes.»

«But why didn't you tell me that when I asked you?», asked the traveller. «Well, how did I know how fast you were going to walk?», retorted the old man.

Words

beauty *'bju:ti*	belleza	seed *si:d*	semilla
cans't *ka:nst*	no podrás	thine *ðain*	tu, tuyo (forma anticuada)
creed *kri:d*	credo		
false *fɔ:ls*	falso	thought *θɔ:t*	pensamiento, juicio
famine *'fæmin*	hambre		
feed *fi:d*	alimentar, dar de comer	thy *ðai*	tu (forma anticuada)
fiction *'fikʃən*	ficción		
fruitful *'fru:tful*	fructífero	true *tru:*	verdadero
glorious *'glɔ:riəs*	gloriosa	truly *'truli*	verazmente
Queen *kwi:n*	reina	victorious *vik'tɔ:riəs*	victorioso
quotations *kwou'teiʃənz*	citas	ye *ji:*	vosotros (forma anticuada)

Nota: «*Cans't*» es una forma anticuada de «cannot»

Quotations about truth

Think truly, and thy thoughts
  Shall the world's famine feed.
Speak truly, and each word of thine
  Shall be a fruitful seed.
Live truly, and thy life shall be
  A great and noble creed.

HORATIOUS BONAR

Tis strange but true; for truth is always strange, stranger than fiction.

LORD BYRON

To thine own self be true,
And it must follow as the night the day,
Thou cans't then be false to any man.

SHAKESPEARE

> Beauty is Truth; Truth Beauty,
> That is all ye know on Earth,
> And all ye need to know.
>
> KEATS

The national anthem   El himno nacional

> God save our gracious Queen
> Long live our noble Queen,
> God save our Queen.
> Send her victorious,
> Happy and glorious,
> Long to reign over us,
> God save our Queen.

My daily prayer

Please, o Lord, teach me to keep my big mouth shut until I know what I'm talking about.

VOCABULARIO

Comprende el presente vocabulario todas las voces que el estudiante pueda necesitar para los ejercicios de versión y tema contenidos en la obra. Sólo deberá tener en cuenta que no figuran en él todos los verbos irregulares registrados en la lista de las páginas 116 a 119. Tampoco incluye los adverbios de uso más frecuente, detallados en las páginas 131 a 135. El vocabulario, desde luego, no suple un diccionario más extenso inglés-español y español-inglés, que resulta indispensable para proseguir el estudio de la lengua inglesa.

1. Inglés - Español

abbey abadía
ably hábilmente
about acerca de, cerca de
above arriba, sobre
abroad el extranjero
abundance abundancia
accept aceptar
accident accidente
accompany acompañar
according to según, de acuerdo con
achieve lograr
acquaintance conocido, amigo
acquisition adquisición
across a través
actor actor
actually de hecho, en realidad
add sumar, añadir
addition suma, adición
additional adicional
address dirección
address dirigirse a, dirigir
admiral almirante
admire admirar
admit admitir
admittance admisión
advance progresar
advance, in por adelantado
advertisement anuncio
advisable aconsejable
aerodrome aeródromo
aeroplane avión, aeroplano

afford permitirse
afraid asustado
afraid (be — of) tener miedo, temer
after después
afternoon tarde
afterwards después
again de nuevo, otra vez
against contra
age edad
ago hace (tiempo)
agree asentir
air aire
airliners aviones de línea
airplane aeroplano
airport aeropuerto
air-sickness mareo
airy aireado
ajar entreabierto
alive vivo, con vida
all todo, -s
alley callejón, caminito
allow permitir
almost casi
alms limosna
alone solo
along a lo largo de, adelante
already ya
also también
altitude altura
altogether en conjunto

always siempre
America América
American americano, -a
amid entre
among entre
amuse divertir
amusement diversión
amusing divertido
analysis análisis
and y
angel ángel
animal animal
Anne Ana
another otro
answer responder
Antarctic Antártico
anxious(ly) impaciente, impacientemente
any algún, -o
anything algo
anyway de todos modos
apparatus aparato
apparently al parecer
apple manzana
apple-tree manzano
approach acercarse
approve aprobar
Arctic Ártico
architect arquitecto
architecture arquitectura
area área
argument discusión
arise levantarse
arithmetic aritmética
arm brazo
arm-chair butaca
army ejército
around alrededor, cerca de
arrange arreglar
arrest detener
arrive llegar
arsenal arsenal
artist artista
as como
as a matter of fact en realidad
ascend ascender, subir (al trono)

ashes cenizas
ashore en tierra firme
ask preguntar
aspirin aspirina
assist ayudar
as well también
at a, en
Atlantic Atlántico
attract atraer
audience audiencia
aunt tía
author autor
automatic automático
Autumn otoño
avenue avenida
avoid evitar
await esperar
awake despertarse
aware enterado
away lejos
axe hacha
axis eje

baby niño pequeño
back espalda
bacon tocino
bad malo
badly mal
bake cocer al horno
baker panadero
bald calvo
ball pelota
ballet ballet
bank banco
Bank Holiday San Esteban
bare liso, desnudo
bargain ganga, trato
bark corteza
barometer barómetro
barren estéril
barrow carretón
bask tostarse al sol
basket cesto
bath baño
bathe, have a bañarse
bathroom cuarto de baño

be ser o estar
be able ser capaz de
beach playa
be allowed estar permitido
bean habichuela
bear soportar
beat pegar, derrotar
beautiful hermoso
beauty belleza
because porque
become devenir, hacerse
bed cama
bee abeja
beer cerveza
before antes, ante, delante
beg rogar
beggar pordiosero
begin empezar
be glad estar contento, satisfecho
behave portarse bien
behead cortar la cabeza
behind detrás
believe creer, pensar
belong pertenecer
beloved amado
below debajo
bench banco
be off salir, marchar(se)
be right tener razón
besides además
be sorry sentir, apesadumbrarse
between entre
be worth valer
be wrong estar equivocado
beyond más allá
bicycle bicicleta
big grande
bill cuenta, nota
bird pájaro
birthday cumpleaños
biscuit bizcocho
bit un poco
bite morder
bitter amargo
black negro
blackberry mora (fruta)

blackboard pizarra
blessing bendición
blind ciego
block tajo
blow soplar
blow golpe
blow away, blow out! ¡saltar la tapa de los sesos!
blow one's nose sonarse
blue azul
blush ruborizarse
boar cerdo
board plancha
boat barco
boating, to go ir de excursión en barca
body cuerpo
boil hervir
bold atrevido
boldly audazmente
bones huesos
book libro
book reservar (un asiento)
booking-clerk empleado
booking-office ventanilla
bookseller librero
bookstall quiosco de periódicos
boot bota
bore taladrar
born, to be nacer
borrow tomar (prestado)
botanist botánico
both a un tiempo, ambos
bother molestarse
bottle botella
bottom abajo
bound obligado
box caja, palco
Boxing Day el día 26 de diciembre
box office taquilla
boy niño, muchacho, chico
brains sesos
branch rama
brandy coñac
brave valiente
bravely valientemente

bread pan
breakfast desayuno
breathing respiración
breeze brisa
bridge puente
bright brillante, vívido, despejado
bring traer
bring forth brotar, sacar
bring up educar
brisk rápido
British británico
brother hermano
brown marrón
brushes cepillos
build construir
building edificio
built construido
bun bollo
burn quemar
bus autobús
busy ocupado
but pero, sino
butcher's carnicería
butter mantequilla
button botón
buy comprar
buzz zumbido
by por, junto a, cerca de
by the way a propósito

cabbage col
cabin cabina
cake pastel
calamity calamidad
calf ternera
call llamar, llamada, llamada telefónica
call box cabina (telefónica)
call out gritar
calm tranquilo
can poder
cap gorra
cape cabo
capital capital
car coche
cardinal cardinal

cards naipes, cartas
care importar
care cuidado
carefully cuidadosamente
careless descuidado
carriage vagón
carry transportar, traer, llevar
carve trinchar
case caso
cash dinero efectivo
castle castillo
catch coger
catch a glipse echar una ojeada
cathedral catedral
cattle ganado
cause causar, causa, origen
cease cesar, dejar de
ceiling techo
celebrate celebrar
celebrated célebre
cell celda
cenotaph cenotafio
cerberus cancerbero
certain(ly) cierto, ciertamente
chair silla
chalk yeso
chance oportunidad
change cambiar(se)
changeable cambiable
charabanc remolque (de un coche para excursión)
characteristic característico
charge atacar, acometer
charming encantador
chat charlar, charla
cheap económico, barato
cheat engañar, estafar
cheese queso
cherry cereza
cherry-tree cerezo
cherub querubín
chest cajón
chew masticar
chickens pollos, pollitos
chief principal
child niño

childhood infancia
chilly frío
chin barbilla
Chinese chino
chips patatas fritas
choose escoger
chooser el que escoge, exigente
chop chuletas (de carne)
chosen seleccionado
Christmas Navidad
church iglesia
cigar puro
city ciudad
clap of thunder trueno
class clase
classroom clase (habitación, aula)
clean limpio, limpiar
clear claro
clear up serenarse, aclarar
clerk empleado
clever inteligente
clock reloj
close cerrar
close by muy cerca
close to cerca de
cloth vestido
clothing ropas
clouds nubes
cloudy nublado
coal carbón
coalfield campo carbonífero
coast costa
coat chaqueta, abrigo
cobbler zapatero remendón
cock gallo
coffee café
coffee house café (bar)
cold frío
collar cuello
collect recoger
college colegio universitario
colliery mina de carbón
colour color
Columbus Colón
column columna
combine combinar

combined combinados, unidos
come venir
come across encontrarse
come back volver
come in entrar
come round pasar(se) (por un sitio)
comfort comodidades
commander-in-chief comandante
commandment mandamiento
comment comentar
commercial comercial
common común, corriente
companion compañero
company compañía
comparatively comparativamente
compared comparado
comparison comparación
compartment departamento
compass brújula
compensate compensar
complain queja
complain of quejarse de
complete total
completely completamente
comprehension comprensión
conceal ocultar(se)
concert concierto
condemn condenar
condition condición
conductor conductor-cobrador
confess confesar
connect relacionar
conqueror conquistador
consent consentir
consider considerar
consist consistir
consulate consulado
consume consumir
contents contenido
contract contraer(se)
conversation conversación
convey conducir, llevar
cook guisar
copper cobre, calderilla, caldera
copy copiar
corn grano, cereal, maíz, callo

corner ángulo, esquina
coronation coronación
cost costar
costume traje
cottage casita, choza
cotton algodón
cough tos
count contar
counter contador
counters fichas (en el juego)
country país, campo
countrymen compatriotas
countryside campo (opuesto a ciudad)
county condado
couple par
course curso, platos (servidos en una comida)
course, of naturalmente
court corte
courtyard patio
cousin primo
cover cubrir
cow vaca
crash catástrofe
crawl arrastrarse
creed credo
crisis crisis
cross cruzar, cruz
cross enfadado, malhumorado
crowd multitud
crowded poblado
crucifix crucifijo
crumble derrumbarse
cry llorar
cry out gritar
cup taza
cure cura, curar
curtain cortina
customer cliente
cut cortar
cut off cortar (comunicación)

daily cotidiano
daisy margarita
dale valle

damage dañar
dance bailar
danger peligro
dangerous peligroso
dare atreverse
dark oscuro
date fecha
datum dato
day día
day-excursion excursión de un día
dead muerto
deadly mortal
deaf sordo
deal tratar en
dean deán, decano
dear querido
dearly cariñosamente
death muerte
decades décadas
decide decidir
deck cubierta
declare declarar
decorate adornar
deer ciervo
degree grado
delight encantar
delightful delicioso
delights delicias
deliver entregar
demand demanda, exigir, pedir
demolish derribar
dentist dentista
department departamento
descend bajar
descendant descendiente
describe describir
deserve merecer
desk caja, pupitre, escritorio
despair desesperado, desesperación
desperate desesperado, furioso
despise despreciar
dessert postre
developed subir
devise planear, idear
devour devorar
dial esfera, marcar (un número)

die morir
difference diferencia
difficult difícil
difficulty dificultad
dilate dilatar(se)
diligent diligente
dine comer
dining room comedor
dinner cena, comida
dirty ensuciar, sucio
disapear desaparecer
disappoint desilusionar
disastrous desastroso
discipline disciplina
disconnect desconectar
discover descubrir
discrimination discernimiento, cuidado
disease enfermedad
disengaged desocupado
dish plato, fuente
disobey desobedecer
display despliegue
distinct(ly) con claridad
distinguish distinguir
distress desgracia
district distrito
ditch foso, hoyo
divide dividir
do hacer
doctor doctor, médico
dog perro
dome cúpula
domestic doméstico
donkey jumento, burro
door puerta
doorkeeper portero
dot punto
dough masa
down abajo
downstairs abajo
dozen docena
drake pato
draught corriente (de aire)
draw dibujar, trazar, arrastrar, correr

drawing room salón
dread temer
dreadful espantoso
dream soñar
dress circle anfiteatro
drink beber
drive conducir
drizzle lloviznar
drop dejar caer
dry seco, secar
duchy ducado
duck pato
due debido
duke duque
dumb mudo
duo dúo
dure durar
during durante
dust polvo
duster borrador
duty deber
dwell residir, permanecer
dying moribundo

each cada
ear oreja
early temprano
ears oídos, orejas
earth tierra
easily fácilmente
east este
Easter Pascua de Resurrección
easterly del este, de levante
easy fácil
eat comer
eccentricities excentricidades
echo eco
Edward Eduardo
effect efecto
egg huevo
eight ocho
either, either... or el uno o el otro
eldest mayor
electric eléctrico
electrical eléctrico
electronics electrónico

elf duende
elope fugarse
elopement fuga
else otro, además, más
Emperor emperador
empire imperio
employ usar, emplear
empty vacío
enclose incluir
end fin
ending final
enemy enemigo
engage comunicar (el teléfono)
engaged ocupado
engagement compromiso
engine motor
England Inglaterra
English inglés
Englishman inglés
enjoy disfrutar
enjoyable divertido
enough suficiente, bastante
enraged irritado
enter entrar
entertainment entretenimiento
entrance entrada
envelope sobre
epidemic epidemia
equal igual
escape escapar
especial(ly) especial, -mente
establish establecer, consagrar
Europe Europa
eve víspera
even pares, incluso, aun, hasta
evening atardecer
even so precisamente
event caso, acontecimiento
every todo, -a, todos, -as, cada
everything todo
everywhere por todas partes, en todas partes
exactly exactamente
examination examen
examine examinar
example ejemplo

excellent excelente
excepting exceptuando
exchange cambio, central de teléfonos
excursion excursión
execute ejecutar
exercise ejercicio
exercise-book cuaderno
expect esperar
experience experiencia
explain explicar
explanations explicaciones
export exportar
export(s) exportaciones
expose expuesto
extra extraordinario
extraordinary extraordinario
extremely extraordinariamente
eye ojo
eyebrows cejas
eye-glasses lentes
eyelashes pestañas
eyelid párpado

fabric géneros, telas
face cara, rostro, esfera
fact hecho
factory fábrica
fair bello, rubio
faithful fiel
fall caer, bajar
fall in love enamorarse
fall into desembocar
false falso
fame fama
family familia
famine hambre
famous famoso
far lejos, completamente, mucho
fare tarifa, precio, billete
farm granja
farmer campesino
fashion moda
fashionable de moda
fast rápidamente, adelantado
fast-train rápido (tren)

fate destino, suerte
father-in-law suegro
feast fiesta, festín
feather pluma
feed alimentar, dar de comer
feel sentir
feeling sensación, sentidos
fellow compañero, chico, muchacho
fence valla
fertile fértil
fetch ir a buscar, traer
fever fiebre
few poco
fiction ficción
field campo
fifteen quince
fight luchar
figure cifra, número
fill llenar
find encontrar
fine hermoso, bello
fine! ¡estupendo!
finger dedo
finish acabar, terminar
fire fuego
first primer(o), -a, principio
fish pescado, pescar
fishing pesca, pesquero
fishing, to go ir a pescar
fit sentar (una prenda)
fit, be a good sentar bien (una prenda de vestir)
five cinco
flag bandera
flail mayal
flake copo
flames llamas
flash relámpago
flatten achatado
flee huir
fleet flota
flesh carne (del ser vivo)
flight vuelo
flood inundación
floor suelo, piso

flour harina
flow fluir
flower flor
flower-bed parterre
flowery florido
fly volar
fog niebla
foggy cubierto, lleno de niebla
follow seguir
following siguiente
fond of, be apreciar, ser aficionado a...
food alimento, comida
foolishly locamente
foolishness locura
foot pie
football fútbol
for para, por
forbide prohibir
forecast previsión del tiempo
foreign extranjero (país)
foreigner extranjero (pers.)
Foreign Office Ministerio de Asuntos Exteriores
form clase, forma
former, the el primero
formerly antes, primeramente
fortnight quincena
forward enviar, reexpedir
foundation fundación
four cuatro
fourteen catorce
fowl pollo
fragance fragancia
free libre
freeze helar
French francés
Frenchman francés
frequently frecuentemente
friend amigo
from de, desde
frost helada
fruit fruta
fruitful fructífero
fruit-tree árbol frutal
fry freír

full lleno, completo
fully enteramente
fun diversión, broma
further más lejano, más lejos, adelantar
future, in en adelante

gaily alegremente
gain adelantar, ganar
gain entrance lograr acceso
gallery galería
game juego
gamekeeper guardabosque
garden jardín
gardener jardinero
gather recoger, juntar
gay alegre
gazes mira
gentle, gently suave, suavemente
gentleman caballero, señor
gentry nobleza, aristocracia
geography geografía
German alemán
Germany Alemania
get obtener, comprar
get a move darse prisa
get back devolver
get in entrar, subir
get into entrar
get off bajar
get on continuar, avanzar
get out bajar, salir
get rid deshacerse
get there llegar
get up levantarse
gift don
girl niña, muchacha
girl cousin prima
give dar, ceder
give back devolver
glad contento
gladly alegremente, con alegría
glass vaso
gloat recrearse
glorious glorioso
glove guante

goat cabra
go back regresar, volver
God Dios
go down bajar
go into entrar
gold oro
golden de oro
goloshes chanclos
good bueno
good-bye adiós
Good Friday viernes santo
good morning buenos días
goods géneros, mercancías
go on continuar, seguir adelante
goose ganso
go out salir
government gobierno
gradually gradualmente
grain grano
grandchildren nietos
grandfather abuelo
grandmother abuela
grandparents abuelos
grant conceder
grass hierba
gray gris
great grande
Great Britain Gran Bretaña
greatly mucho
greatness grandeza
green verde
greet dar la bienvenida, saludar, felicitar
grey gris
grieved apenado
grievous(ly) penoso, penosamente
grind moler
gross gruesa (medida)
grow crecer
grow bright aclarar, animarse
guard guardar, guardia, guarda, jefe de estación
guest huésped
guide guía
guitar guitarra

gums encías
gun escopeta

hail ¡salve!, granizar
hair cabello
half medio
hall sala
hallo hola
halo aureola
ham jamón
hand mano, manecilla, alargar, presentar
handful puñado
handkerchief pañuelo
hang up colgar
happen ocurrir
happiness felicidad
happy feliz
hard mucho, duro
hard time pasarlo mal
harm daño
haste prisa
hat sombrero
have haber, tener
have better ser preferible
hay heno
head cabeza
headache dolor de cabeza
heading encabezamiento
heal sanar
health salud
healthy sano, saludable
hear oir
hearing oído
heart corazón
hearth hogar
heat calor
heavy pesado
heedless desatento, desoyendo
heir heredero
help ayudar, (con negación) evitar
helpful servicial
hen gallina
hence desde aquí
Henry Enrique
her su, -s (de ella)

here aquí
hereafter en lo futuro
hero héroe
high alto
hiking, to go ir de excursión a pie
hill colina
him le, la (a él, a ella)
his su, -s (de él)
history historia
hitherto hasta aquí
hoist alzar, izar
hold caber, coger, sujetar, sostener
hole agujero
holiday día festivo, (en plural) vacaciones
home casa, hogar
homeless sin hogar
honour honrar
hope desear, esperar
horrified horrorizado, aterrorizado
horse caballo
hosiery calcetería
hospital hospital
hostel parador
hot muy caliente
hotel hotel
hotel-keeper hotelero
hour hora
house casa, albergar
how como
however sin embargo
how many? ¿cuántos?
how much? ¿cuánto?
huge(ly) grande, enorme, enormemente
hum zumbar
humour humor
hunger hambre
hungry hambriento
hunter cazador
hurricane huracán
hurry prisa, apresurarse
husband marido

hymn himno
hysterics histerismo

ice hielo
idea idea
idle ocioso
idly perezoso
illness enfermedad
imagine imaginar
immediately inmediatamente
immense inmenso
impair dañar, empeorar
import importar
important importante
improve enmendarse
improvement mejora
imprudent imprudente
in en
include incluir
inconvenience molestia
indeed verdaderamente
Indian Ocean Océano Índico
indicate indicar
indoors en casa (en el interior)
inferior inferior
influenza, 'flu gripe
inform informar
inhabitant habitante
injure lesionar
injury lesión
ink tinta
in order that para que
inside dentro
insist insistir
instance, for por ejemplo
instead of en lugar de
instrument instrumento
interesting interesante
interference interferencia
intermittently intermitentemente
interrupt interrumpir
interval intervalo
intimately íntimamente
into en, dentro de
introduce introducir
in turn a su vez

invitation invitación
invite invitar
iris iris
Irishman irlandés
iron hierro
ironfoundry fundición de hierro
island isla
isle isla
its sus, -s (de ello)

jam mermelada
Jane Juana
Japanese japonés
jar jarro -a; tarro
jersey jersey
John Juan
join unir, reunirse
journey viaje
joy goce, alegría
joyful alegremente
jump saltar
just justamente, sólo, justo

Kate Catalina
keep tener, guardar, conservar
keep in touch estar en relación, en contacto
keep out apartar, contener
Kew Kew (nombre propio)
key llave
kill matar, morir
kind amable, clase, especie
kindness amabilidad
king rey
kingdom reino
kiss beso
kitchen cocina
knead amasar
knee rodilla
kneel arrodillar
knife cuchillo
Knight templar templario
knit hacer punto
knock llamar (a la puerta)
know saber, conocer
knowledge conocimiento, saber

label etiqueta
lack falta de
lady señora
lair guarida
lake lago
lamb cordero
lame cojo
land tierra, continente
landscape paisaje
lane sendero, callejón
language lengua
large grande
lark alondra
last último, fin, últimamente, pasado
late tarde
later más tarde, después
latest último
Law Courts Palacio de Justicia, Tribunales
lawyer abogado
lay yacer, estar tumbado
lazy perezoso
lead conducir, llevar, guiar, plomo
leap-year año bisiesto
learn aprender
learning ciencia, cultura
leafe hoja, salir, dejar, abandonar, restar, marchar de
lecture conferencia
left izquierda
leg pierna, pata
legend leyenda
lend dejar, prestar
lesson lección
lest no sea que, por miedo a
let alquilar
letter carta, letra
lettered marcado con la letra...
level nivel
library biblioteca
lie mentira, mentir, yacer, tumbarse, echarse
lier embustero
life vida
life, for perpetuamente

lift levantar, ascensor
light iluminar, encender, luz, ligero, claro
lightning-rod pararrayos
like gustar, como, igual, semejante
lily lirio
limbs miembros
line clase, calidad, línea
lips labios
list lista
listen escuchar
little pequeño, poco
live vivir
loaf pan (hogaza)
local local
lofty altivo, elevado, alto
Londoner londinense
look parecer, aspecto, mirada
look after cuidar
look at mirar
look for buscar
look of, by the por el aspecto
Lord Señor
Lord justice presidente del tribunal
Lord Mayor alcalde
Lordship señoría
lose perder, atrasar
lot lote, cantidad, todo
lot (a — of) mucho, -s
lots muchos
louse piojo
love amar, gustar, amor
lovely encantador, delicioso, bonito, lindo
low bajo
luck suerte
lucky, luckily afortunado, afortunadamente
luggage equipaje
lunch(eon) almuerzo
lying mentira, mentiroso

machine máquina
mackintosh impermeable

madam señora
magic mágico
magnificent magnífico
maid-servant criada
main principal
mainly principalmente
Majorca Mallorca
make hacer, convertir en
maker fabricante
make sure asegurarse
make up formar
male macho
man hombre
manage llevar, cuidarse, dirigir
manager gerente
Mandarin mandarín
manhood virilidad, edad viril
manner manera
man-servant criado
Mansion-House residencia oficial del alcalde de Londres
manufacture fabricación, manufacturar
many muchos, -as
map mapa
Margaret Margarita
mark marcar
marmalade mermelada de naranja
marry casarse
Mary María
mason albañil
master maestro, amo
masterpiece obra maestra
match unión, boda, partido (deporte)
material material
matter motivo, asunto
may poder
me a mí, me
meadow pradera
mean querer decir, significar
means medios
measles sarampión
meat carne (para comer)
medal medalla, condecoración

medicine medicina
meet encontrar (persona)
memorable memorable
mention mencionar
menu menú
merchant comerciante
mercy misericordia
merry alegre
message mensaje
metal metal
microphone micrófono
midday mediodía
middle medio
midnight medianoche
Midsummer day el 24 de junio
mighty poderoso
Milanese milanés
mild templado
mile milla
mill molino, fábrica
miller molinero
million millón
mind importar
mine mina
minute minuto
misery infortunio, desgracia
miss perder (tren, etc.), señorita
mist neblina
mistake error
mistress dueña, señora
mix mezclar
model modelo
monarch monarca
money dinero
monk fraile, monje
monster monstruo
month mes
monument monumento
moon luna
morning mañana
mortally mortalmente
motion movimiento
motor-car automóvil
mountain montaña
mouse ratón
mouth boca

move into cambiarse, trasladarse
multiply multiplicar
murder asesinar, asesinato
museum museo
music música
must deber
mutton cordero
my mi, -s
mythology mitología

nail-polish barniz de uñas
name nombre
narrow estrecho
nasty asqueroso, malo
nation nación
national nacional
natural natural
naval naval
navigator navegante
navy flota
near cerca
nearly casi
necessary necesario
necessity necesidad
need necesitar
neighbour vecino, prójimo
neighbouring vecinos
neither... nor ni... ni
nephew sobrino
nest nido
never nunca
new(s) nuevo, noticias
new-found recién hallado
newspaper diario (periódico)
New Year año nuevo
New York Nueva York
next próximo
nib plumilla
nice(ly) bonito, agradable, con esmero, bien
niece sobrina
night noche
nine nueve
no no, ningún
noblemen nobles
nobody nadie

noise ruido
none ninguno
nonsmokers no fumadores
nonstop directo (tren)
noon mediodía
northern nórtico
nose nariz
not no
not at all en absoluto
note nota, billete
nothing nada
nothing else nada más
notice notar
nought cero
novel novela
now ahora
nowadays actualmente
nowhere en ninguna parte
nuisance fastidio, molestia
number número
nurse enfermera
nursing cuidados

oatmeal copos de avena
obedient obediente
obey obedecer
observe observar
obtain obtener
occasion ocasión
occasional intermitente, ocasional
occur suceder, aparecer
Ocean océano
odd impar
Oedipus Edipo
of de
of course naturalmente
off lejos, a la altura de (mar)
offer ofrecer, oferta
office oficina
officer funcionario
official oficial
often a menudo
old viejo
omit omitir
on en, encima de, sobre
once una vez

one uno
only solamente, solo
onto en, encima
open abrir, abierto
opera ópera
opera-glasses gemelos de teatro
operator telefonista
opposite opuesto (delante), contrario, delante de
or o
orange naranja
orange(tree) naranjo
orchestra orquesta
order encargar, ordenar, mandar, orden, pedido, organización
Order of Merit Orden del Mérito (condecoración)
ordinal ordinal
organ órgano
organization organización
oriental oriental
orphan huérfano
other otros
ought debería
our nuestro, -a, -os, -as
out fuera
outing excursión, paseo
outlook previsión
out of fuera de
outside fuera
oven horno
over sobre
overhear oir, espiar
overnight durante la noche
own propio
ox buey

Pacific Ocean Océano Pacífico
pack of cards baraja
page página, paje
pain dolor, dificultad
painted pintado
painter pintor
painting pintura
pair par
palace palacio

palate paladar
pane cristal
pansy pensamiento (flor)
pantry despensa, alacena
paper papel, periódico
paradise paraíso
parcel paquete
parched reseco, tostado
pardon perdón, perdonar
Paris París
park parque
Parliament Parlamento
part parte
particular detalle
partly parcialmente
party fiesta
pass pasar
passenger pasajero
passport pasaporte
past pasado
pasture pasto
patient paciente
patronage protección, patrocinio
pattern modelo
Paul Pablo
pause pausa
pavilion pabellón
pay pagar
pea guisante
pear pera
peasant campesino
pen pluma
pence peniques
pencil lápiz
penholder mango
people gente
peopled poblado
perched posado
perfect perfecto
perfectly perfectamente
perform cumplir, realizar
performance representación
performer actor
periods períodos
persuade persuadir
Peter Pedro

phone teléfono, telefonear
phrase frase
physics física
pick coger, recoger
pick out coger, seleccionar
pick up coger
picture grabado, cuadro, retrato, película, cine
piece pedazo
pierce romper, forzar
pig cerdo
pigeon paloma
pile amontonar
pinnacle cumbre, pináculo
pitch tono
pity lástima
place colocar, poner, lugar, sitio
plague plaga
plan plan
planet planeta
plant planta
plate plato
platform plataforma, andén
play jugar, tocar, representar
pleasant agradable
please complacer, agradar, satisfacer, por favor
pleasure gusto, placer
plenty of abundante, mucho
plum ciruela
plum-tree ciruelo
plus más.
pocket bolsillo
point punto, señalar
pole polo
Police policía
policeman policía
polite educado
politics política
pond estanque
poor pobre
popularity popularidad
population población
populous populoso
pork puerco
porridge gachas
porter mozo
Portuguese portugués
port wine vino de Oporto
post echar al correo
post office correo
potato patata
pottery alfarería
poulterer avicultor
poultry aves de corral, volatería, caza
pound libra
pound-note billete de una libra
pour llover a cántaros
power fuerza, poder, poderío
practically prácticamente
praise alabanza
pray rogar
precede preceder
precious precioso
prefer preferir
prepare preparar(se)
prescription receta (medicina)
present presente, actualmente, regalo, regalar
presently en seguida
press apretar
pressurized presión acondicionada
pretty bastante
price precio, lista de precios
prima ballerina primera bailarina
prince príncipe
principal principal
prison prisión
prisoner prisionero
private particular
proceed proceder
produce producir
product producto
production presentación
professor profesor
profit provecho
programme programa
promise prometer, promesa
prone predispuesto
pronounce pronunciar
proof prueba

propeller hélice
proper adecuado
properly correctamente, bien
protect proteger
proud orgulloso
prove probar, demostrar
proverb proverbio
provide proveer, abastecer, suministrar
provided siempre que
province provincia
provision provisión
public público
public holiday fiesta oficial
pudding budín
pull tirar de
pull out arrancar, sacar
punish castigar
pupil alumno
purchase comprar, compra
purge purgar
purpose propósito
purse monedero
pursue perseguir
pursuit ocupación
put poner
put down depositar, entregar
put off posponer
put on poner(se)

quarter cuarto
queen reina
quickly de prisa, rápidamente
quiet tranquilo
quit largarse, salir de
quite completamente
quotations citas

rack red (del vagón)
radio radio
rage rabia, coraje
rail ferrocarril, rail
railway ferrocarril
rain lluvia, llover
rainbow arco iris
raise elevar

rapid(ly) rápido, rápidamente
rare raro
rather más bien, bastante
raw en bruto
read leer
reading lectura
realize darse cuenta, comprender
really realmente
reap segar
reaper segadora
reaping-machine segadora
receiver receptor
recently recientemente
recommend recomendar
record registrar, informe
recover restablecerse
recreation recreo, descanso
recurrence recaída
red rojo, encarnado
refuse negar
regain recobrar
regain control volver a controlar
register registro
reign reinar, reinado
rejoice alegrarse, regocijarse
relative pariente
rely confiar
remain permanecer
remark observación
remarkable notorio
remember recordar
render volver(se), quedar(se)
renowned renombrado, conocido
repair arreglar, preparar, componer, reparación
repeat repetir
reply contestar, replicar
report explosión, detonación
request petición, ruego
require necesitar, requerir
residence residencia
resident huésped
resolute decidido
resolve resolver, decidir
respectfully respetuosamente

rest descansar, descanso, restante, resto, soporte
restaurant restaurante
resting-place morada
retire retirarse
retort replicar
return volver, regreso, billete de ida y vuelta
revolution revolución
revolve girar
reward recompensar
rhythmic rítmico
rich rico
Richard Ricardo
riches riqueza
riddle acertijo
ride paseo, montar
right derecha, correcto
right away en seguida
ring the bell tocar el timbre
ring up telefonear
ripe maduro
rise salir (el sol), levantarse, nacer (un río)
risk riesgo, arriesgar
risky arriesgado
river río
road camino, carretera, calle
roast beef asado
roll panecillo
Roman romano
Rome Roma
roof tejado
room habitación
rose rosa
rotate girar
rotation rotación
round redondo, alrededor
rubber goma
rule regla, gobernar
run correr
run a temperature tener fiebre
run away escapar
run over atropellar
rushed corrió, se precipitó
rye centeno

sack saco
sacred sagrado
sad triste
safe seguro
sail hacer(se) a la vela, navegar
sale venta
salesgirl dependienta
salesman dependiente
salty salado
sample muestra
satchel cartera
satisfied satisfecho
save ahorrar
say decir
saying dicho, proverbio
scarce escaso
scarlet escarlata
scarlet-fever escarlatina
scene escena
scenery escenario, vista
school escuela, colegio
school-boy colegial
schoolroom clase
scissors tijeras
Scotland Escocia
Scots, Scotch escocés
Scotsman escocés
scrape (money) juntar, recoger (dinero)
screen biombo, mampara de chimenea
scythe guadaña
sea mar
sea(s), over allende el mar
search registrar
seaside playa
seaside resort lugar de veraneo en la costa
season estación (del año)
seat asiento, butaca
second segundo
secretary secretario
see ver
seed semilla
seem parecer
seldom raramente

self mismo
sell vender
send mandar, enviar
send for enviar a buscar
senses sentidos
sentence oración, frase
series serie
serious serio, importante, grave
seriously seriamente, gravemente
servant criado
serve servir
service servicio
set colocar, poner
set out partir
seven siete
several algunos, varios
severe severo, grave, doloroso
shade sombra, tonalidad
shape forma
sharp puntiagudo
sheaf gavilla
shed dejar caer, desprenderse
sheep cordero
shelf estante
shelter cobijo, guarecerse
shilling chelín
shine brillar
ship barco, buque
shirt camisa
shiver tiritar
shocking chocante, espantoso
shoe zapato
shop tienda
shopkeeper tendero
shopping ir de tiendas
shopping-centre centro comercial
shore costa, ribera
short corto
shot tiro
shout grito
show enseñar, mostrar, indicar
shower chaparrón
shut cerrar
sick enfermo
sickle hoz
side lado

side-door puerta lateral
sight vista, mirada
sign firmar, señal
signature firma
signify significar, querer decir
silence silencio
silent silencioso
silver plata
similar semejante
since desde
sincerely sinceramente
sing cantar
singer cantante
singing canto
single uno, solo, único, billete (de ida sólo)
sir señor
sister hermana
sit sentarse
sit down sentarse
site lugar, emplazamiento
situated situado
six seis
size tamaño, medidas
skate patinar
skates patines
ski patinar
skilfully hábilmente
skull calavera
sky firmamento, cielo
sleep sueño, dormir
sleeping-car coche-cama
slight ligero, delgado
slip resbalar
slippery resbaladizo
slot ranura
slow(ly) despacio, atrasado, lentamente
smack pegar
small pequeño
smash estrellarse, romper
smell olor, oler
smile sonrisa
smoke fumar
smokers fumadores
snatch arrebatar

sneeze estornudar
snow nieve, nevar
so así, por lo tanto
soar elevarse, volar
soft blando
socks calcetines
soldier soldado
sole right monopolio
solid fuerte, sólido
solve resolver
some algún, alguno
something algo
sometime alguna vez
so much tanto
son hijo
son-in-law yerno
soon pronto
sore throat dolor de garganta
sorry sentir (lamentar)
sort especie, clase
sound sonido
soundly profundamente
sound-prove insonorizante, a prueba de ruido
soup sopa
South Sur
Spain España
Spaniard español
speak hablar
special especial
spectacles lentes
speed velocidad
spell deletrear, escribir
spend pasar (el tiempo), gastar (dinero)
sphynx esfinge
spin hilar
spinning hilatura
splendid espléndido
spoil estropear
sponge esponja
spoonful cucharada
spread extenderse
spring surgir, primavera
square plaza
staff palo

stage escena
stall platea (butaca de)
stammer balbucear
stand alzarse, estar situado, estar de pie
stand up levantarse, erguirse
star estrella
start empezar
state indicar, afirmar
statesman hombre de estado
station estación
stationer's tienda de objetos de escritorio
statue estatua
stay estar, permanecer, detener
steamboat vapor
step-son hijastro
step this way por aquí
sternly severamente, duramente
stick palo, bastón, pegar
still todavía, aún, inmóvil
stitch punto
stockings medias
stone piedra
stop parada, pararse
story historia, cuento
straight recto
straight ahead derecho, recto
strange extraño
strawberry fresa
stream corriente
stretch estirar
street calle
strike golpear, dar (en el blanco), dar la hora
stroke golpe, campanada
stroll una vuelta
strong fuerte, resistente
struggle lucha, pelea
student estudiante
study estudiar
subscriber abonado
substantial substancial
subtract restar
succeed tener éxito, salir bien (una cosa)

succession sucesión
such tan
such as tal
suddenly súbitamente
suffer sufrir
sufficient(ly) suficiente, suficientemente
suit ser conveniente
sultry sofocante
Summer verano
sun sol
sunny soleado
sunshine sol
superb soberbio
superior superior
supper cena
support aguantar
suppose suponer
sure seguro
surely seguramente
surface superficie
surplus superproducción
surprised, to be sorprenderse
survive sobrevivir
swallow golondrina
swarm enjambre, hormiguear, bullir
sweep barrer, arrasar
sweet dulce
sweets caramelos
swim nadar
swine puerco
Swiss suizo
sword espada
symbol símbolo
symptom síntoma

table mesa
tact tacto
tail cola
tailor sastre
take tomar, sacar
take back devolver
take care cuidar
take out sacar
tale cuento, relato

talk hablar
tall alto
taste gusto, sabor, gustar, saber, saborear
tea té
teach enseñar
teacher profesor
teapot tetera
tea-set juego de té
telephone teléfono
television televisión
television set televisor, telerreceptor
tell decir
temperature temperatura
tempt tentar
ten diez
tender tierno
tenor tenor
terribly terriblemente, (fig.) enormemente
thank dar las gracias
thankful contento, agradecido
thanks, thank you gracias
that ese, esa, aquel, -lla
theatrical teatral
their su, -s (de ellos)
them a ellos, los, les
then entonces, luego
there allí
therefore por lo tanto
thereupon a lo cual, entonces, después de esto
thermometer termómetro
these estos, estas
thief ladrón
thin delgado
thine tu, tuyo (forma anticuada)
thing cosa
think pensar, creer
thinly débilmente
third class tercera clase
thirsty sediento
thirteen trece
this este, esta
Thomas Tomás

thoroughfare vía pública
those aquellos, -as; esos, -as
though aunque, a pesar de
thought pensamiento, juicio
thrash trillar
thrasher trilladora
thrashing-machine trilladora
thread hilo
three tres
throne trono
through por, a través
throw echar, arrojar
thumb pulgar
thunder trueno, tronar
thunderbold rayo
thunderclap trueno
thunderstorm temporal, tormenta
thus así, de esta manera, así pues
thy tu (forma anticuada)
tick golpear, tictac
ticket billete, entrada
tie corbata
tight fuerte
tiles tejas
till hasta
timber madera
time tiempo, vez
tin estaño
tiny diminuto
tip propina
tired cansado
title título
to a, para
toast tostada
tobacco tabaco
to-day hoy
toe dedo del pie
together juntos
tomato tomate
to-morrow mañana
tongs tenazas
tongue lengua
too demasiado, también
too much demasiado
tooth diente
top arriba, en lo alto

torrent torrente
touch tacto
touch of ataque ligero (de enfermedad)
tough duro (de alimento)
tour excursión
tower torre, alzarse
town pueblo, ciudad
toy juguete
tract trecho
trade comercio
trader comerciante
train tren
training entrenamiento
tram-car tranvía
translate traducir
travel viajar, viaje
traveller viajero
treason traición
treasure tesoro
treat obsequio, obsequiar
tree árbol
trick truco
trip viaje, excursión
trouble molestar
trousers pantalones
true verdadero
truly verdaderamente, verazmente
trunk tronco, baúl
trust confiar, creer
truth verdad
try intentar, tratar, juzgar
try on probar
tube metro, ferrocarril subterráneo
tunnel túnel
turn turno, volver(se), vuelta
turn away echar, hacer marchar
turn on encender la luz
turtle-dove tórtola
twice dos veces
two dos

ugly feo, -a
umbrella paraguas
unbearable insoportable
uncle tío

uncomfortable incómodo
under debajo
undergraduate estudiante universitario
underground metro, ferrocarril subterráneo
understand comprender
undertake emprender
underwear ropa interior
undisturbed tranquilo
undone sin hacer
undoubtedly indudablemente
unequal desigual
unfortunate desdichado
unfortunately desgraciadamente
unhappily desgraciadamente
unhappiness desgracia
unit unidad
united unido
United States Estados Unidos
unless a menos que
unnecessary innecesario
unripe verde (fruta)
unsettled inseguro
until hasta
unusual extraño, inusitado
up arriba
upper alta
upright derecho
upset trastornado
up to hasta
up-to-date moderno
us nos, a nosotros
use uso, usar, soler
useful útil
usual, as de costumbre
usually generalmente, corrientemente

vacant vacío, vacante
valley valle
valuable valioso, de valor
value valor
varied variado, diverso
variety variedad
various varios
vast vasto
veal ternera
vegetable(s) verdura, vegetales
venerable venerable
very muy
victorious victorioso
victory victoria
view vista, ver, contemplar
villa villa
village pueblo
violet violeta
virtue virtud
visit visita, visitar
visitation visita
vitality vitalidad
voice voz
volunteer prestarse, ofrecerse
vow juramento

wait esperar
waiter camarero
wake up despertarse
walk andar, paseo
walk back volver andando
wall pared, muro
wander vagar
want querer
want of falta de
war guerra
ward sala de hospital
warehouse almacén
warm caliente, templado, caluroso
War Memorial monumento a los caídos en la guerra
warning aviso, advertencia
warrior guerrero
watch reloj (pequeño, de bolsillo, de pulsera, etc.)
watch over vigilar
water agua
watering place balneario
waterproof impermeable
wave ondear, agitar
waves olas, oleadas
way camino, modo, manera

wealthy rico
wear llevar, usar
wear well durar
weather tiempo
weaving textura
week semana
well bien
West Oeste
wet húmedo, lluvioso
wet through calado, mojado
wharf muelle
what que, lo que
whatever cualquier cosa
wheat trigo
when cuando
whenever siempre que, cuando
where dónde
where... from? ¿de dónde...?
whether... or tanto si... como si...
which cual, el cual
while mientras
whip látigo
whistle pito, silbato
white blanco
Whitmonday lunes de Pentecostés
who quien
whole todo, entero
wholly completamente
whomsoever cualquiera que sea
why? ¿por qué?
wide ancho
wife esposa
wild silvestre, salvaje
William Guillermo
willow sauce
win ganar
wind viento
window ventana
window (shop-) escaparate
windy hacer viento, ventoso
wings alas
Winter invierno
wipe limpiar, borrar
wire telegrama
wireless radio

wise prudente, sabio
wish desear, deseo
witches brujas
with con
within dentro
without sin
witness ser testigo, atestiguar, testigo
wittier más ingenioso, más chistoso
wolf lobo
woman mujer
woman-servant criada
wonderful maravilloso
wore usaba, llevaba
work trabajo
working trabajando, funcionando
world mundo
worm gusano
worry preocuparse
worst peor
worth valor
wound herir
wounded herido
wrist muñeca
write escribir
writer escritor
writings escritos, obras
wrong equivocado, mal

yard yarda, unidad de longitud
yawn bostezo, bostezar
ye tú (forma anticuada)
year año
yellow amarillo
yes sí
yesterday ayer
yet todavía
yon, yonder aquel (a lo lejos)
young joven
your tu, -s; su, -s; vuestro, -s
youth juventud

zero cero

2. Español - Inglés

a to, at
abierto open
abogado lawyer
abrigo overcoat
abrir open
absoluto, en at all
absurdo absurd
abuelo grandfather
abundancia plenty of
acabar end
a causa de because of
accidente accident
accidente (de aviación) air crash
aceptar accept
acercar approach, go near
acompañar accompany
actor actor
actriz actress
adelantar gain
adiós good-bye
admirablemente wonderfully
admirador admirer
admitir admit
adonde where, wither
a eso de about
afeitar shave
afición, diversión favorita hobby
aficionado fond of
afortunadamente luckily
agradable pleasant
agua water
ahora now
ahorrar save
aire air
alcanzar obtain

alegrarse be pleased
alegre gay
alegría mirth gaiety
algo something
alimento food
almuerzo lunch
a lo largo along
alrededor around
alto tall, high
alto (en lo) top (on the)
alumno student
allí there
amable gentle, kind
amasar knead
a menudo often
América America
amigo friend
Ana Anne
anciana old woman
anoche last night
antes first, before
antiguo ancient
anuncio advertisement
año year
Año Nuevo New Year
apearse get out of
aplauso cheering
aquello that
aquí here
árbol tree
arriba up
arrojar fling
arroyo stream, rivulet
arte art
así thus

Español-Inglés

asombrarse de, preguntarse wonder (at)
asunto matter
asustar frighten
atrasado slow
atrasa (reloj) loses
aún yet
aunque although
auto car
autobús bus
a veces sometimes
avena oat
avena, copos de oatmeal
avergonzarse be ashamed
ayudar help
azúcar sugar
azul blue

bailar dance
bajo low, short
bajo, lo base, contemptible
banco bench
barato cheap
batalla battle
baúl trunk
bautizado christened
bebidas drinkables
bello beautiful
bicicleta bicycle
bien well, right
bisiesto leap
blanco white
boca mouth
bolsillo pocket
bonito nice
borrador duster
borrar wipe
brazo arm
brillar shine
buenos días Good morning
buscar look for

caballero gentleman
caballo horse
cada each
caer fall down

caer(se) fall
café coffee
caja box
calle street
campesino farmer
campo country, field
cansado tired
cantante singer
cantar sing
caramelo sweet
carbón coal
carnero mutton
caro expensive
carta letter
cartera satchel
casa house, home
casarse marry
castigar punish
catedral cathedral
católico catholic
cazador hunter
cazar hunt
centeno rye
cerca about, near
cerdo pig
cereza cherry
cerezo cherry-tree
cero zero
cerrado shut, closed
cerrar shut, close
césped grass
cielo sky
ciertamente certainly
cinco five
cine cinema
circunvecinos all around
ciudad city
claro clear
clase classroom schoolroom, kind, sort of
cobrador ticket collector
cocer bake
coche car
coger pick, take catch
colección collection
colegio school

colgar hang
colina hill
colocación employment
color colour
combatir fight
comer dine, have dinner, eat
comida food, meal
como as
cómo how
compañero companion
comprar buy
comprender understand
conducir drive
conferenciante lecturer
conocer know
conocimiento knowledge
con que provided
consecutivamente consecutively
conseguir reach, get
contar tell
contentar please
contento gay
contestar answer
contra against
conversación talk
convertir en become, change
corbata tie
corral, patio yard
correos Post Office
correr run, draw
cortar cut
costar cost
costumbre habit
crecer grow
creer think,
creer en trust
criado servant
cristiano Christian
cuaderno copy-book
cualquier any
cualquiera anybody
cuánto how much
cuántos how many
cuarto room
cuatro four
cubrir cover

cuchillo knife
cuenta bill
cuento story
cuerpo body
cuidar to take care of
cumpleaños birthday

chal shawl
chica girl
chico fellow
chimenea hearth
chino Chinese

daño damage
daño, hacerse hurt
dar give
dar de comer feed
dar la hora strike
de of
debajo under
deber must, owe
débil weak
decir say, tell
dedo finger
delicioso delightful
demasiado too much
de nuevo again
deportes sports
de prisa quickly
derecho right
derrotar defeat
desayunar breakfast
descansar rest
descanso rest
descuidado careless
desde from
desde (hace) since
desear wish
desesperado despair
desesperarse despair
desgraciadamente unfortunately
desgraciado unhappy
desobediencia disobedience
despacio slowly
despacho office
despejado bright

despertar awake, wake up
después afterwards, after
detrás behind
día day
diablo devil
dichoso happy
diente tooth
dientes teeth
diez ten
difícil difficult
dinero money
dirección address
discípulo pupil
donde where
dormir sleep
dos two
dueño owner, landlord
durante during

echar throw
eje axis
ejercicio exercise
empezar begin
empujar push
en in
encantador charming
encarnado red
encender light
encerrar shut
encima on
encima, por over
encontrar find, meet
enfermo ill
enfrente de opposite
enfriamiento chill
Enrique Henry
en seguida immediately
enseñar show
entender understand
entrada entrance
entrar come in, enter, go into
entre between, among
entreabierto ajar
entregar deliver
en vez instead of
equipo team

equivocado wrong
escalera staircase
escaparate shop-window
escribir write
escritor writer
eso that
esperar expect, wait for, hope
esponja sponge
esquiar ski
estación (del año) season
estar be
estar apesadumbrado be sorry
estar de acuerdo agree
estilográfica fountain pen
esto this
estornudar sneeze
estrella star
estudiante student
estudiar study
examinar examine
excelente excellent
excepcional exceptional
éxito success
experiencia experience
explicar tell
exportación exportation
exportar export
extensión surface
extranjero foreigner
extranjero, en el abroad
extraordinario extraordinary

faltar miss
famoso famous
feliz happy
fiel faithful
fiesta holiday
fin end
física physics
flor flower
forma shape
fotografía photograph
francés French
frecuentemente often
freir fry
frío cold

fruto, -a fruit
fuego fire
fumar smoke
fútbol football

galería gallery
gallina hen
ganado cattle
ganar gain
ganso goose
gato cat
gavilla sheaf
generalmente usually
géneros goods
gente people
geografía geography
girar turn
globo globe
gol goal
golondrina swallow
goma rubber, gum
gordo fat
grado degree
grande big
granizar hail
granja farm
granjero farmer
grano grain
grave severe
gris grey
guante glove
guardar keep
guerra war
guisar cook
gustar like

haber be
habitación room
habitante inhabitant
hablar speak
hace (tiempo) ...ago
hacer do
hambre hunger
harina flour
hasta till
helar freeze

herido wounded
herir wound
hermana sister
hermano brother
hermoso beautiful
heroína (fármaco) heroin
hierro iron
hoja leafe
hombre man
hora hour
horno oven
hospital hospital
hotel hotel
hoz sickle
huerta kitchen-garden
huevo egg

iglesia church
igualmente equally
importación importation
importancia, tener mind
importar import
Inglaterra England
inglés English
inmediatamente immediately
inocente guiltless
inteligente clever
intentar try
interesante interesting
interesar interest
invierno Winter
invitación invitation
invitar invite
ir go
ir a caballo ride
isla island, isle

jabón soap
japonés Japanese
jardín garden
jarro jug
jaula cage
joven young
Juan John
juego play
jugador player

Español-Inglés

jugar play
juguete toy
juicioso sensible
jump brincar
junto by
justamente just

ladrón thief
lápiz pencil
largarse quit
largo long
lástima pity
lavar wash
lección lesson
leche milk
leer read
lejos far
lengua language
lente lens
león lion
lesión injury
levantarse get up, rise
librería bookshop
librero bookseller
libro book
limosna (pedir) beg
loco foolish
Londres London
love amar
luego then
luna moon
luz light

llamar call
llegar arrive
llegar a ser become
lleno full
llevar bring
llorar cry
llover rain
llover a cántaros pour
lluvia rain

madurar ripen
maduro ripe
maíz corn

malo bad, wicked
maltratar ill-treat
mandar send
manecilla hand
manera manner
mano hand
mantequilla butter
manzana apple
mañana morning, to-morrow
mapa map
mar sea
maravilloso wonderful
marcar mark
marcharse go away
María Mary
marrón brown
matar kill
matemáticas mathematics
materias subjects
me me
médico doctor, physician
medio half
mediodía mid-day, noon
menos less
menú menu
mercado market
mercancías goods
mes month
mesa table
metal metal
miedo fear
miel honey
mientras while
mineral mineral
minuto minute
mirar look, see
mismo same
moderno modern
modo manner
mojado wet
moler grind
molino mill
moneda coin
montaña mountain
morar dwell
morder bite

morir die
mover(se) move
muchacho fellow
mucho a lot
muerto dead
mujer woman
mundo world
muñeca doll
museo museum
música music
musulmán Moslem
muy very

nacer to be born
nacer (un río) rise
nación nation
nacional national
naranja orange
naturalmente of course
Navidad Christmas
necesario necessary
necesitar need
necio foolish
negro black
nevar snow
nido nest
niebla fog
nieto grandson, grandchild
nieve snow
niña girl
niño boy
no, ningún no
noche night
Noche Buena Christmas Eve
Noche Vieja New Year's Eve
nombre name
noticia news
nuestro our
nueve nine
nuevo new
número (del reloj) figure
nunca never

obedecer obey
obra play, performance
obtener obtain, get

ocupación, trabajo work
ocuparse apply oneself to
ocurrir happen
ocho eight
oficina office
ofrecer offer
oir hear, listen
ojo eye
oler smell
olvidar forget
ópera opera
oprimido oppressed
oración sentence
orden order
orgulloso proud
oro gold
orquesta orchestra
otoño Autumn
otra parte elsewhere
otro other, another, else
oveja sheep

paciente patient
pagar pay
página page
país land
pájaro bird
palacio palace
palo staff
pan bread
panadero baker
panecillo roll
pañuelo handkerchief
par pair, couple
para for, to
parada stop
paraguas umbrella
parar stop
parecer seem
pared wall
París Paris
parque park
partido party
pasado last
pasar (ocurrir) to be the matter
pasear walk

paseo walk
pastor shepherd
pata leg, foot
patatas fritas chips
patinar (resbalar) slip
patio yard
pausa pause
pecho chest
pedazo piece
pedir ask for, beg
Pedro Peter
película film, picture
pelota ball
pequeño small
pera pear
percha coat-stand
perder lose, spend
perdón pardon
perezoso lazy
periódico newspaper
permitir let, permit, allow
pero but
perro dog
pertenecer belong
pesado heavy
pescado fish
pie foot
piedra stone
pierna leg
pintura picture
piso floor
pito whistle
pizarra blackboard
placer pleasure
plantar plant
plato course
plaza square
plomo lead
pluma feather, pen
pobre poor
poco little,
pocos few
poder can
poesía poetry
policía policeman
pollito chick, chicken

poner put, set
por by, through
porción part, piece
por consiguiente consequently
por lo tanto so
porque because
portería porter's lodge
portero doorkeeper
postre dessert
precaución precaution
precioso precious
preferir prefer
preguntar ask
premio reward
presentar hand, introduce
prestar lend
primavera Spring
primero first
primo cousin
princesa princess
principalmente mainly, principally
príncipe prince
principio beginning
prisionero prisoner
probar try, taste
probarse try on
profesor teacher
progresar progress
progreso progress
pronunciar pronounce
protestante Protestant
proverbio proverb
próximo next
prudente, sabio wise
puerta door
puerto harbour
puesto que because of
pulgar thumb
punto point
pupitre desk

¡qué...! what a...!
quedar rest
quedarse stay, remind
quemar burn
querer want

queso cheese
quién who
quincena fortnight
quizá perhaps

rabia rage
rama branch
raqueta racket
rara vez seldom
ratón mouse
realmente really
redondo round
regalar give, offer
regalo present
regañar scold
reino reign
reir laugh
relámpago flash
relampaguear lighten
reloj clock, watch
repetir repeat
representación performance
representar play
resfriado cold
resistente strong
restaurante restaurant
retrato portrait
rey king
ribera bank
Ricardo Richard
río river
robar steal
rodear surround
rojo red
romper break
rosa rose

saber know
sabiduría knowledge
sabio wise
sacar take out
sala hall
salir go out
salir (el sol) rise
salir go out
salir para to leave for

saltar spring, jump
salud health
salvaje wild
sanar cure
sano healthy
sano (mentalm.) sane
sastre tailor
satisfecho pleased
secar dry
seco dry
segar reap
seguido consecutively
seguir go on
segundo second
seguramente probably
seis six
semana week
sentarse sit down
sentir(se) feel, be sorry
señalar point
señorita miss
separar, quitar(se) take off
sí yes
Sicilia Sicily
siempre always
siete seven
significar mean
silbato whistle
sin without
sol sun
solamente only
soldado soldier
solo alone
sólo only
sombrero hat
sonarse blow one's nose
sonido sound
sonreir smile
soñar dream
sopa soap
soplar blow
sorprender surprise
sótano cellar
súbditos subjects
sublime sublime
suceder happen, take place

Español-Inglés

suelo floor
suponer suppose

también also
tan so
tanto mejor so much the better
tanto tiempo so long
taquilla box office
tarde late, afternoon
taza cup
teléfono telephone, phone
televisión television
televisor (telerreceptor) television set
tempestad storm
templado warm
temprano soon
tenedor fork
tener have
tener aspecto look
tener razón be right
tenis tennis
tenor tenor
tentar tempt
terminar finish
termómetro thermometer
tía aunt
tiempo weather
tienda shop
tierra earth
tigre tiger
tijeras scissors
tímido, vergonzoso shy
tinta ink
tintero inkstand
tiza chalk
tocar touch, play (music)
todavía yet
todos every, all
tomar take
Tomás Thomas
tormenta storm
torre de iglesia steeple
toser cough
trabajar work
traducir translate

traer bring
traje dress, costume
traje (hombre) suit
tranvía tramway, tram
trato bargain
travieso naughty
tren railway
trepar climb
tres three
trigo wheat
tronar thunder

último last
una vez once
único only
Universidad University
uno one
útil useful

vacaciones holidays
valer cost
valiente brave
valioso valuable
valor courage, value
varios some, several
vaso glass
veces, a sometimes
vecino neighbour
vencer defeat
vender sell
venir come
ventana window
ver see
verano Summer
verdad truth
verdad, ser be true
verdadero true
verde green
verde (fruta) unripe
verdura vegetable
viajar travel
victoria victory
viejo old
viento wind
vino wine
violeta violet

virtud virtue
visita visit
visitar visit, call on
vista sight
víveres food
vivir live
volar fly
volcán volcano

volver go back, come back
vuelta (dar una) (take a) stroll

y and
ya already, ...no more

zapato shoe
zorra fox
zurdo left-handed